CHAMPAGNE-ARDENNES
& BURGUNDY

PASSPORT'S REGIONAL GUIDES OF FRANCE

Auvergne & the Massif Central
Rex Grizell

Brittany
Frank Victor Dawes

The Dordogne & Lot
Arthur & Barbara Eperon

The Loire Valley
Arthur & Barabara Eperon

Languedoc & Roussillon
Andrew Sanger

Normandy, Picardy & Pas de Calais
Barbara Eperon

Paris
Vivienne Menkes-Ivry

Provence & the Côte d'Azur
Roger Macdonald

The Rhône Valley & Savoy
Rex Grizell

South West France
Andrew Sanger

Also available:
Passport's Regional Guides of Italy
Passport's Regional Guides of Portugal

CHAMPAGNE-ARDENNES &BURGUNDY

Arthur and Barbara Eperon

Photographs by Joe Cornish

PASSPORT BOOKS
a division of *NTC Publishing Group*
Lincolnwood, Illinois USA

Published in 1997 by Passport Books,
a division of NTC Publishing Group,
4255 West Touhy Avenue, Lincolnwood
(Chicago), Illinois 60646–1975 U.S.A.

Originally published by
Christopher Helm (Publishers) Ltd,
a subsidiary of A & C Black (Publishers) Ltd,
35 Bedford Row, London, England

Photographs © Joe Cornish
Maps and plans by Robert Smith,
© A & C Black (Publishers) Limited

ISBN 0–8442–9926–X

Library of Congress Catalog, Card Number:
95–71160

Typeset in 9 on 11 pt Optima

Printed and bound in Italy by Printer Trento.

Contents

Practical Information   228

Phone Number Changes **228;** Tourist Information Offices **229;**
Hôtels and Restaurants **229;** Events **240;** Châteaux, Museums,
Castles, Abbeys, Exhibitions **242;** Metric and Imperial Conversion
Tables **246**

Maps and Plans

1. Introduction

For 40 years we have followed a wine lovers' route to the South of France. Spurning the horrors of the Paris périphérique and its bewilderment of signs and escape routes, we have aimed for Reims through the St Gobain forest, weaved through the little Champagne villages to Epernay and Troyes, then crossed into Burgundy at the welcome little town of St Florentin to visit the Chablis vineyards and caves. We have stopped for at least a meal at the delicious hilltop town of Auxerre above the river Yonne, then wandered along the valleys of the river Cure, fast flowing and rich in trout, and the little Cousin, bubbly and sometimes turbulent, to another fascinating hilltop town, Avallon, and eastward across charming Côte d'Or countryside of hills, woodlands, waterways and pleasant villages to Dijon, one of our favourite towns in France. Burgundy's powerful Dukes made Dijon their capital and brought in Flemish artists, craftsmen and architects to beautify it, so today it is still a beautiful, interesting town of historic buildings, fine wines, great works of art and excellent meals, from low-priced true Burgundian farmhouse-style meals to the superbly cooked, balanced meals of renowned chefs.

At Dijon, of course, the great Burgundian wine route begins. Here we have old friends to meet and new and old wines to taste in a dozen famous villages—Fixin, Vougeot, Vosne-Romanée, Nuits-St-Georges, Beaune itself (overcrowded always, but still a vinous and historic delight), Meursault (where our elder daughter says we should live in our old age), and down into the Chalonnais to Rully, which Parisian wine addicts discovered 30 years after we did, Buxy, a treasure-house of lesser-known wines, then on to Mâcon, the twin villages of Pouilly and Fuissé, and the twisting lanes of Beaujolais, which the bureaucrats in Paris insist is in Rhône département but where the wine is still called Burgundy and will ever remain so.

Our route is not as eccentric as you might think. Champagne and Burgundy are the backbone of France—the very body which holds the north and south together. True, our route takes time. But the treasures you meet by the wayside are ample reward, and by the time you reach Provence you are already relaxed and content.

That is what Burgundy offers—timelessness. You feel that no one is going to hurry you, jostle you, nag you from a car telephone or rush you through a decision, a meal or a bottle. Burgundians say that they learn patience from waiting for their red wine to mature in cask—which takes anything from 16 months to two years.

New motorways and new faster trains are changing the map of Europe. Suddenly the British have found that Reims and Epernay are within as easy week-ending distance as Paris or Brussels, and Auxerre, Dijon and Beaune within driving distance for experienced continental drivers. Dijon is 612km (382 miles) from Calais. Arthur (then aged 74) made it in five hours. Motorway gaps have been filled. You can pick up the A26 at Calais and follow it past Reims, Châlons and Troyes, switch to the A5 near Langres and on to the A31 to Dijon. Four important motorways pass near to Dijon, but none near enough to spoil the charm of the old capital.

It was the fast train, the TGV, which made us realise that Dijon, our favourite food town in France, was within range for a relaxing weekend. We caught the 17.19 TGV from Gare de Lyon in Paris and by 19.30 we had our knees under the table at Jean-Pierre Billoux's restaurant in Dijon's place Darcy, sipping a true Kir of double-crème de cassis and Aligoté wine and choosing from the brilliant young chef's modern dishes inspired by old Burgundian recipes. Take the three-hour Eurostar train from London to Paris Gare du Nord and nip over to Gare de Lyon to catch the TGV (another 1hr 36 min). Alternatively, catch the Eurostar 15.23 from London to Lille, change platforms for the TGV train to Dijon, arriving at 21.11.

These fast journeys, of course, give you no idea of the variety of scenery, the beauty of the countryside or the village life hidden behind the trees, hedges or embankments. Even experienced travellers still talk of the Champagne's 'monotonous flat countryside and unappealing grey villages' and of Burgundy as if it were mainly made up of the tempting Route des Grands Crus south from Dijon. They could not have wandered far from Autoroutes and Routes Nationales.

For such close neighbours, these two regions of Champagne-Ardennes and Burgundy have widely different histories, traditions, scenery and artistic backgrounds. Even their wines, of course, are spectacularly different. But they do have one common philosophy—that the route to Paradise is downwards into a cellar and kitchen.

The people of Champagne, especially those living or working in the bigger centres such as Reims, Châlons, even Troyes and Charleville, seem to have the unsettled urgency of Parisians, the harried feeling that they must keep ahead or be trampled underfoot. Even on the way to heaven or hell, it is said, the true Burgundian would find time for a chat and a glass of wine.

Champagne villages are very different from the towns—even the wine-producing villages. To go from the enormous, brilliantly organised caves of the big Champagne companies like Ruinart, the oldest in Reims, and Moët et Chandon in Epernay to the caves of family producers in villages such as Ambonnay, Bouzy or Cuis is like suddenly switching centuries. Yet the wine they produce is as precious and desirable, and often bought by the big companies to add a powerful bouquet and strength to their blend.

The Champagne region has indeed had an unsettled, often turbulent history. Though their ruling Counts came under the French crown by the 13th century, that brought little peace to the province. The Burgundian Dukes

The wonderful Grey-Poupon mustard shop in Dijon

ruled more land than the Kings of France for some time, after Duke Philip the Bold pawned his possessions to pay for his courtship and steeled himself to marry an ugly widow, Margaret of Flanders, to get his hands on her rich province, plus Artois, Nevers, and the Franche-Comté. Later Dukes added much of what is now Holland, land in Germany, Lorraine and Upper Alsace.

Invasions of Champagne continued through the centuries. The English, Burgundians, Spaniards and Germans of Charles V's Empire, French Catholics and Protestants all used it as a battle field, so did Napoleon I. Invading Prussians smashed the Empire of Napoleon III there in 1870, the Germans occupied most of it in 1914–18 amid battles which left hardly a village intact or a building in Reims unharmed. The Germans were back in 1940–44, leaving a trail of destruction. Peasants and wine-growers must have wondered through generations if it was worth rebuilding farms or houses and to this day the Champagne is one of France's most sparsely populated regions.

Most vineyards can look bare, cold and lonely under dull clouds of winter but the gently curvaceous vineyards of Champagne come alive with greenery in spring and under the summer sun, with the deep mauve Pinot Noir grapes and the yellow-green Chardonnay tugging in heavy bunches at the vines, the vineyards make a great sea of green almost to the grey walls of the village churches. Then in autumn they turn to red, bronze and gold as the villages and vineyards become fiendishly busy around vintage time.

Nearly all the vineyards are in the biggest département of Champagne, Marne, around Reims, whose Gothic cathedral is one of the finest religious buildings in the world, the wine town of Epernay and the important commercial centre Châlons. Aube, the département stretching from way south of Reims to the Burgundy border, has a few vineyards, producing mostly Coteaux de Champagne, a pleasant still table wine. It is a thinly populated area, but its medieval capital, Troyes, is beautiful. It was here that Queen Isabella of France signed a treaty with England's Henry V after his great victory over the French army at Agincourt. Henry married Catherine, daughter of Isabella and her ailing husband Charles VI and was declared heir to the French throne. To the English, this was a sensible move to ally France and England and put an end to centuries of bloody wars. To the French it was a sell-out. The 'mad' Jesuit who murdered Henry undoubtedly received political urging. The land of northern Aube was dry and poor until the 19th century when pine trees were grown so successfully that the soil gradually became one of the richest in France, and since 1945 has produced sugarbeet, wheat and barley. South from Troyes to the Burgundy border is called Champagne humide, a narrow strip of woodlands and pastures where dairy cows are raised and cheese is made, including the softly nutty *chaource*, known since the 14th century.

Haute-Marne, the south-east département of Champagne, is wooded, with valleys, rivers and four large man-made lakes produced for water supply, used for fishing and watersports. Though a poor area, it lures holidaymakers, especially walkers and cyclists, looking for peace and attractive country. The old city of Langres, which has kept its medieval walls despite centuries of wars and invasions, is one of the most attractive and interesting in Northern France.

Though the fourth département of the Champagne gives the whole region its official name, Champagne-Ardennes, the département of Ardennes-Français is a mysterious land driving a wedge into Belgium and leaning on the border of Luxembourg. It is true wanderers' country, sometimes steep with narrow paths, very beautiful and wild, often awesome, even eerie with dark ravines, threatening cliffs and thick forest carpets of deciduous trees. A different world from the pine forests of the Belgian Ardennes a few kilometres north, it harbours the same wild boar (*sangliers*) and deer. Winding slowly but strongly through the valleys below is the Meuse river, making leisurely 'meanders', so that it seems to be going back for something it has forgotten. Seeing it in summer, you cannot believe that this is the same river whose wild flooding put the capital Charleville 6 metres under water in January 1995. It is a little known corner of France, visited mostly in summer by French and Belgian 'wanderers' on foot, on mountain bikes, paddling canoes down the Meuse, just fishing, or climbing energetically to mysterious rocks which have inspired legends of witches and werewolves, sorcery and magic, heroism, treachery and infidelity, with the Devil never far away. They still tell these stories in the villages.

A handful of expensive hotels have been converted from old châteaux or abbeys but towns and villages are small and simple and you stay in 1 or 2-star logis, family-run, clean, simple and serving family-style meals of local products from freshwater fish, lamb and pork to game in autumn, or in village rooms or the odd gîte or cabin. Seasonal campsites are fairly comfortable. Derelict iron foundries and forges near the forests are gradually disappearing under greenery. Until the late 1940s, they were an important part of France's industry—especially the arms industry, centred in those days in the charming capital, Charleville-Mézières. Until the 1960s these were two towns divided by the Meuse. Mézières was a medieval fortress, Charleville an important commercial centre, trading by road and by river and canal with much of Europe, and town planned in 1606 with a huge square around which you can still see the 17th century buildings. It is an elegant, pleasant town and still important commercially, with roads to Liège, Metz, Luxembourg, Reims, Paris, Lille and Calais fanning out through its green countryside of cattle farms, cereals and vegetables. Ardennes-Français meets Marne département only 19km (12 miles) north of Reims.

Despite their many differences, there are no noticeable boundaries between Champagne and Burgundy. Burgundy has a centre in Dijon but has no logical frontiers. History, not geography, shaped it. The one natural border is in the west, where the river Loire south from Briare and then its tributary the Allier divide Burgundy from the Loire region. The wine town of Pouilly-sur-Loire is on the Burgundy side of the river, but its Pouilly-Fumé is called 'Loire wine' and is similar to the wine of its rival Sancerre over the river and therefore just inside Loire region.

In the 15th century when Philip the Good, Duke of Burgundy, ruled an area bigger than that of the French king, he had dozens of titles, some high flown, some truly important, but his proudest was 'Lord of the finest wine in Christendom'. After the Revolution the new government actually abolished the name of Burgundy when they divided France into 90 départements. But the people still called their land Burgundy. After all, their wine was still Burgundy and that was what mattered. Then De Gaulle brought back the name in 1964 when he grouped départements into regions for economic planning. So Burgundy now consists of the départements of Côte-d'Or, Saône-et-Loire, Yonne and Nièvre. Though the Beaujolais wine area is in Rhône, not Burgundy, it is on every Burgundy wine list, the wine is Burgundy and Beaujolais wine and its countryside are in this book.

As you wander down the D122 Route des Grands Crus from Dijon to Beaune, to wonder at the magnificent roof of the medieval charity hospital, l'Hôtel Dieu, ablaze with coloured tiles, and to taste the wine in the Convent of the Visitation, you can forget quite easily that Burgundy has only 6130 ha (15,150 acres) of vineyards to its 1,000,000 ha (2,471,000 acres) of forest. The forests are richest in the plateaux of the north—in the Sens lands bordering Champagne and the Ile de France and in the Morvan west of Dijon, secret hideout of the Burgundians in war and peace, a land of damp, dripping winters when narrow forest roads turn to mud and of blissful shade and sudden views in the heat of summer—a delight to walkers and to seekers after solitude. On surrounding pastures they breed cattle but, alas, the old red-coloured local cattle have given way to the big white Charolais which promise such fat profits to breeders and wholesalers. In the Charollais itself in Saône-et-Loire west of Mâcon, where Charolais beef cattle originated there are now about three million. Goodness knows how or when they lost an 'l' in their name, but they have spread far and wide across the world.

Burgundy has 1207km (750 miles) of navigable rivers and canals, which until 1945 were vital to the region's trade, especially the wine trade. Henri IV started the canal system with the Briare canal connecting the Seine and Loire valleys. He planned to connect Paris with as many parts of France as possible. The greatest was Canal de Bourgogne joining Paris to Dijon—started in 1775 and finished in 1833. When goods moved on to the roads, some canals closed. On others commercial traffic thinned to a trickle and the rivers were left empty, their little ports decaying. But as the holiday boom hit Western Europe, the great potential of inland waterways for recreation was spotted in every Western European country and the beautiful rivers and convenient canals of Burgundy, forming a great linked network, were just asking to become a playground for cruisers, converted canal boats, canoes and fishing boats.

Pleasure cruising has brought a whole new dimension to exploring Burgundy, so that we have given it a separate chapter in this book. The four main rivers, the Loire, Saône, Yonne and Seille, their many tributaries and the great canals have delightful villages and hamlets on their banks and some pass through or flow through the valleys below superb old cities, as the river Yonne flows beneath the truly delightful and very Burgundian old city of Auxerre (usually pronounced 'osserre'), or pass nearby beautiful old historic

Beaune: Pierre Meurgey of Champy Père et fils tastes his wine

buildings as the Canal de Bourgogne passes the two superb Renaissance châteaux of Tanlay and Ancy-le-Franc below Tonnerre. The Canal du Nivernais is the most peaceful and cuts through the loveliest countryside of orchards and vineyards, with many charming châteaux and manor houses. You can cruise from St Florentin on the Champagne border in Yonne to Dijon in about ten days.

Looking after vines is a full-time job every month of the year, and unlike Bordeaux, most Burgundy holdings are small and family-owned, with no outside help except during the vendange. So for much of the year villages are truly dead during the day.

Grape-picking machines are quite new in Burgundy. It is not economic for small growers to buy one, despite the rising cost of paying, feeding and sometimes lodging pickers, mostly French and foreign students. Margaret Loxton, a Kent artist who has a way of portraying French country life, has painted some delightful and evocative pictures of well-fed, strong-armed Burgundian men and women picking the grapes, with famous Burgundian wine villages in the background. Burgundy would lose a lot of its traditional lifestyle and social life if machines replaced pickers. The vines might not be happy either, and Burgundian wine-makers spend their lives keeping vines happy and healthy.

The Vendange

Midsummer can be very hot in Burgundy, winters cold, so May, September and October are pleasant times to be there. For the wine village the *vendange*, the grape harvest, is a wonderful time, but you need help from the growers, the oenological stations which test the amount of sugar in the grape and the Almighty to guess when that will be. It could be early September; it could run into October. We once waited for three weeks, with everyone telling us that it would be 'any time now'; then we had to leave a day before it began. In 1976 it started on 30 August in Côte de Beaune. We would gamble on 23 September—our wedding anniversary. Anyway, at this time the villages will be in action, even if they have finished picking and are drinking to celebrate a good vintage or drown their sorrows for a bad one. And there are often the little local wine festivals, *paulées*, after the picking is finished. Then the villages are great fun.

Burgundians love to put out flags, turn out the village band, feast, drink and dance. Almost every wine village has at least one annual fête and outside wine areas they find other excuses, like water-jousting at Clamecy, which used to live on river trade, a goose fair at Toucy, a snail festival at Blaisy-Bas and the oldest horse race in France at Semur.

Beaune's annual Les Trois Glorieuses three-day festival has become a great international event. It is based on the wine sale for the Beaune Hospice. The Saturday night in November before the sale the Chevaliers du Tastevin, an order of wine producers and wine lovers whose motto is 'Jamais en vain, toujours en vin' (never in vain, always in wine) dress in their spectacular costumes and hold a banquet in their ancient Clos Vougeot vineyards built originally by St Bernard's Cistercian monks. After the wine sales, a candlelit dinner is held in one of the huge cellars of Beaune's town walls. On Monday, the feasting moves to our favourite little village of Meursault, where 300 growers each take two of their best bottles and demolish them at another banquet. But Les Trois Glorieuses is no longer just a celebration by local growers and their best clients: it has become a prestige occasion for the famous, the rich and well-connected, and that weekend Beaune is no place for ordinary enthusiastic wine bibbers, for every hotel bed and restaurant seat is booked months ahead.

The festival of small growers, vineyard workers and visiting wine lovers is St Vincent Tournante in January—a true one where we are *all* welcome (see box, p 37).

2. A Little History

Burgundy

The wars between Burgundy and France

Wars between Burgundy and France started with a family squabble. For centuries afterwards most people of Burgundy thought of themselves as Burgundians first and Frenchmen by accident. The Nazis were so sure that Burgundy longed to be free of France again that when they occupied the region in 1940 Himmler wanted to form a Burgundian state, based on the old Duchy and consisting of Burgundy, Belgium, Luxembourg, Franche-Comté and Switzerland, with its own army, currency and laws. 'What has France done for Burgundy except pickle it in wine?' he asked. He had, of course, completely misunderstood the Burgundian people. He could hardly have done more to encourage recruitment in the Resistance movement, which was already being organised by the socialists and communist steelworkers of Nièvre, the supporters of De Gaulle in the socialist Morvan and the Catholic followers of Dijon's courageous cleric-mayor, Canon Felix Kir.

The original argument which split France and Burgundy started in the French Valois royal family. The death of the Capetian Duke Philip of Rouvres in 1361 had ended Burgundy's Ducal line and France ruled the region. The great victory of the English Black Prince at Poitiers in 1356 had resulted in the French King John the Good being taken prisoner. With him was his fourth son, 14-year-old Prince Philip, who slapped the face of an English knight for not showing deference to the King of France even when in captivity. It was the King of England, Edward III, who nicknamed the lad Philip the Bold. For his courage in captivity, his father gave him the title of Duke of Burgundy when it fell vacant. The King and his son were ransomed but France was so poor after its disastrous wars and the horrors of the Black Death that King John could not keep up the instalments on his ransom so, in the chivalrous tradition of the time, he returned to England and gave himself up. In the same courteous tradition, Edward gave a great banquet for his returned royal prisoner, but he was too hospitable with the drink. King John dropped dead at the height of the party.

Philip's elder brother, Charles V, became King of France and Philip was left with a hollow title to a near-bankrupt dukedom and no means of support. Margaret, daughter of the Count of Flanders and one of the richest heiresses in Europe, was widowed. When her father died, she would inherit the rich province of Flanders, which included much of what is now Belgium and Holland, plus Artois, Nevers and Franche-Comté. However, she was rather ugly. Resigning himself to this fact, Philip pawned his gold plate and jewels and borrowed wherever he could find money for the wedding, and set about pleasing the old Count (her father) by putting down uprisings of Flemish citizens, especially the independent townsmen of Ghent. He was rewarded in 1384 when the Count died. He lived in Dijon and spent a lot of Margaret's money extending and improving the Ducal Palace, and bringing in Flemish craftsmen and artists to beautify his capital.

His brother, Charles V of France, had died in 1380 and Philip, who was by now esteemed as a statesman, became the leader of the Regency Council which ruled France for the new King Charles VI, who was only 12 years old. Even after Charles became of age, it was obvious that he was unbalanced and could not rule without regents. He suffered frequent attacks of paranoid delusions, finally deciding that he was made of glass. Duke Philip the Bold of Burgundy virtually ruled France until his death in 1404—which he found very convenient because he was able to pay himself a 'salary' of about half the royal income from rents and taxes! Despite this looting of France's exchequer and his wife's vast assets, Philip died owning vast lands but with no cash. His gold and silver plate was sold to pay for his funeral.

When he died, the Regency of France was taken by Charles VI's brother, the notorious but popular rake Louis, Duke of Orléans, who counted among his mistresses Queen Isabella of France, Charles VI's wife and his own sister-in-law.

His cousin, John the Fearless, the new Duke of Burgundy, was determined to be Regent. The cousins hated each other and in 1407 John of Burgundy had Louis of Orléans ambushed in a dark alley and bludgeoned to death. This started a near civil war in France as Louis' father-in-law, Bernard of Armagnac, took up the fight. All Frenchmen were divided between Burgundians and Armagnacs in a most extraordinary way. In Paris, the University backed the Burgundians, the clergy backed the Armagnacs. To make life more complicated, Henry V of England invaded France, claiming back the old English lands, and his crushing victory at Agincourt in 1415 left France in chaos.

In Paris, John of Burgundy had recruited the butchers of Les Halles, the great market, as strong-arm men, using them as bodyguards and gangs to attack and frighten Armagnac supporters. They led the *coup* in 1418 when John won control of Paris, with great slaughter of Armagnacs.

On 10 September 1419 a meeting was held on a bridge over the Yonne at Montereau, south of Paris, to try to arrange peace between John and the Dauphin (Joan of Arc's 'gentil' Dauphin, who later became Charles VII of France). Charles, in his 'gentil' manner, arranged for one of his knights to murder the Burgundy Duke with a hachet.

The new Duke, John's son Philip the Good, set out to avenge his father's murder. He made an alliance with England, signing a treaty with Henry V and

Queen Isabella, wife of the mentally deranged Charles VI, declaring that the Dauphin Charles was the illegitimate son of the Queen's adultery and therefore was *not* the Dauphin. The treaty recognised Henry of England as the true heir to the French throne, arranged Henry's marriage with Charles VI's daughter and made him Regent of France until Charles VI's death. Henry, however, was murdered by a fanatical Jesuit monk.

The Dauphin Charles himself had doubts about his own legitimacy—not surprising, considering his mother's reputation—and hid in the Loire valley. It took the peasant girl from Lorraine, Joan of Arc, to persuade him that God had told her he was the true heir and that he was to give her an army to drive out his enemies and put him on the throne. It was the Burgundians who finally captured Joan of Arc at Compiègne and sold her to the English.

The Dauphin made peace with Philip the Good by recognising the virtual independence of the Burgundian Duchy, which stretched through Artois and Picardie to Flanders, nearly all of what is now Belgium, much of Holland and Luxembourg, Burgundy itself and Franche-Comté. Philip had palaces in Lille, Ghent, Brussels, Bruges and Hesdin, and although in documents he referred to Dijon as his capital, he in fact ruled from Brussels, for his power and wealth were centred in the Netherlands. His son, Charles the Rash, extended his empire to the rest of Holland into what is now Germany, Lorraine and Upper Alsace. But he overreached himself: in 1477 he was killed in a battle to hold Lorraine. His heir was his 19-year-old daughter, Mary. It was a wonderful opportunity for the cunning Louis XI of France to invoke the French Salic Law, which stated that women could not inherit, and to grab all the Burgundian lands his army could occupy. He took the Duchy of Burgundy, Artois, Picardie and Franche-Comté. Mary quickly married the German Emperor Maximilian of Hapsburg, whom she had intended to marry earlier. The Emperor failed to hold Burgundy against Louis but held Flanders and Mary's non-French lands.

Louis was clever enough to grant Burgundy special privileges, and as the people were not very keen to become part of the Holy Roman Empire—the German empire—Burgundy reverted to the French crown.

Burgundy's early history

The first Burgundians came from the Baltic Scandinavian island of Bornholm (Burgundarholm). The Romans called them Burgundiones. They crossed into the Middle Rhine around the fifth century as the western Roman Empire was in decline, but in AD 436 were utterly defeated by Attila's Huns and their King Gunther was killed. The defeat is described in the first story of the 13th century poem of the legend of the *Niebelungenlied*. The survivors of the tribe settled near Lake Geneva and became allies of the Romans in their fight against the invading German tribes. By AD 470 they were strong enough to take Lyon and then took over most of Switzerland and much of what is now Eastern France.

They did not mix with other people in the area but were Romanised quickly and by AD 500 had produced a version of Roman law for their people. They adopted Arian Christianity—Arians believed that the son of God was not divine—in preference to Catholicism. But the Merovingian kings took them over with the whole of Gaul and they became part of Charlemagne's huge empire. Burgundy, now much smaller, came under the Franks. The murderous raids by Scandinavian Norsemen in the 9th century drove monks from the western areas to take refuge in Burgundy and the great Burgundian abbeys became powerful, their schools spreading learning and culture through Western Europe. The abbey at Cluny put Burgundy at the head of Christendom. It had 1450 dependent abbeys and monasteries around Europe, with 10,000 monks, and was also one of the greatest artistic centres. The abbeys' wealth made Burgundy prosperous.

The dukes of Burgundy

In 1031 Robert, second son of the French king, was made Duke of Burgundy, starting the 300-year line of Capetian Dukes, named after the Capets, kings of France. They were a colourful lot. The first, Robert, contemporary of William the Conqueror, divorced his wife in a great scandal, killed his father-in-law, then walked to Rome to receive absolution from the Pope. Another suddenly gave up the job of Duke and became a monk; most of them fell out with the church and were excommunicated; and two married into the French royal family. Suddenly, in 1361, the young Duke, Philip of Rouvres, died of the plague and the French kings came to power again.

When King John of France rewarded his son Philip the Bold for his courage as a fellow prisoner in England by making him the first Valois Duke of Burgundy, no one would have believed that both the Burgundian dukes and Burgundy itself were to become great enemies of France.

Though Philip the Bold lived ostentatiously and ran through vast fortunes he did not outpace his grandson Philip the Good in showmanship. Philip the Good had palaces in six towns. The greatest artists of the time worked for him; painters and sculptors decorated his palaces, poets and musicians were kept at his Court. The painter Jan van Eyck was an important courtier, treated like a noble and entrusted with delicate diplomatic missions.

To celebrate his marriage with Isabella of Portugal, Philip founded the Order of the Golden Fleece, still one of the most exclusive in Europe. It was created in honour of 'God, the Virgin Mary, and St Andrew' (his patron saint), and its motto was 'Autre n'auray' (not for others). Members dressed in scarlet tunics trimmed with squirrel fur and similar long cloaks. When a member died, his heirs had to send his necklace medallion and fleece costume back to the Grand Master of the Order.

As well as great works of art, Philip collected practical jokes, such as bridges that collapsed and dropped you in the water if you stepped on them, or sprays which wet ladies from underneath if they trod on the pad. He also collected mistresses—30 were publicly acknowledged. His son Charles the Rash led a flamboyant daily life. Each meal was a banqueting ceremony. He

Swearing on a Pheasant

Duke Philip the Good's banquet of the Vow of the Pheasant, which he gave at Lille in 1454, made even the most ostentatious Hollywood parties of the 1950s and 1960s seem like mere picnics. The Turks had recently captured Constantinople and Philip held the party to boast that he would lead a crusade to get it back. He and all the knights present competed to make fanciful vows of what great deeds they would perform.

The decorations were living tableaux. The writer Olivier de la Marche appeared as the Holy Church, riding in a tower on an elephant's back. The tables were centred on extraordinary live scenes, such as a wood with wild animals, a meadow, rocks and fountain, a fully rigged ship, Lusignan castle, a church with an organ and choir, sharing the music with a 28-piece orchestra concealed in a pie.

Eating and drinking must have ranged from the hazardous to the intolerably noisy. Then the King-at-Arms brought in a live pheasant wearing a necklace of precious stones and each knight had to announce what remarkable feats he would perform. Philip himself swore to challenge the Grand Turk to single combat. What he *did* do was to impose such heavy taxes on his people to pay for his extravagances that the city of Ghent started a revolution in his Flemish provinces. He killed 20,000 people to put it down. Philip the Good was not good for all his subjects.

had musicians and poets to sing or tell stories of chivalry, romance and heroic deeds for an hour or two each night before he went to bed. He played several musical instruments. He must have been the only Burgundian Duke, almost the only Burgundian, to water his wine. His court thought him odd for not having a mistress. He longed to be a conquering hero and a king, and he resented deeply the cunning King of France, Louis XI. He did extend his Empire into what is now Germany, Lorraine and Upper Alsace. He married an English princess, Margaret of York, to gain an English alliance, but Louis bribed Edward IV of England not to invade France.

Charles once tricked Louis into visiting him for a conference to forge an alliance, met the French king personally on his arrival, and on pretence of showing him to his lodgings, locked him up in a tower. He then had Louis driven in a simple cart through the streets, forcing him to shout 'Long Live Burgundy!'

Charles's mistake was that, instead of killing his enemy, he treated the whole thing as a joke and released Louis, who, of course, never forgot the insult.

The Hapsburg Emperor Frederick, desperately short of money, with his German Empire besieged on one side by the Turks, suggested that Charles's daughter Mary should marry his son Maximilian to cement a massive alliance. All was arranged. Charles was to be crowned King of Burgundy. The guests had arrived from all over Europe. Lavish and very expensive entertainment had been provided. Then, for some reason, Frederick and his son slipped away in the night. Perhaps Frederick guessed that Charles was a spent force. Soon Louis XI bribed Swiss mercenaries to do France's fighting against Charles in Lorraine. Louis's armies won the battle. Charles's stripped body, partly eaten by wolves, was found in a frozen pond.

Burgundy's losses

During the Revolution, the destruction of the beautiful and once-powerful old abbeys of Burgundy was zealously wanton. Cluny, greatest of all, was sold to a property asset stripper from Mâcon who pulled it down systematically for building materials. The very name of Burgundy officially disappeared under the Revolutionary division of France into 90 départements.

Champagne-Ardennes

Invaders

Before 58 BC, when the Romans made the river Meuse the boundary of their Gaulish empire, then later from the end of Charlemagne's rule until the Nazi defeat a thousand years afterwards foreign invaders from the north and east have poured into the Champagne. Here in battle after battle, the history of Europe and even the world was changed.

The Roman roads soon built up prosperous trade, with Reims and Langres as the main centres. Then in the middle of the third century St Remi, bishop of Reims, converted Clovis, king of the Franks, to Christianity and in AD 451 these Gallo-Roman Christians, under a Roman General Aetius, achieved the extremely rare feat of beating the invading Huns of Attila, the 'Flail of God', in a big battle near Châlons.

Finally the French were obliged to fortify the Ardennes to keep out the armies of the Hapsburg German-Spanish Empire. Vauban, Louis XIV's great military architect, who surrounded the French kingdom with a cordon of fortresses, built some of his strongest defences here.

At the top of the spur of land at the north of the French Ardennes, which pokes provocatively into Belgium, is the charming old town of Givet, beside the Meuse. Dominating it is a less charming but extremely formidable fortress called Charlemont. It was built in 1555 by Charles V, the powerful Hapsburg ruler of the German-Spanish Empire, who had made a treaty with England's Henry VIII in opposition to France's François I. Southward, François' successor Henri II built an equally formidable star-shaped fort at Rocroi, scowling defiantly towards Charlemont.

Vauban turned both fortresses into complete towns, able to withstand a long siege or the strongest attack. Rocroi, and the French crown, had had a

The Coronation of the Virgin from the gable of the central portal of Reims Cathedral—a copy of the original which is in the Palais du Tau

very narrow escape in 1643. Louis XIII had died a few days before and the five-year-old Louis XIV had succeeded him as King of France. His mother, Anne of Austria, was Regent and Cardinal Mazarin, her favourite, had taken power. The German-Spanish Empire grabbed the chance to invade from the north.

The French forces were commanded by the 21-year-old Duke of Enghien, future Prince of Condé and known in history as Le Grand Condé. The Spanish were commanded by a renowned soldier, Francisco Mellos. Their experienced infantry were believed to be invincible. Soon the French left flank was surrounded and the battle already seemed lost. In a manoeuvre which military experts then and since have called foolhardy, the young Condé moved all his right-flank reserves across the Spanish army and threw them in on the left. Twice they were thrown back. The third time they broke through, utterly defeating the Spanish and killing Mellos. Condé won one big battle after another, even changing sides after falling out with the powerful Cardinal Mazarin, then returning to fight for France. Military experts still insist that his successes came from fiery energy, not military talent.

The excellent Ardennes-Français tourist office in Charleville-Mézières offers a series of historic routes for visitors. The Route des Fortifications, which includes Givet and Rocroi, is much more interesting than it sounds and gives a very clear picture of what the people of Champagne have suffered through generations. In Bazeilles south of Sedan is the Maison de la Dernière Cartouche, where a company of French soldiers fought to the last cartridge in the Franco-Prussian War of 1870 after being ordered to cover a retreat by a Command which had failed to blow up a vital bridge over the Meuse. The bullet-ridden house contains a most interesting collection of period military equipment. At Sedan you can see the largest medieval castle in Europe, at readiness for centuries for attacks which never came. The most modern of the historic fortresses on the tour was not built until 1939—a sad monument to outdated thinking and obstinate optimism. Near Villy-la-Ferté, a village south of Carignan on the north-eastern border of Ardennes and Alsace, the French built a large pillbox fort called *Ouvrage 505*. This was part of the 'invincible' Maginot Line—the string of concrete forts and underground passages which, despite all the warning books and articles already written about modern mobile warfare and 'blitzkrieg', the French High Command believed would save France from Hitler.

The invading German armoured divisions came this way in 1940 on their rush to Paris and the Channel ports. Fort 505 was one of a handful which defied their tanks. Armed only with a 7.5cm gun against the heavy armoured guns of the Germans, the 104 French soldiers withstood days of shelling, though every hatch was blown out. Ironically it was not this battering that beat them. Their air-filtration system broke down. All of them were killed by carbon-monoxide fumes from grenades.

Warring countries, warring religions

Like much of France, the Champagne was devastated during the Hundred Years War, not only by the invading English troops, who nearly took Reims in 1360, but by looting French troops and above all by Les Routiers, the mercenaries of the French robber barons who fought for anyone who would gain them money or loot and terrorised the French countryside. And the great plague, the Black Death, left whole villages completely abandoned and the countryside overgrown. The towns became half-deserted, too. Only 2000 people remained in Châlons and 3000 in Troyes by 1480.

When Joan of Arc finally persuaded the Dauphin to be crowned Charles VII in Reims cathedral in 1429, the tide had turned against the English, although peace did not come to all France until 1453. Just over 100 years later war broke out again—between France's Catholics and Protestants. And the spark that lit the fire came with a visit by the belligerent, ardently Catholic soldier François, Duc de Guise. Returning from a visit to his mother at the family château in Joinville, he went to the village of Wassy which he owned. It was Sunday, 1 March 1562. The villagers had been converted to the Reformed Religion and had been holding a prayer meeting in a big glade. The duke's soldiers broke up the meeting and massacred anyone they could catch. The Protestants of France, already suffering persecution, were enraged, and combat flared into battle and one of France's bloodiest wars.

Bubbles of success

After Louis XIV was crowned at Reims in 1654, relative peace came to Champagne and in a cellar of the Abbey of Hautvillers, 6km north of Epernay, a monk made a discovery which brought almost as much good to Champagne as constant wars have done harm. Dom Pérignon discovered the secret of double fermentation in bottles of wine. Champagne bubbles have brought more fame and prosperity to the region than any other industry.

The man who saved Louis XIV from bankruptcy as his chief minister, Jean-Baptiste Colbert, was born in Reims of a successful local money dealer. He forced most Frenchmen to pay their taxes, imprisoned dishonest administrators, encouraged arts and science, built up industries (including the arms industry in Charleville), and gave France a very powerful navy. Alas, his efforts were thwarted by the extravagance of the court and especially of Louis himself.

Napoleon's skirmishes

Napoleon fought battle after battle in the Champagne against the Prussians and Austrians, in 1814, but most of them were skirmishes. Outnumbered, he lost a battle in March 1814 at Arcis-sur-Aube (birthplace of the Revolutionary leader Danton—see box, p 96) and the Allies were able to march on Paris, which capitulated.

In 1870 Napoleon III was forced to fight *his* battles against the Prussians in Champagne, too. He had hoped to cross the Rhine and challenge them there. The short campaign was a French disaster. Napoleon, with 83,000 other Frenchmen, was taken prisoner after capitulating at Sedan.

Battles and bombardments

Sedan was where the Nazis broke through in May 1940. It was occupied by the Germans in World War I, when two decisive battles were fought in the Marne. After the north of Champagne had been devastated, the battle settled into trench warfare from September 1914 to May 1918 along a line from near Verdun westward through Vitry-le-François, Coulommiers and Meaux (the Brie cheese area). To hold the line in 1914, reinforcements were rushed in 600 Paris taxis and a fleet of London buses. A British breakthrough forced the Germans back to river Aisne. A huge attack in June 1918 by the Germans broke through in the centre to the edge of Château Thierry. It was a very dangerous situation for the Allies and only advances nearly everywhere else held the line until the Armistice in November 1918.

Reims was always about a mile from the German line and suffered terrible artillery bombardment for 49 months. Only 3000 of its 15,000 houses survived. The people who remained spent much of their time hiding in the massive wine caves under the city, and at one time the city was evacuated. On 14 September 1944, the French army under Général de Lattre de Tassigny, which had landed in Provence from North Africa with the British and Americans, met up with Général Leclerc's Armoured Division, which had landed just after D-Day on the Normandy coast near St Lô. They met at a hamlet called Nod-sur-Seine, just south of Châtillon-sur-Seine. From there they drove towards the Champagne vineyards. A wartime legend says that there was a hold-up before the Allied Forces reached them. A French liaison officer warned against rushing headlong into a Nazi trap. By a strange and fortuitous coincidence, by the time the French agreed that it was safe to drive ahead, the Champagne harvest was safely gathered. It was fitting, perhaps, that on 7 May 1945 General Eisenhower, Allied Supreme Commander, received the German Surrender in Reims—in a technical college. Most of his Allied fighting men would have chosen the caves of Pommery Champagne as being more appropriate.

3. Wines

Champagne

We were once drinking Champagne before luncheon at Moët et Chandon's delightful Château de Saran near Epernay when an urbane Frenchman said to us suddenly 'I have just had a terrible thought. If you Protestants had beaten Richelieu at Rochelle, we should never have had champagne to drink.'

'Why ever not?' Arthur asked.

'You would have closed the monasteries. Dom Pérignon would never have had the chance to discover the champagne method in his abbey cellars.'

We feel sure that *somebody* would have discovered the way to 'marry' wines and control the second fermentation, even if he had been a Protestant, but Château de Saran is too delightful a place and the champagne was too good to start an argument. But we have often wondered whether the patient old 17th century monk cellarman of the Abbey of Hautvillers would have approved of the image that his wonderful wine has gained through the centuries. He was surely not seeking the wine of celebration and seduction—the perfect appetiser for food and love.

In the wild days of Versailles, under the Regency of Philippe, Duc d'Orléans, champagne seems to have been a compulsory accompaniment to promiscuity. Strange that it was used later to toast the bride and groom! Edward VII's *affaires* prospered under the influence of Joseph Perrier champagne. More recently the film star Marilyn Monroe blossomed for long on Piper-Heidsieck, taking a quarter-bottle for breakfast, a half-bottle for luncheon and a bottle or two for dinner. Winston Churchill loved Pol Roger so much that when he died Madame Odette Pol Roger put a black edge round the label. Before Waterloo, Napoleon said of champagne 'In victory you deserve it. In defeat you need it.' When he visited Moët et Chandon's cave in Epernay he so enjoyed the wine that he left his hat behind. It is still there, in the little wine museum. The Duke of Wellington took *his* hat with him. He might have drunk less Moët, or perhaps he was used to something stronger—port, which he did not water as Napoleon watered the superb Chambertin Burgundy which he even took to Moscow.

Three grapes are used for champagne—Pinot Noir black grapes which give the wine body and life, Pinot Meunier black grapes which bring quicker ageing, and Chardonnay white grapes, which give it lightness, freshness and elegance. Most wines are a blend of black and white but Blanc de Blancs is made solely from white grapes. It is lighter, and makes a splendid apéritif.

About 1.66kg (3½lb) of grapes are needed to produce one bottle. The grapes are grown on a chalky soil, well drained, and they are hand-picked, only the best being used for champagne. They they are pressed and left to ferment in large metal vats (205-litre/54 gallon oak casks were used in our youth!). They ferment for several weeks, producing a still, cloudy wine. During the winter, the lees separate and fall to the bottom.

Now the blenders assess the young wine from each vineyard. Nearly all the champagne we drink is a blend of many vineyards. If the wine is quite exceptional, a 'vintage' is declared and you will see the year of production on your bottle. After the blending a little cane sugar and yeast is added, the wine is bottled, corked and stacked on its side *sur lattes* in the dark cool cellars. A second slow fermentation starts in the bottle, the sugar is turned into alcohol and carbonic gas which gives the champagne its fizz. The wine stays like this for a minimum of 12 months but for around three years for top grade champagnes.

This second fermentation causes a deposit to form. To remove this the bottles are placed in racks with the necks tilted slightly downwards. Each day, over several months, an expert (called *Le Remueur*) shakes the bottle gently, gives it a 45 degree turn and gradually increases the tilt until the bottle is nearly vertical, cork down. To watch these men working at high speed, using both hands, is almost bewildering. They can handle 20,000–30,000 bottles a day. But, alas, that is not considered to be enough, and already someone has invented a 'riddling' machine called a *gyropalette*—a cage holding 40 dozen bottles set to do the work electronically. Riddling is followed by the *dégorgement* (getting rid of the deposit). This was very tricky until someone thought of freezing the neck of the bottle. A small block of ice forms, containing the deposit. When the cork is removed, the ice block shoots out. The space in the bottle is then filled with *liqueur* (old champagne mixed with cane sugar)—called the *dosage*. The amount of sugar controls the type of champagne—*brut* (very dry, once called the Englishman's champagne), *sec* (medium dry), *demi-sec* (sweeter) or *doux* (sweet). Then a new cork is put in, wired, and the champagne is ready to drink—or to be kept lying down in a cool, dark place.

Champagne rosé (pink champagne) popular in Edwardian days and again in the 1920s, was back in fashion in Paris a few years ago, mostly for the improbable reason that pink had become a fashionable colour for clothes and magazines could headline stories 'La Vie en Rose'! The British and American magazines fell quickly into line. Pink is made usually by leaving the two black-skinned grapes, Pinot Noir and Pinot Meunier, in contact with the original grape juice to produce a pale rose-coloured wine. We find non-vintage rosé champagne a poor substitute for a Chardonnay Blanc de Blancs, but we have had vintage Moët and Rothschild rosés which were worthy to be drunk with cold red meat.

The village of Bouzy produces a much more definitive rosé champagne by adding during blending some of its famous Bouzy still red wine. The result is surprisingly pleasant. We have grown to like the red Bouzy though it is lighter than most Côte d'Or reds of Burgundy and pricier than most Côtes de Nuits or Côte de Beaune.

Still white wines of champagne may not be called champagne these days but must be called Coteaux Champenois. They are pleasant, refreshing, and have more body than the ordinary run of A.C. Chablis from Burgundy, although made from similar Chardonnay grapes grown on the same lime-stone-clay soil of the Kimmeridgian clay which runs through many of the champagne villages to Chablis. Coteaux Champenois is not a cheap wine, so beware the mistake of an editor we know who thinks that anyone who drinks anything better than a simple Vin de Pays is a wine snob. He walked into a village inn on the N51, brusquely ordered Vin de Pays and found himself paying about £10 for a vintage Coteaux Champenois. We *did* enjoy it!

About 220 million bottles of champagne are made each year. About 15,000 vignerons grow the grapes and more than half of those own less than 1 hectare. Nearly half of the grapes grown are sold to the big champagne houses, the négociant-shippers such as Moët et Chandon, Mumm, Lanson and the rest, or to cooperatives of small growers who have not the capital to produce and market wine. Until recently very little land was actually owned by the big négociant-shippers, but they have increased their stake lately, especially in areas where the grapes are officially ranked as grand cru ('hors classe'). They are Ambonnay, Avize, Ay, Beaumont-sur-Vesle, Bouzy, Chouilly, Cramant, Louvois, Le Mesnil-sur-Oger, Oger, Oiry, Mailly, Puisieulx, Sillery, Tours-sur-Marne, Verzy and Verzenay. Of these, Bouzy produces particularly powerful, intense wines, rich in bouquet, body and alcohol—so outstanding that the leading champagne houses have found it necessary to own their own vineyards in or around the village so that they do not have to compete in bidding for the grapes or wines. These are particularly vital for blending into richly flavoured wines such as Bollinger, Veuve-Cliquot and Pommery, although Moët, Lanson, Mumm and Heidsieck are among those who find it necessary to own Bouzy vineyards to use the wine for blending. We love to drink the Bouzy champagne neat. You can taste the Herbert Beaufort wines in its pleasant little tasting room in rue des Tours, Bouzy, including its renowned still Bouzy red.

The first of the three major routes around these villages starts at La Montagne de Reims, south of Reims, and passes through Rilly-la-Montagne, then Ludes, where Canard Duchêne has its caves and receives casual visitors on weekdays. Next come Mailly-Champagne, a big vineyard with an excellent cooperative of growers; Verzenay, where the Pinot Noir grapes give its wine a flavour to rival Bouzy; Verzy and the Ambonnay, with excellent local wines which can be tasted at Margaret Vonnerave's rather posh cave and shop 100m from *Auberge St Vincent*, where the food is excellent. Then Bouzy, from where you can choose between a route through Louvois in a forested valley protected with vineyards on the slopes or joining the Marne canal and river at Tours-sur-Marne with vineyards to the north and the champagne house of Laurent Perrier in the village. You follow the Marne to Ay, home village of Bollinger, Ayala and Deutz, then on to Epernay.

Marc Herbrart uses traditional machinery for corking his champagne at Mareuil

The valley of the Marne route has fewer champagne villages but many other interesting sights. You can start at Tours-sur-Marne, then follow the D1 to Ay (see above) and Dizy, taking the RD386 to Hautvillers, where Dom Pérignon tamed the bubbles in a bottle. We have been lucky enough to see the abbey cellars where he performed his miracle, though few guests are invited. There is not room for them. There is a new museum which you might see by applying to the owners, Moët et Chandon in Epernay (see p 85). But local producers are open for *dégustation et vente* (tasting and sales). Southward at Cumières are champagne producers and *Le Caveau*, a restaurant in an old wine cave which is popular with people from Epernay. The route continues north of the Marne to Châtillon, with the well-known cave of Jacky Charlier at Montigny-sous-Châtillon, and three small producers at Vandières. Route D1 continues through Verneuil and Vincelles to Dormans.

The third route south of Epernay is through the Côtes des Blancs, the mainly Chardonnay-growing area which produces excellent Blanc de Blancs champagne. From Pierry on the N51, where Gobillard has a wine cave in the château, you turn south-east along the D10 through a series of champagne-producing villages. In Cuis, we have found excellent wine at De Blémond cave. Cramant produces wines with a striking bouquet, and most big houses own vineyards here, including Moët, Mumm, which produces a renowned Crémant de Cramant (not quite so fizzy) and Perrier Jouet, Queen Victoria's favourite. Avize's Chardonnay grapes are much praised in the wine business and you can buy several single-village champagnes there, including Agrapart et Fils. Union Champagne is a cooperative of 1000 growers. Alas, the village has dropped its pagan custom 'Salut au Soleil du 1er Mars' when on 1 March the young ladies encouraged the coming of spring by lying naked on the slopes of Mont Aimé. The villages of Oger and Mesnil-sur-Oger are said to produce the best Chardonnay champagne (Blanc de Blancs) and certainly Veuve Cliquot and Krug have had vineyards there for years. Krug produces a single-village wine called Clos de Mesnil which is excellent. Several local producers are in avenue de la République and welcome visitors. At Bergère-lès-Vertus, follow the RD33 to Etoges where a minor road takes you to Congy (visit Breton et Fils) and Courjeonnet (visit Ragot Nomine). Go west to the RD51 main road to Epernay, where there are many wine producers on or near the road.

You can get a map and pamphlet of the three routes in Epernay from Comité Interprofessionel du Vin de Champagne, 5 rue Henri Martin, 51200 Epernay (tel. 26 54 47 20) or Office de Tourisme, 7 ave de Champagne, 51200 Epernay (tel. 26 55 33 00).

Very many of the small producers offer tastings and sales. Of the big companies, some do organise visits for wine enthusiasts, others offer visits by arrangement (mostly for the trade) and many only accept trade visitors. You can get a list at the Epernay wine and tourist offices (see above) and in Reims from the Office de Tourisme, 1 rue Jadot, 51100 Reims (tel. 26 47 25 69).

Moët et Chandon in Epernay (18 ave de Champagne, tel. 26 54 71 11) is best organised for visits. This was founded in 1743 by Moët, which took over after the French Revolution the very vineyards and cellars in the Abbey of Hautvillers where Dom Pérignon worked. Moët still owns them and the monk's statue stands outside its Epernay caves. Moët is the biggest champagne company and now part of the Moët-Hennessy empire, which owns also Hennessy brandy, Mercier and Ruinart (the oldest champagne négociant, founded 1729) and part of Christian Dior perfume, plus huge vineyards in Napa Valley, California. Moët is the most popular champagne in France, Britain and the US and is exported to 150 countries. 'Somewhere in the world, a Moët et Chandon cork pops every two seconds', and we do our little bit to help. Visits are excellently organised, with tastings at the end (Mon–Fri all year 09.30–12.30, 14.00–17.30; 1 Apr–31 Oct also Sat, Sun). Conducted tours are in French, English, German, Spanish, Dutch, Polish or Russian, and you learn a surprising amount about champagne making. There are 28km of maturing bottles but you skip some and go round by train.

Champagne Secret

Initials on a champagne label can tell you secrets of its production. If it was made by a grower from his own grapes, the label will be marked RM (recoltant-manipulant), R means a grower's special brand limited to 500 bottles, SR means made by a company of growers from the same family, NM (négociant-manipulant) means that it is made by one of the champagne houses—by far the majority of champagnes, CM (cooperative-manipulant) means made by a growers' cooperative. MA (marque acheteur) means buyer's own brand (or BOB in Britain— such as brands with supermarket names or big wine merchants). The initials are printed very small, usually in a corner.

Mercier (75 ave de Champagne, tel. 26 54 75 26, same opening times as Moët) has a mere 18km of galeries, but still takes you round by train. Beside a museum of wine presses is the largest wine cask in the world. Made in 1899 for the Paris Exposition, it is beautifully carved and needed 24 oxen to pull it through Paris streets. It holds 200,000 bottles—the perfect birthday present.

In Reims, a visit to Pommery is most rewarding, 5 place du Général Giraud; take bd Henri Vasnier towards Châlons—tel. 26 05 05 01—phoning helps, but is not necessary. (Open weekdays 09.00–11.00, 14.00–17.00, or weekends at 10.00, 11.00, 14.30, 15.30, 16.30.) The huge cellars, reached by 116 steps, are decorated with chiselled bas-reliefs. They are beneath the old château headquarters built in the last century by Louise Pommery, widow of the founder. Opposite is the later Pommery family residence and park, now housing Gérard and Elyane Boyer's superb hotel-restaurant *Les Crayères*. In the cellars is a cask beautifully sculpted in 1903 by Gallé and holding 100,000 bottles.

Louise Pommery pioneered dry and brut champagne when others made only sweet. Its famous wine is now Brut Royal.

Near to Pommery is Piper Heidsieck where you tour cellars, containing 16 million bottles, in an electric train (51 bd Henri Vasnier—tel. 26 85 01 94. Open weekdays 09.30–11.30, 14.00–17.30, also weekends from end March to early November. English-speaking guides). Some unusual cuvées are produced, such as *Champagne Rare*, made only in the greatest years. The first bottle was presented in 1775 to Queen Marie-Antoinette, who lost her head in the Revolution. Another unusual wine is *Champagne Sauvage*, absolutely brut-dry with no topping-up sugar at all, aged in opaque bottles to retain its delicacy.

Sauvage was produced originally for *La Tour d'Argent*, the Paris restaurant where they number ducks and you choose your own before it is cooked. Piper-Heidsieck has run its own wars against German occupying forces. The family refused to collaborate with occupying Prussians in 1870, so Prince Hohenlowe let his troops pillage the cellars. In 1916 German artillery deliberately shelled the cellars. In 1943 the boss of Piper-Heidsieck, the Marquis d'Aulan and his staff hid in the cellars arms dropped by the RAF for the French Resistance. They were betrayed to the Nazis and mostly killed or deported to concentration or labour camps. The Marquis escaped to North Africa where he was killed as a pilot in the Free French Lafayette squadron. His son, Marquis François d'Aulan, lived to revive the company. Britain's Queen Mother, it seems, drinks their rosé champagne with soup while the Queen drinks sweet champagne after her meal. That, anyway, is what Prince Charles told the Marquis.

Châlons-sur-Marne has two champagne houses. Joseph Perrier, which Queen Victoria drank, still produces flowery, delicate, easy-to-drink wine in its 18th century building with cellars in a chalk quarry dug, like most in champagne, by Roman slaves. You must phone to visit (26 68 29 51).

In Aube, around Bar-sur-Aube, Bar-sur-Seine, Mussy-sur-Seine and Les Riceys, are more than 2200 wine growers, of whom 370 grow to produce champagne. More than half their grapes are bought by houses around Epernay and Reims, but just under ten million bottles are made locally, mostly by small family producers. Many did not start making champagne until the 1960s. Among the biggest producers are Cheurlin et Fils at Gye-sur-Seine near Mussy-sur-Seine, a fortified medieval town, Drappier at Urville, Bar-sur-Aube, Bernard Robert Voigny at Bar-sur-Aube, and René Huillier at Fontette near Essoyes, a fortified village where the artist Renoir is buried. The other Aube growers produce mostly still white Coteaux Champenois wines.

A handful of champagne houses are outside the Champagne-Ardennes region in Aisne. The best known is Baron Albert of Porteron, which is in a bend of the river Marne on the D969 south-west of Château Thierry. Baron Albert has been a grower since 1677.

The French are quite bureaucratic about what you should or should not do with champagne. We are in favour of banning those Victorian saucer glasses, from which the bouquet and bubbles soon escape. A traditional *flûte* or a tulip-shaped glass is better. So you are not supposed to ask for a *verre* of champagne but a *coupe* or a *flûte*. We agree with the French way of opening a bottle because it seems to work best. You hold the bottle at 45 degrees, hold the cork firmly in one hand and turn the *bottle* round with the other hand. This should be done nonchalantly, preferably making a joke. According to current Paris-inspired fashion you are not supposed to let the cork pop out with a bang. If you do, you are 'English', 'American' or 'a peasant'. Nonsense! Do as you like—it's your champagne.

Listening to a group of enthusiastic amateurs giving their opinions on different champagnes can be as tiresome as Question Time in the House of Commons. As Jacques Mercier said to Arthur as amateurs argued: 'Let us not *talk* about champagne—let us drink it.' He was absolutely right. The clock pointed to 11.30 am.

Burgundy

No one knows how wine came to Burgundy. Pliny and Plutarch told a story that the Gauls invaded Italy because they thirsted for its wine and when thrown back across the Alps they took vines and the secrets of making wine with them. A Roman romance, it seems. The popular modern belief is that the vine came to Burgundy from the Greek colony of Massilia (Marseille) around 600 BC and that after importing wine from the Aegean in amphorae for some time the Gauls were persuaded to bring back cuttings. Now there is a suggestion that they themselves, in their wanderings, brought back the vine and developed it.

We are just very grateful indeed that wine did come to Burgundy, whoever brought it, and that the Gauls invented the wooden barrel to replace the amphora.

We are also grateful to the monks to whom we owe the beginnings and rise of many of the great vineyards of Burgundy. When parcels of land were given to their monasteries by kings and nobles trying to buy their way to paradise, the monks found that wine was a great cash crop, and they needed cash to build and extend their great monasteries. The monks of the Monastery of Cluny created and extended the vineyards of the Mâconnais in the 10th and 11th centuries, and the strict Cistercians of Pontigny built up Chablis in the 12th century. The Cistercians became renowed as wine producers, showing that poor soil, fit for little else, could produce superb wine. They established a branch of their order at Clos Vougeot.

The harsh order of the Cistercian nuns founded the Abbey of Notre-Dame-du-Tart and bought a vineyard at Morey which they owned until the Revolution and which still produces superb wine. It is called Clos de Tart—an unfortunate name for a nunnery wine when marketed in Britain.

A far earlier claim is made for Aloxe-Corton. Emperor Charlemagne gave

Aloxe (pronounced Alosse) to the monks of Saulieu in AD 775 when he rebuilt their abbey, which had been destroyed by raiding Saracens. Charlemagne drunk so much Aloxe that when he was old his white beard was stained red. It is said that his wife nagged him so much that to appease her he ordered part of the vineyard to be planted with white grapes so that he could drink a non-staining white wine!

Beaune wines were claimed to be the finest reds in France by the beginning of the 13th century, and when the Popes moved their court from Rome to Avignon in 1309, the wines of Burgundy became renowned at the Papal Court, despite the rival claims of Rhône wines. In fact, Petrarch accused the Cardinals of delaying their return to Rome for love of Burgundy wines.

When the Revolution came, the monasteries were disbanded, the nobles who did not lose their heads lost their lands and the big vineyards were broken up and sold to farmers and vineyard workers. Unlike Bordeaux, where the nobles later got back their lands, Burgundy vineyards are still divided among many small growers and often they own parcels of land, sometimes kilometres apart. French inheritance customs, whereby all the children inherit instead of just the eldest son, have helped to keep properties small.

Last century, Burgundy, like all French vineyards, was struck by two disastrous diseases. A powdery mildew (oidium) cut yields right back until the remedy of dusting vines with sulphur was discovered. Then there was the terrible vine louse (phylloxera) in 1875 which killed the vines. It came from the United States and ironically was only cured by grafting on vine stock also imported from the US, which was immune to the pest. Burgundy still has only a quarter of the vine area that it had in 1875.

The growing, production and naming of wines are very strictly controlled under AOC (Appellation d'Origine Contrôlée) laws, including maximum yields for each half hectare, so that abundant harvests do not bring increasingly abundant quantities of wine. The grape varieties are limited: red wines must be made of Pinot Noir grapes or of Gamay, white wines of Chardonnay or Aligoté.

Pinot Noir is used for all the great red wines of Côte de Nuits (just south of Dijon to just north of Beaune), for Côte de Beaune (down to Santenay) and Côte Chalonnaise (further south and including Mercurey). Two-thirds of the red grapes of Mâconnais are Pinot Noir, the other third are Gamay. Pinot Noir, incidentally, produces a white juice—the colour of the wine comes from the skins, which is why the juice can be used for making champagne.

Gamay, the grape of Beaujolais, produces a lighter wine, which is drunk younger and brings quicker cash to the producer, the négociant and even the retailer. In the Côte d'Or, a wine called Bourgogne Passe-Tout-Grains is made of one-third Pinot Noir, two-thirds Gamay.

The best white wines of Chablis, Côte d'Or, Côte Chalonnaise and Mâconnais are made from Chardonnay, the grape which has become so popular in wines of Australia, New Zealand and the US in recent years. It is one of the main grapes of champagne, too. In Chablis it is known locally as Beaunois. Other great Chardonnay wines are Pouilly-Fuissé, Meursault and

Puligny-Montrachet. Chardonnay has spread to south-west France, and although the wines are not of Burgundy standard, they are cheaper and quaffable, so have hit the Burgundy market.

Aligoté is the other white grape used in Burgundy. Wines are not sold under village names, simply as Bourgogne Aligoté, except in the case of the village of Bouzeron, outside Chagny, but you can often tell where it comes from when the producer also bottles it and puts his village on the label. Aligoté is drunk young.

Sparkling wines have been made by the champagne method in Burgundy since 1822, but recently a good Crémant de Bourgogne has been produced. Pinot Noir or Pinot Gris (white), Chardonnay and Aligoté grapes are used. Rully was until recently the great centre for Crémant.

The grades of wine are grand cru, premier cru, Villages AOC (village's name is allowed), and Régional. In the last grade are wines called Bourgogne Hautes Côtes de Beaune, Bourgogne Hautes Côtes de Nuits, Bourgogne Passe-Tout-Grains, Bourgogne Aligoté, Bourgogne Aligoté de Bouzeron, Bourgogne Grand Ordinaire, Bourgogne Rosé and simply Bourgogne. Chablis AOC and Mâcon AOC are regional names, too. Fixin (Côte de Nuits) is allowed its own appellation. Beaujolais has a different system.

Although Pouilly-sur-Loire and its neighbouring wine areas are in Burgundy, the wine is officially a Loire wine.

Some of the villages with great individual vineyards have added the vineyard name to their village name. They include Puligny-Montrachet, Gevrey-Chambertin, Aloxe-Corton and Vosne-Romanée.

Côte de Dijon and Côte de Nuits (Côte d'Or)

The great wine road of Burgundy, from Dijon south, is called Route des Grands Crus, starting on the D122, then joining the N74.

Marsannay, a village of 6000 people, is the only village producing a quantity of wine in the old Côte de Dijon. It produces rosé, and is allowed to use its name—Bourgogne-Marsannay-Rosé. The Pinot Noir grape is used but the skins are removed quickly from the vat. Domaine Clair-Daü and Domaine Bruno Clair both produce a wine with a lovely strawberry flavour and robust enough to stand up to Burgundian dishes. The red also has an earthy flavour. For tasting, Regis Bouvier, 52 rue de Mazy (tel. 80 52 21 37) produces a fruity red called Clos du Roi, in a vineyard known since the Middle Ages and owned by kings of France. Fixin, where the Côte de Nuits begins, is just west of the D122. It produces red wine often underestimated because it is not kept long enough. It can be coarse (*sauvage*) when young, and should be kept five to ten years; then it becomes robust and reliable and goes very nicely with red meats and cheese.

Gevrey-Chambertin on the D122 has more grand cru wines in its commune than any in Burgundy. The sprawling village of Gevrey added the name of its greatest vineyard, Chambertin. The monks of the abbey of Bèze started making wines here and the monks of Cluny controlled the abbey in the Middle Ages and built the château to store and protect their wines. A local story says that a peasant named Bertin copied the methods of the monks in Bèze and his wine became as good as theirs. His vineyard was called Champ de Bertin (Bertin's field) then Chambertin. Le Chambertin is now a truly full-bodied wine, superb with game and roasts. Clos de Bèze is the only wine as great as Chambertin itself and is allowed the title of Chambertin-Clos de Bèze.

Certain surrounding parcels of land are allowed to add the name Chambertin to their own. Latricières-Chambertin is not so powerful as Chambertin but has a lasting flavour. Charmes-Chambertin is best known, less tannic and almost too easy to swallow. It can be drunk younger than the others. Chapelle-Chambertin, with a small production, is very fruity. Other grand cru wines are Griotte-Chambertin, Mazis-Chambertin and Ruchottes-Chambertin. There are 24 premiers crus Gevrey-Chambertin and some, like Clos St Jacques, are almost equal to grand cru wines. The Gevrey vineyards cover 506 ha (1250 acres) and produce 1,900,000 bottles a year.

They proudly tell you in Burgundy that Napoleon loved Chambertin and took a wagon-load of it in his baggage-train wherever he went. What they don't say is that he usually put water in it! Anyway, it must have tasted a little shaken up, especially when he got to Moscow.

Our favourite accolade was given by that great Anglo-French bon vivant Hilaire Belloc, novelist, essayist and poet, who died in 1953. He wrote when he was old that he had dreamed of confessing his sins to St Peter at the Gates of Heaven, though his memory was fading. 'I'm sorry, St Peter,' he said, 'I cannot remember now the name of the French village, nor of the girl, nor even what we ate for dinner. But, my God, the wine was Chambertin!'

The Burgundy poet, Gaston Roupel, a Gevrey man, wrote of the wine, too. 'It blends grace and vigour. It unites firmness with power and finesse ... an admirable synthesis of unique generosity and complete virtue.'

Gevrey spreads so far south that its slopes stretch to those of Morey-St-Denis and Morey shares the same geological make-up. Before the laws of Appellations Contrôlées were passed, Morey wines were sold as Gevrey or as Chambolle, the commune which borders it to the south. So Morey-St-Denis wine is less known than most, underestimated by many and well worth buying.

Clos de Tart, of the old Cistercian convent, and the premier cru wine Clos de la Bussière are both produced in a typical medieval abbey close, completely surrounded by walls to which the old buildings are attached. Clos de Tart has been owned since 1932 by the Mommessin family of Mâcon and Beaujolais fame who use 100 per cent new oak casks every year. The grapes are destalked and undergo long vinification with their skins. This all makes for tannin from the oak when the wine is young. When kept long enough, it has a superb spicy strength of flavour. You can't drink a good Côte de Nuits Burgundy young.

Another Clos owned by a single proprietor is Clos des Lambrays. Watch this wine. It was only made a grand cru in 1981 after a programme of replanting had begun.

Clos St Denis, founded in 1203 as College of St Denis de Vergy, was added to the title of Morey in 1927. It produces a charming wine with finesse. The premiers crus wines have a lot of flavour but are not quite so rich as grands crus. The ordinary Morey wines really taste of fruit and can be absolutely delicious. One of the most respected producers is Jean Taudenot (tel. 80 34 35 24). The main wine route now joins the N74 with sorties westward a few kilometres for some vineyards.

Chambolle-Musigny added the name of its best vineyards, Le Musigny, out of sheer pride. Grand cru Musigny wine has received all the accolades. And, of course, it is very expensive. There are other good wines, too—elegant, not powerful, but having a subtle taste and a gorgeous bouquet. Bernard Amiot produces a straight Chambolle wine with a lovely taste, charming bouquet and a sensible price. The premier cru wines of Les Amoureuses vineyard have more than a charming name.

Clos Vougeot has been famous in Europe since the Hundred Years War. There are 50 ha inside its stone walls. The Cistercian monks who owned them built a fort in 1367 to protect them from roving bands of thirsty French and English soldiers and above all from les routiers, the freelance mercenaries who would fight for either side so long as the loot was good.

In 1790 in the Revolution, all church property was confiscated and auctioned for the nation. Before he handed over the keys, the monk in charge of the cellars, Dom Goblet, is said to have smuggled out enough of the last vintage to satisfy him for life. We feel sure that St Peter forgave him at the Golden Gates. The Clos was bought as a single vineyard, but in 1889 it was broken up. There are now just under 80 owners. This means that even Clos Vougeot wines can vary considerably and picking one, even if you have the money, is not easy. There is a snob value, too, in owning a parcel of the vineyard.

The fine old building is well preserved. Vineyard owners have to keep up the old walls and the rest is the headquarters of a prestigious brotherhood started in 1934 to boost sales of Burgundy during a slump. The Confrérie des Chevaliers du Tastevin originated when wine merchants and growers met at Nuits-St-Georges. In 1944 they bought the Renaissance château of Clos Vougeot as a meeting place for their 'chapters'. Dressed in scarlet and gold robes, the officers of the brotherhood initiate new members at gastronomic banquets with superb wines. They hold about 20 chapters a year. The greatest banquet is on the eve of the Hospice de Beaune sales. On the Monday is the Paulée de Meursault. These events are called Les Trois Glorieuses (three glorious days). The Confrérie also chooses the best wines to carry the Tastevinage label. (Clos open daily except 25 Dec to 2 Jan from 09.00, evening closing time seasonal, tel. 80 62 82 75. Guided half-hour tours followed by a quarter-hour audio-visual story of the Confrérie.)

The Clos is 270m up with a gradual slope to vineyards beside the N74 road. On the whole, higher vines produce better wine. Clos wines are rich. Premier cru wines have less body but still have finesse. Vougeot Village wines are, of course, much cheaper and pleasing, but not exciting.

You are not likely to be asked to taste Clos Vougeot wines but you can taste some very good premier cru wines at Domaine Bertagna in rue du Vieux Château (tel. 80 62 86 04, open 08.00–19.00 every day including Sunday). Les Petits Vougeot wine has superb fruit and a lovely bouquet, Clos de la Perrière is rich.

The village of Flagy-Echézeaux is across the plain between the N74 and the A31 motorway. There are two grand cru wines—Echézeaux and Grands Echézeaux, and straight Flagey wines sold as Vosne-Romanée.

The village of Vosne-Romanée, just off the N74, 2km before you reach Nuits-St-Georges, produces some absolutely magnificent grand cru wines which are extremely pricey. Burgundians say 'If Chambertin is King of wines, Romanée is Queen'. Certainly it is delicate in fragrance, subtle in taste and outstandingly seductive.

Most highly praised is Romanée-Conti, a wine that we have never had the luck or money to taste, though we have tasted La Tâche, which in some years is regarded as better. For over two centuries the Romanée vineyard was owned by a family called Croonembourg and when it was sold in 1760 there was a great rush of buyers. Louis XV's grabbing mistress, La Pompadour, intended to get it but for once was outwitted by the Bourbon Prince of Conti. Now it is owned by a company (Domaine de la Romanée Conti) who own other vineyards of Vosne-Romanée. We have had an excellent Romanée-St-Vivart 1985 (another grand cru Vosne-Romanée).

Richebourg runs Conti and La Tâche very close in some years. Serena Sutcliffe has called it 'velvet come to life'. Arthur remembers especially the sumptuous 1983 of Domaine Jean Gros, also a premier cru Clos des Réas 1985 of the same Domaine—lovely smell and full of flavour. Jean Grivot makes a gorgeous Richebourg, too, and other wines, including a premier cru Les Beaumont. (You can taste some of his wines if you phone 80 61 05 95.) Buying is inevitably costly and you will have to keep it a few years, but what a splendid drink it will be!

Nuits-St-Georges is a delightful town. We love staying in it. It is second to Beaune as a wine trade centre. The wine area stretches for 6.5km, so there is a great deal of wine produced. The best wines have real depth of flavour. They should be kept four to eight years.

When Jules Vernes' heroes landed on the moon, they celebrated by opening a bottle of Nuits-St-Georges. One giant gulp forward for mankind, perhaps.

Louis XIV was advised to drink glasses of Nuits or Romanée with each meal, as a tonic. He probably needed a bottle of two after his activities—the Sun King was so addicted to love-making that when a mistress took a long time preparing her toilette, he would bed her lady-in-waiting to pass the time. Perhaps that is where the title lady-in-waiting came from! Anyway, Louis seems to have had no trouble taking his medicine, and, of course, both wines became fashionable at Court. Wine has been produced from the vineyards since AD 1000.

Nuits wines are rich and intoxicating. Do try a mature Les Vaucrais. Les

St Georges has strength and finesse and is considered to be the supreme Nuits wine. As in Beaune, the hospice owns vineyards and sells its wines at auction each year, usually on the Sunday before Palm Sunday. There is also a white made from Pinot Noir grapes, nothing like Burgundy Chardonnay, nor so good.

Henri Remoriquet produces some of the most respected Saint Georges premier cru and an ordinary AOC Les Allots. Both are fruity and age well. (You can taste Monday to Friday, at his caves, 25 rue de Charmoise, tel. 80 61 08 17.) His grandparents were vineyard workers who saved up to buy a few parcels of vines in 1892. Now he and his son have also started a vineyard in Hautes Côtes de Nuits in the south hills. The family of Xavier Dufouleur, 17 rue Thurot, have been vignerons since the 16th century and made excellent wines traditionally, matured in oak casks and reaching their best in ten to 20 years. (Tastings cave open 08.30–12.00, 14.00–18.00. No need to phone.)

Côte de Beaune (Côte d'Or)

The first great vineyard of the Côte de Beaune is Aloxe-Corton, just north-west of the N74 on the pretty little D18 which runs up into the hills. The village of Aloxe-Corton itself lies beneath a hill (the Massif du Corton) and its beautiful little manor house Château de Corton is almost hidden by vegetation. It is a true working Burgundian wine village, with vines so close to the houses that you could almost pick grapes from the windows.

Le Corton vineyard itself is a narrow strip just beneath the wood which crowns the hill, but the vineyards around it are also able to use the title Corton before their name as they produce such superb red wines. The Corton area, however, spreads around the hill to the other side, which is in the prettier village of Pernand-Vergelesses, and this, too, has vineyards producing grand cru Corton wines, as do some small vineyards in the twin villages of Ladoix-Serrigny. They also take a part in growing grapes for the magnificent white wine Corton Charlemagne—flinty, slow in maturing and a true rival to the best Montrachet. The other good wines are all red. Red Corton is more powerful than other Côtes de Beaune and it starts off very tannic. It really does need time to develop and soften—a good ten years. Considering its price, it would be ridiculous to drink it too young. It is very rich.

Premier cru wines are not usually as rich, but are ready to drink much sooner and are attractive and satisfying. Outstanding and rich is a Pernand-Vergelesses Ile des Vergelesses, which must be mature. Pernand Village wines can be earthy, even harsh, but are good value. Ordinary Aloxe is a good buy, too. Pernand makes a lot of Aligoté white.

Aloxe and Pernand had been producing wine for a long time when Charlemagne, who rebuilt their abbey, gave some of his vineyard to the monks of Saulieu and he, of course, is credited with first making white wine so that his beard would not be stained red. Voltaire liked the red. It was sent to him by the man who built the Château de Corton. Voltaire kept the Corton for himself; to his guests he served Beaujolais.

The Château is now called Château Corton-André after the André family who bought it in 1927. The family has an estate of 70 ha in Burgundy and another in Côtes-de-Rhône. The old Château cellar is a splendid place to taste wine. It is better to phone first but not necessary (tel. 80 26 44 25).

Savigny-lès-Beaune, on the little D2 road 6km north-west of Beaune, is an absolutely delightful village at the entrance to the lovely valley of the tiny river Rhoin. The attractive D18 runs north to Pernand, just missing Aloxe-Corton, and the D2 itself follows a pleasant route to Bouilland. Just beyond, you can turn right along the D25 for a charming drive to Nuits-St-Georges.

After Beaune and Pommard, Savigny produces more red wine than anywhere on the Côte de Beaune and its wine matures fast, which pleases the wine trade. The wines have a superbly rich perfume of fruit and flowers and those produced south of the river are mostly seductively light. A little white is made from Chardonnay grapes or from Pinot Blanc.

Like Beaune, Savigny lives by and for wine. The motto of La Cousinerie de Bourgogne, the wine producers' brotherhood, is 'All gentlemen are cousins', and they meet in the communal cellars, over the door of which is written in Latin, 'There are five reasons for drinking: the arrival of a guest, a thirst, an oncoming thirst, an excellent wine and any other reason you care to think of'.

Chorey-lès-Beaune, once a quiet village just off the N74 north-east of Beaune, finds itself these days within 2km of the meeting of the A6 and A31 motorways. It produces no premier cru wines, most of its wine is sold as Côte de Beaune-Villages, which is best drunk fairly young to keep its fruitiness.

Beaune is the heart and metropolis of the Burgundy wine trade. It has such a rich heritage of beautiful historic buildings and streets that to know them truly you would have to live there for a long time. And the wine and the heritage are so closely knit that it is difficult to describe one without the other. So please also read the story of Beaune the town on pages 177–181.

The hospice, of course, is mainly kept going by the famous sale of wines from vineyards presented to it over centuries. But many producers and négociants are in historic buildings and you can visit them not only for their wines but to see the surroundings. Patriarche Père et Fils, for instance, has one of the biggest cellars in Burgundy in what was the convent of the nuns of the Visitations, founded by the grandmother of the Marquise de Sévigné and bought by Jean-Baptiste Patriarche in 1796 when his cellars at Savigny-lès-Beaune became too small. The nuns' cellars have been joined to other underground passages, including the 14th century cellars of the monks of Chartreuse. Patriarche is a négociant, but also owns vineyards and the Château Meursault.

Using the little silver flat Burgundian cup called a tastevin, you can taste 21 wines the proper way, not gulping down 21 glasses! You are given a comment card, which says 'taste sensibly'. The visit (1 Mar–15 Dec, 09.30–11.30, 14.00–17.30) takes 40 min and a fee is charged, which is given to charity. The building itself is beautiful, with elegant 17th century arcades.

J. Calvet, the great international wine company founded in 1818, exporter to Britain for more than 150 years, has superb cellars in the medieval fortifications of Beaune and you taste wine in a 15th century tower. (Visits daily except Monday 08.00–11.00, 14.00–17.00, 6 bd Perpreuil, tel. 80 22 05 32.)

One of the most interesting visits in Burgundy is to the cellars of Bouchard Aîné, 39 rue Ste Marguerite (tel. 80 22 07 67; 09.00–12.00, 14.00–16.30). You cannot *taste* unless you are in the wine trade but you will learn a great deal about Burgundy wine, and drink a Kir (one part crème de cassis, alcoholic blackcurrant liqueur, to four parts Aligoté white wine). You can buy a choice of wines. So many people wanted to visit these family-owned cellars that Terry Price, the English PR man, has been forced to ask would-be visitors to phone. It's worth the trouble.

Cave Exposition de la Reine Pedauque, Porte St Nicolas (tel. 80 22 23 11) is in ancient caves with hundreds of thousands of bottles and barrels, including the greatest crus of Burgundy and some of the oldest wines. It was set up by the owners of Clos des Langres near Nuits-St-Georges and in Mâcon and Beaujolais. Visits and tastings are welcome in business hours and English is spoken.

It is worth remembering that the appellation Beaune on a wine is different from Côte de Beaune, which is wine from certain small parcels of land on the Beaune 'mountain', and from Côte de Beaune-Villages, which is a blend of two or more red wines from 16 picked wine villages, such as Savigny-lès-Beaune, Puligny-Montrachet and Meursault.

Wines simply called Beaune are produced on the slopes around the town, up to about 330m. Most are red. The vineyards are cut in half by the D970 and near the Savigny border the A6 motorway cuts right through some vineyards, such as Les Marconnets, which produces some of the best premier cru wines, of which there are more than 30. They do vary enormously, but some are delicate and can be drunk youngish (four–five years), others are more robust and need longer. One of the very best is Bouchard's Grèves wine from its tiny vineyard Vigne de l'Enfant Jesus. You will notice that most of the vineyards are owned by négociants. Beaune has for centuries been the main centre for the sale and shipping of Burgundy wines and when the big estates owned by the church and aristocrats were taken away and sold in the Revolution, the wholesalers and shippers moved in quickly and bought the vineyards before the peasants could.

Ordinary Villages-Beaune is underrated in many cases. Some wines are fruity when quite young but most of the wine is at its best at five years old and goes very well with richer food which would kill the taste of a fine Côte de Nuits. White wines often have a coarse, rustic flavour, not unpleasant.

We tell the story of the Hospice de la Charité in Chapter 14 on Beaune. Through centuries rich men and women have left vineyards to the hospice, perhaps in exchange for a little parcel of land in Heaven, and the list of vineyards they own and wines they produce is formidable. The wines are sold, of course, at the huge annual auction held on the third Sunday in November, but you cannot attend unless you can ingratiate yourself with somebody in the trade and persuade him to take you as a personal guest.

It is an old-style traditional auction: a taper is lit and when it goes out it is replaced with another until the bidding stops. When the second candle has gone out, the wine is sold. Prices are high because there is prestige in bidding and in having the wine on your trade list when it has been raised and matured. But the prices paid are a relative guide to the price level that year. Usually the biggest money-spinner is a white. In the evening a candlelit dinner is held in one of the huge cellars of the town walls. On the Saturday night before the sale is the banquet of the Chevaliers du Tastevin at Clos Vougeot. On Monday the eating and drinking moves to Meursault, where 300 growers take two of their bottles each and demolish them at another banquet. The three events are called the Trois Glorieuses. It is no time to be in Beaune unless you are well connected with the wine business—every hotel bed and restaurant table has been booked long before.

Pommard, the next village, astride the D973 and stretching to N74, is the tough guy of Burgundy—producing a full-bodied, sometimes unsubtle and rather tannic mouthful which goes splendidly with old Burgundy dishes like *boeuf á la bourguignonne*. There is such widescale production that there are great variations in quality. It takes time to open out. Some wines from good vineyards made by good wine-makers are wonderful with old-fashioned man-size meals. Like modern cooking, modern Burgundy can be too light for a winter's night. The best Pommard wines are generally reckoned to be Les Grands Epenots and Les Rugiens and there is a movement to have them promoted from premiers crus to grands crus. Most of the vines are grown by small vignerons with caves beneath their old houses in the village.

The Château de Pommard used to have a huge notice outside just after World War II reading 'Free tasting every day'. It was next to a warning notice saying: 'Safe driving demands sobriety'. So many people visited that a nominal charge was introduced, to cover something of the cost of the wine tasted. The wines must be kept four to ten years according to the vintage. (Visits Easter to third Sunday in November, 08.30–18.30.)

The Parent family, in place l'Eglise by the church with an oddly shaped belfry, has owned Pommard vineyards since 1740, supplied wines for Thomas Jefferson when he was US Ambassador to France and still uses the old traditional methods. Its Clos Micault, aged for at least ten years, is the sort of beefy, old-style Pommard that we love. Its Les Epenots wines are fruity and elegant (to taste, telephone 80 22 15 08).

Pommard was named after Pommona, Roman goddess of fruits and gardens. Friends of Pommard included Henri IV, Louis XV and especially Victor Hugo.

The wine of Volnay, 2km along the D973, could hardly be more different—a gorgeous perfume, delicate, elegant. It has a definite scent of violets. The dukes of Burgundy had one of their most beloved vineyards there and a favourite country house. When Louis XI's force of Swiss mercenaries beat and killed the Burgundy Duke Charles the Rash, Louis celebrated by looting the whole 1477 vintage and having it taken to his château of Plessis-

St Vincent Moves House

Each January we try to help St Vincent move house—the least we can do for him, for he is the patron saint of wine-growers. St Vincent Tournante, this festivity is called, and it is held on the first weekend after St Vincent's Day (22 January). Each year he moves to a different wine village in the area and local wine-makers blend a wine to be drunk at the fête. Meanwhile the schoolchildren spend many hours making a wine, grape and vine motif to decorate the trees, houses, caves and the Mairie.

On the Saturday around 08.00, members of the St Vincent de Paul Societies of all the villages in the area gather at the chosen village to carry their various statues of St Vincent in procession round the streets, through the vineyards and back to the church for mass. The St Vincent of the chosen village rests in the church for a year. Then the caves are opened and the feasting begins, while folkloric groups and musicians perform old Burgundian dances and songs.

For about 20 francs you buy a handsome Burgundy goblet inscribed with the village coat of arms and you can fill it, free, with 'cuvé St Vincent' wine as often as you can empty it. Stalls and caves offer freshly made snacks, such as cheese *gougères*, parsleyed ham or ham sandwiches, or you can book for the Repas Gastronomique of traditional Burgundy dishes. Around 21.00 a dance begins and goes on until around 05.00. But most people dance in the street. It's a true Burgundian feast. And it continues through Sunday.

Obviously, the wine varies every year according to the village. The weather varies, too. We have stamped our feet in frost and wandered in the sun. One year at Aloxe Corton it rained through day and night, so the caves were truly crowded and a local entrepreneur made a few francs selling dustbin liners to the unwary who had no raincoats or umbrellas.

With no discourtesy to our other hosts over the years, 1992 was our vintage year for wine. We were in Vosne-Romanée.

lès-Tours. Far too good for him! Volnay is a hamlet of only about 500 people, most of whom live in solid old Burgundian houses standing proudly above the vineyards. Do try the wines of Hubert de Montile's Domaine if possible.

The lovely old hamlet of Monthélie has only 200 people and until 1937 its wines were sold as either Pommard or Volnay. It is rather similar to Volnay, with an attractive scent, but even lighter and noticeably cheaper. It is a splendid luncheon or summer dinner wine. There is a white wine which you may be able to taste in the village café, and you may also get a chance to taste the best of Monthélie by phoning Robert de Suremain at Château de

Monthélie caves and asking for an appointment (tel. 80 21 23 32). Burgundians pronounce Monthélie 'Mon-tli'.

Meursault, a little town between the D973 and the N74, produces what some people, especially the people of Meursault, believe to be, with Puligny and Chassagne Montrachet, the best white wine in the world. With its ripe-grape and cinnamon perfume and hint of hazelnuts in its strong, long-lasting flavour, it can be difficult to decide how dry it is. But it *is* dry, and some wines are actually flinty, while others are very rich. We wish that we could afford to drink it more often—such as every day. Louis XV's Cardinal de Bernis would celebrate mass with no other wine because, he said, he did not want his Creator to see him pulling a face when he made his communion. Good red wines are produced, too.

Patriarche Père et Fils owns the 16th century Château de Meursault, which until recently belonged to le Comte de Moucheron. The cellars, holding half a million bottles and one thousand oak maturing casks, were partly dug by the monks of Cîteaux abbey in the 13th century. The white wines produced here are gorgeous even by Meursault standards. The great park with ancient trees was partly replanted with Chardonnay grapes in 1975. Visitors may taste wines and walk round the park (every day including Sundays, 09.30–11.30, 14.30–17.30). It is one of the most rewarding visits in Burgundy.

Back on the D973 is Auxey-Duresses, at the entrance to a gorge dominated by Mont Melian. There are many pretty roads around here, and although most vineyards are too high to make great wine, they produce red and white wines which are very good value, having not yet become fashionable. Most red is similar to Monthélie. Alain Gras produces a nice one. White is very pleasant drunk young.

The attractive D973 continues to La Rochepot. Equally attractive is the little D17 west to St Romain, a hamlet with a ruined castle high on a spur and the highest vineyards on the whole Côte d'Or, producing an excellent fresh apéritif white Chardonnay and a very quaffable rustic red with the flavour of cherries.

Puligny-Montrachet, a charming place, is the next village you reach near to the N74 after Meursault, but take the little D13A vineyard road, then follow it across the N6 to Chassagne-Montrachet. From a mere 7.5 ha Puligny and Chassagne produces sheer nectar—almost certainly the best white wine in the world. Alexandre Dumas, gastronome and wine worshipper as well as a best-selling novelist, said that Puligny should be drunk on bended knee and with head bared. The greatest grand cru wines are Le Montrachet, Bâtard-Montrachet, Chevalier-Montrachet and Criots-Bâtard-Montrachet. 'It is really a vinous crime to drink Le Montrachet at under ten years of age', says Serena Sutcliffe, and although the other grands crus can be drunk earlier, they do need to be kept until the lovely greenish-yellow colour of the young wine turns to gold in the bottle and the full taste of honey and fruit develops. They should be served at 13°C (55°F) cellar temperature—not from a fridge. Most Chassagne can be drunk younger than Puligny. Many wine experts say that grands crus Puligny should be drunk without food, for they are too powerful for fish.

All this talk, of course, can be academic to many of us, for they cost enough to warrant the bended knee. But if you cannot taste the grand cru wines there are some premiers crus wines such as Les Pucelles and Les Folatières which are a delight, and the village wines are good and inexpensive. A virus called fan leaf appeared on a few vines recently, making wine scarcer and even dearer. Chassagne-Montrachet red is underrated, more is produced than white and although the French drink them both two to four years old they do get smoother with age.

Alongside Chassagne-Montrachet on the N6 is the village of St Aubin whose old vignerons' houses are so interesting that it is an historic monument. If you want to drink wine with a true Burgundy flavour but lighter, fresher and considerably cheaper, this is the place to stop. The reds taste of strawberries and are drunk at around three to four years old; the best whites have a distinct affinity to Puligny-Montrachet. The village of Gamay alongside gave its name to the Gamay grape—the 'Beaujolais grape'.

The last vineyards are at Santenay, west of the little industrial town of Chagny. Santenay is really a string of three hamlets along the banks of the little river Dheune, beneath a mountain. Its wine has changed a great deal in our time. The old vignerons produced dark, earthy, beefy wines from old vines more like those from Côte de Nuits. Now more modern methods have also produced a light and fruitier wine, drunk much younger. You can taste the excellent wines of the Prieuré family, which has made wine here since 1804. Do try its La Maldière in the 15th century caves at Domaine Prieuré-Brunet. This is a good Domaine to visit because there is no need to phone and the family owns vineyards producing great and good wines all over the Côte de Beaune, including a superb white Bâtard-Montrachet (tel. 80 20 60 56; visits 10.00–12.00, 15.00–19.00).

Côte Chalonnaise

The long line of vine-covered hills from Dijon breaks up at Santenay. From there, vines are grown on favourable slopes and the area is called Côte Chalonnaise after the town of Chalon-sur-Saône out on the plain. The best wine villages are mostly on tiny winding roads just west of the D981 from Chagny, and are well worth seeking. Though the wines are not in the class of the best Côte d'Or wines, they are improving greatly and can be good value. Bouzeron, the first village, produces very good Aligoté white wine, so good that it is allowed to use the name Aligoté de Bouzeron on the label.

Rully's red wines and most of its white were for long made by the champagne method into sparkling wines just called Burgundy. Then trade buyers came looking for a substitute for overpriced Chablis. Now 70 per cent of Rully white is still wine, which has gone up in price as people have realised how good it is. Red wines are real Burgundy Pinots, quite light in colour and with a raspberry flavour.

Nearby Mercurey produces nearly all reds, which are heavy, sometimes rustic, and go well with old local dishes such as *boeuf à la bourguignonne*.

A lighter, more elegant wine is produced by the Marquis de Jouennes d'Herville. It is best after four to five years and is called Château de Chamirey after his 17th century château, which is a national monument, well worth visiting. Phone if possible (85 45 22 22); they speak English.

Givry, only 9km from Chalon (on the D981), was for centuries a very important wine-producing town. In the 6th century, Gregory of Tours was already praising 'the wine of Chalon'. In the Middle Ages it was rated with Beaune and equally heavily taxed in Paris. It was on the table of many monarchs, but the one who matters to Givry is inevitably Henri IV, le Vert Galant, who loved wine as much as he loved women. Before you reach the village, notices on the D981 tell you that it was his preferred wine, as do the bottle labels. We must blame the 18th century Burgundy poet and historian Courtépée who wrote that Henri got to like the wine when his favourite mistress Gabrielle d'Estrées was staying in the nearby Château of Germolles and that he made it his daily tipple back in Paris, exempting it from duty. However, when ten times more wine than Givry could ever produce suddenly appeared for sale duty free, the tax had to be put back.

Givry wine kept its popularity until World War I. Then it fell so low in people's estimation that it still does not have a premier cru. But it does produce very good light red wines with a pleasant smell, a lingering taste and delicate flavour which goes well with old-fashioned sauces. They are reminiscent of Loire wines. Caves left over from its heyday are enormous—the biggest belonged to the family of the late Baron Louis Thénard who worked hard to get Givry back on the map. One red, Le Cellier aux Moines, was described aptly by Serena Sutcliffe as 'having the smell of all the herbs of Provence'. The white wine is pale and fruity, like a lightweight Meursault.

Buxy, 8km down the D981, is an old, busy, pleasant little town which, with the village of Montagny 3km west, produces the delicious Montagny white wine that we will go far out of our way to buy at local prices. It is greeny-gold in colour and tastes like a crisper version of Pouilly-Fuissé. It is said to keep the mouth fresh and the head clear and it was the drink of the learned monks of Cluny, not of roistering kings. Drink it between two and three years old.

Cave des Vignerons de Buxy is much respected in the trade in France and Britain. We have found it excellent for Montagny and for other ordinary Burgundy wines. Buxy, by the way, is another of the towns with an 'x' in it that the French say you should pronounce 'ss'—Bussy. Not all the locals do. The town's market is on Thursday.

The Mâconnais

The Mâconnais vineyards stretch for 50km from Tournus on the river Saône to St Vérand in the south and are about 15km wide from the river Grosne valley to the valley of the Saône, but to tour them would be a winding, circuitous route.

The great abbey of Cluny was north-west of the town of Mâcon and the

Cluny monks planted the first grapes in the area. Now the grapes grown are Chardonnay for white wines, which are the most important, and Gamay, the grape used in Beaujolais for most of the reds, with some Pinot Noir.

Most Mâcon Blanc is made without using oak casks—kept in a vat and bottled young. But in the cellars of the greatest Mâcon wine, Pouilly-Fuissé, you will see barrels and even old traditional wooden vats.

Nowadays an increasing number of the Gamay red wine-makers are copying Beaujolais and making wines by the semi-Macération Carbonique method, which means that they can and should be drunk young. The Gamay grapes, which are black with white juice, are never crushed in making the wine. The fermenting juice at the bottom of the vat induces fermentation within each individual grape, which lasts for four to six days. In the full Macération Carbonique method, the vat is saturated with added carbon dioxide. However, grapes are still pressed by many producers. Macération Carbonique does accentuate the beautiful bouquet of the wine while losing none of its fruitiness.

Mâcon for the King

The hero of the Mâconnais was a wine-grower from Charnay-lès-Mâcon, a little village now almost on the western edge of the town. Claude Brosse was an ordinary wine-grower but a giant of a man, who decided that the wine of Mâcon deserved to be better known. So he loaded two hogsheads of his best wine on to an ox-cart and took it to Versailles, hoping to attract the custom of some noblemen. He arrived after 33 days and went to Mass in thanks for his safe journey. King Louis XIV was there and was annoyed to see a man still standing when everyone else was kneeling in prayer. He sent one of his staff to tell the man to kneel, only to discover that the Burgundian giant *had* been kneeling. Louis sent for Brosse and asked what had brought him to Paris. Brosse explained and asked the king if he would like to taste the wine. Louis did and exclaimed that it was far better than the Suresnes and Beaugency wines being drunk at Court. So, of course, all the sycophantic courtiers wanted Mâcon to serve at their tables. Brosse took his wine to Versailles every year—and became rich. No doubt he bought in his neighbours' wines, too!

If you want to see something of the Mâconnais vineyards in a short time, you could start at Mâcon, forgetting the northern stretch from Tournus, and make straight for the Pouilly-Fuissé villages (Pouilly, Fuissé, Solutré, Vergisson and Chaintré), then for Loché and Vinzelles. But you would be missing some superb scenery west of the Saône.

Mâcon is a busy place on the Saône with a river port used for centuries to transport wine. The town adopted the Spanish St Vincent, who became patron of vignerons, and it holds the French National Wine Fair in the last two weeks of May, so if your wine bottle has a round golden sticker saying that it has won a Gold, Silver or Bronze medal at Mâcon, there are few higher accolades in its class.

Pouilly-Fuissé is a gorgeous white wine, made with Chardonnay, rich but with a lovely flavour which makes it more refreshing than Chablis or Puligny-Montrachet. Alas, it is too popular, especially with Americans and Japanese, and the price is too high for some of its old supporters.

Good cheaper substitutes are Pouilly-Vinzelles and Pouilly-Loché, named after nearby villages, but production is small and they are hard to find, though the great Georges Duboeuf offers them (see Beaujolais). The wines are more rustic than the real thing but are luscious.

A Fuissé substitute more easily obtainable is St Véran, from seven different villages, including Chasselas, which also produces the famous dessert grapes, and a village confusingly called St Vérand with a 'd'. Although it matures more quickly than Pouilly-Fuissé, it should be two to four years old to enjoy its full nutty flavour.

Mâcon-Blanc-Villages is made by 43 villages, mostly being produced by cooperatives. Best known are Lugny, Clessé, Viré (easy to reach because it is 3km west of the N6, 19km north of Mâcon) and Chardonnay (8km south-west of Tournus) where the Chardonnay was probably developed, some say by the monks of Cluny. The wines are fruity, with a flowery perfume, and are often drunk when only one year old in France. They sometimes have the musky taste of some Australian Chardonnays. The cave-cooperative at Viré makes a good wine, fresh and fruity. It has a mural showing Viré's twinning (jumellage) with another village—Montmartre in Paris! You can taste there, in business hours, paying by the glass. No need to phone, but the number is 85 33 11 64.

Mâcon Rouge and Mâcon Supérieur Rouge (1 per cent more alcohol) are best drunk young (two years) when they are fruity and fresh. They go well with charcuterie or poultry. Like all Gamay wines, they are often drunk cool or cold (not iced) in France. A wine of Gamay mixed with a third or more Pinot Noir is called Bourgogne-Passe-Tout-Grains. Mâcon Rosé is not much good.

You can taste wine in Mâcon at the Comité Interprofessionel des Vins de Bourgogne et Mâcon, Maison de Tourisme, avenue Marechal-de-Lattré-de-Tassigny.

Beaujolais

Nearly all the Beaujolais is in the département of Rhône, in the Lyonnais, not in Burgundy, but the Beaujolais wine *is* Burgundy and the little wine villages of the Beaujolais produce enough grapes to make about 150 million bottles of wine a year!

Beaujolais must be drunk young. Only a few cru wines are better for

Beaujolais vineyards at Roche de Solutré

keeping five to six years. Nor is it a wine for a lot of deep thought and pretty words after solemn tasting. The great wine producer, négociant and writer Alexis Lichine said 'Forget the delicate sniffs and sips, the ruminatory gargles, the suspenseful silences with which we approach the great Burgundies and Bordeaux. The wines of Beaujolais are meant to be swallowed and gulped and unabashedly enjoyed!' But please allow yourself a sniff long enough to enjoy that lovely fruitiness of the Gamay grape at its best.

All this fuss about Nouveau Beaujolais is bewildering and we are glad that the silly fashion is fading. It all started in Lyon and Paris in the old days when cheap bistros served the wine direct from barrels, kept in the smoky bar, and by November it was going pretty nasty and vinegary. So when the new wine arrived, the bistro owners happily announced, 'Le Nouveau Beaujolais est arrive!' Even in the late 1940s and early 1950s much Beaujolais never reached a bottle. In Lyon the joke was that three rivers flowed into the city, the Saône, the Rhône and the Beaujolais.

The earthy Beaujolais growers would drop their tastevins laughing if they could see snob amateurs of Paris and London solemnly going through a tasting ritual, then pronouncing wise words on the merits of the year's Nouveau when the wine has not had time to stop revolving round the bottle after its journey.

Georges Duboeuf, who is variously called the King or the Pope of Beaujolais and who is known personally to every great chef and wine-trader in the world, has improved Nouveau Beaujolais greatly and sends a lot of his carefully chosen wines to be independently tasted and analysed to make sure which are suitable for drinking young. Despite that, one nasty November night a few years back, Arthur arrived at his cave to taste and take away the new wine, but after a smell, a swirl and a swallow had to admit that he didn't want to drink any more because it gave him hiccups and an acidic stomach. Georges disappeared into the cellar and brought back a bottle of Fleurie which was two years old, flowery, soft and delicious. That is another advantage of Beaujolais—it can be drunk at cellar temperature when not accompanying food. In fact that is the current fashion.

Fleurie is one of the cru wines—made by single villages which may sell under their own names and which are all in the north of Beaujolais, where the granite-based soil produces a better, fruitier Gamay wine than any we have tasted even from Touraine.

Nearly half of red wines produced are ordinary AOC Beaujolais. They are light, fruity, very quaffable and should be drunk at one year old or younger. Beaujolais Supérieur can be kept a little longer. Most of the wines that are seen outside France are Beaujolais-Villages, which are more full-bodied and satisfying but still fruity and easy to drink. They are best from one to two years old.

Many bigger wine villages making Villages wines have tasting bars of some sort. Some open only in tourist season, others on Friday, Saturday and Sunday. At most you must pay a nominal amount for a glass or a tasting. A pleasant place to taste a light Villages wine is Château de Corcelles, a 15th century fortress with Renaissance galleries in its courtyard, fine wood-carvings in the chapel and a 17th century Grand Cuvier, 80m long, with wine maturing in huge casks. It is at Corcelles-en-Beaujolais, just west of the N6, 8km north of Belleville (tel. 74 66 00 24—check opening times). Another is La Cave Beaujolais at Château de Loges, Le Perreon. From St Georges-de-Reneins on the N6, north of Villefranche, go west on the D20 and the D49 to just north of Vaux-en-Beaujolais (Clochemerle). Wine-making equipment is modern, wine is fruity and light except Château de Loges (full-bodied, maturing excellently) and you taste in the fine old 18th century caves of the château. (Pay for tastings; 09.00–12.00, 14.30–19.00; tel. 74 03 22 83.)

Georges Duboeuf, négociant par excellence and the man with 'the best nose and palate in Burgundy', is at Romanèche-Thorins, just west of the N6, 15km south of Mâcon. Everyone wants to visit him, so you must make an appointment (tel. 83 35 51 13) and visits are for serious buyers. He travels through Beaujolais and Mâcon each year, tastes 8000 wines and brings back 3000 for exhaustive laboratory analysis.

First of the cru wines you meet coming from Mâcon is St-Amour at St-Amour-Bellevue. The wines are sprightly, fruity and delicate. They take about three years to ripen, as true Amour should. Wines of Château de St-Amour are outstanding—as are the aptly named Domaine du Paradis, bottled by Georges Duboeuf.

The wine of Juliénas, the neighbouring commune named for Julius Caesar, is said to be the epitome of Beaujolais. Deep purple, gloriously fruity at six months to a year, spicy as well at two to four years. Slopes are very steep, making picking difficult and expensive. Its producers' association has a convenient tasting cave, Cellier de la Vieille Eglise, in a fine old church with coloured frescoes devoted to Bacchus and his worshippers. You can taste Juliénas and St-Amour (every day in June, July, August; shut Tuesdays rest of year, 10.00–12.00, 14.30–18.30). Château de Juliénas wines are excellent.

Chénas wines are less known and not quite so good as Moulin à Vent. If kept for a few years they have a lovely flowery smell and super fruitiness which stays a long time in the back of the throat. The cooperative in a Louis XIV château is one of the best places to visit in Beaujolais. Its wines are outstanding and you have a chance to compare Chénas with Moulin à Vent. (Visits Monday to midday Saturday, 08.00–12.00, 14.00–18.00; also on Saturday afternoons from 1 April to 30 October. Tel. 74 04 11 91, but there is no need to phone. Tastings free.)

On the road from Chénas to Romanèche-Thorins you can see the windmill of Moulin à Vent on a hill overlooking the vines—a symbol of Beaujolais. And there is a tasting cave at the bottom of the hill. Deep in colour, smooth and rich, Moulin à Vent is best drunk after three or four years. Good vintages improve for ten years. The wine is often more like a Côte d'Or wine than a Beaujolais, which is why it is served at around 15°C (60°F) and not 13°C (55°F).

Fleurie, west of Romanèche-Thorins, is 'easy to say, easy to drink', and is a favourite luncheon wine. It is charming, very fruity and can easily seduce you into drinking more than you intended. Parisians drink it within 18 months of the vintage. Burgundians often keep it three years. It has real style. Happily there is quite a lot of it. The Cave des Producteurs de Fleurie was made famous by its president for many years, Mlle Marguerite Chabert, 'Queen of the Beaujolais'.

Chiroubles, Cinderella of the Beaujolais Crus, has gone to the ball, by courtesy of Nouvelle Cuisine, and is light, fragrant, tasty, and ready before the others! It was hardly known 15 years ago, now it is the favourite Beaujolais of the young French who, alas, drink so much of it by the February after it is made that it is difficult to find by summer, when it would be so refreshing with salads or at picnics.

Morgon wines have a different bouquet and a different taste from the others. The vineyards are around the villages of Bas-Morgon and Villié-Morgon, with the best wines said to come from the hill between, Mont du Py. They used to be made so that they seemed dead when young, rich, robust and mouth-filling when kept two to four years, and they were so popular that the wine trade would say of wines that improved with keeping, 'Ils morgonnent'. Now, wine-makers are aiming at lighter wines. Jean Descombes is the great grower. Domaine Lieven, bottled by Duboeuf at the Domaine, belongs to Princesse de Lieven, who is Mrs Charles Piat (a name you may have noticed on Beaujolais bottles of an unusual shape!). You can taste (small charge) in Caveau de Morgon at Villie-Morgon in the attractive cave of the Louis XVII Château de Foncrenne, in a big, pretty public park. There is a display of old wine-making tools and a small zoo. Tasting daily 09.00–12.00, 14.00–19.00. If you phone (74 04 20 99) you can see a 17-minute film in English on Morgon wines and taste the wine of the year.

A new cru was added in 1988 called Régnié. The wine comes from the vineyards around the two steeples of Régnié-Durette, villages south-west of Morgon close to the D47. The cherry-coloured wine has a slight taste of redcurrants and is often served cold 13°C (55°F) with pâtés, terrines or hot starters.

The D43, a pretty road south from the D47, which joins Belleville to Beaulieu, leads you to Mont Brouilly and the village of Brouilly, home of the most southerly cru Beaujolais, Brouilly and Côte de Brouilly. Mont Brouilly rises to 500m and the vineyards are on all slopes. Vines for Côte wine grow on the south-facing slopes. It is a better wine than Brouilly itself, very rich and grapey. Brouilly produces more wine than any of the other crus. It is normally light, fruity, simple and very quaffable, but some are luscious and heavier, like Château de la Chaize, a splendid Brouilly produced in a cuvage 110m long in the château outside Odenas. Château de la Chaize was built by François de la Chaize, brother of Louis XIV's confessor. It stands in a huge property and in its vaulted caves, the largest in Beaujolais, is an antique *pressoir* famous in Beaujolais. The château is now a private home, almost enclosed by vineyards.

Odenas is on the fairly wide and modern D43, 16km north-west of Villefranche-sur-Saône, the end of Beaujolais. You must turn left 5km after

'Homage to wine makers', a contemporary relief outside the cellars at Château de Foncrenne, Villié-Morgon

leaving Odenas on the little D49 to reach Vaux-en-Beaujolais—the village of Clochemerle (see Chapter 15, Beaujolais).

Lyon is only 31km down the N6 from Villefranche. But it is on another planet from the Beaujolais villages.

Chablis

Chablis is produced in 20 communes in the northernmost part of Burgundy, around hills of limestone. The white wines made from Chardonnay are a lovely pale yellow with a greenish tinge and are drier, crisper and fruitier than most other Chardonnay. They are often gorgeous. Alas, there is a lot of variation and different views on how they should be made. The ordinary AOC Chablis can be drunk after one or two years, but ages well. The fine premiers and grands crus need at least three to five years. It is always stressed that Chablis is perfect with shellfish, which it is, but it goes splendidly too with any delicate fish, with hors d'oeuvres, with smoked salmon and with white meats such as chicken, turkey, guinea fowl and cold pheasant.

The seven grands crus are all on the slopes of the big hill across the little river Serein from Chablis town. They are Blanchot, Bougros, Les Clos, Grenouilles, Preuses, Valmure and Vaudésir.

Apart from the grands and premiers crus and ordinary Chablis wines, there is some Petit Chablis which is really an AOC Chablis from a few villages around Chablis town.

Spring frost has always been the great enemy here, any time from the end of March to mid-May. Two protective methods used are spraying to give the vines an insulating coat of ice and using oil burners. The water method needs great skill and experience and no wind, and oil burning is expensive in fuel and labour. Oddly, weedkillers have lessened the danger, as fewer weeds mean less humidity. Whole vintages have been lost to frost and the danger is still there. Owing to unlucky harvests and world demand, Chablis prices shot up between 1993 and 1995.

Most growers now use stainless steel or lined cement vats for fermenting, but there are many arguments about maturing wine. Some use old oak casks, others new oak and some modern makers use no oak casks but bottle younger wine straight from the vat, producing a young, fresh wine delicious with oysters or most shellfish, but no good for chicken or other poultry. We prefer the traditional old Chablis, kept in vat until the spring after the picking and then aged in barrel for a year. Grands crus and good premiers crus made like this improve for several years. It is best if you buy in Chablis to ask when a grand cru or premier cru should be drunk. My 1985 premier cru was not ready until 1990. Nor was a 1983 grand cru Preuses.

You can taste at La Chablisienne, the cave-cooperative to which 200 growers send wine. Formed in 1923, it has done much to see Chablis through bad years of frost. It produces many wines, including the excellent Grenouilles (9 bd Pasteur, tel. 86 42 11 24. Mon–Sat 08.00–12.00,

14.00–18.00). Simonnet-Fèbvre (La Maladière, 9 ave d'Oberwessel, tel. 86 42 11 73. Phone if possible in office hours), is not only a grower but an excellent *éleveur*, buying *must* and bringing up wines. They produce young bottled wines, superb long-keeping grand cru Preuses and magnificent rich and delicate Fourchaume, plus an interesting red Irancy (see below). Domaine Laroche has won many awards, produces lovely premier cru wines matured in oak and superb grand cru Les Clos to be kept ten years. Some wines are kept in the original cellars of the monks who fled here in the 9th century and started it all. There is also a 13th century wine press (10 rue Auxerroise, tel. 86 42 14 30; 09.00–12.00, 14.00–18.30).

Irancy is a red or rosé wine from the Yonne made with Pinot Noir with a little rustic grape called César added. The wine has been known since the 12th century. In good years it is full-coloured with fruitiness, rustic at first, smoother with age. Simonnet-Fèbvre carries this wine and also a lighter red from Coulanges-la-Vineuse.

St Bris-le-Vineux, south-west of Chablis, produces a white from Sauvignon grapes—light, dry and quite fruity. A VDQS wine (Vin Délimité de Qualité Supérieure) which is one below an AOC wine, it is a good apéritif, goes with shellfish, light fish and hors d'oeuvres and is also used for Kir.

Pouilly-sur-Loire, on the Burgundy side of the river Loire, just north of La Charité-sur-Loire, produces similar smoky Sauvignon wine (Pouilly-Fumé) to the wine Sancerre produces on the other side of the river. The wine is all called Loire but Pouilly is in Burgundy. Pouilly-Fumé has become so popular recently that prices have risen greatly. A dry white wine called Pouilly-sur-Loire is made from Chasselas grapes. It is fruity, light and quaffable. Drink it very young. Guy Saget makes magnificent Pouilly-Fumé.

A cooperative cave making good wines, Caves de Pouilly-sur-Loire, is opposite the Relais Fleuri on the old road through the village, branching off the N7. Try its dry and fruity Moulin à Vent and the Vieilles Vignes, which has more body (tel. 86 39 10 99; Mon–Sat 08.00–12.00, 14.00–18.00).

Information on wines

Comité Interprofessionnel des Vins de Bourgogne et Mâcon, Maison de Tourisme, ave Maréchal-de-Lattre-de-Tassigny, 71000 Mâcon. Tel. 85 38 36 70.

Comité Interprofessionnel de la Côte d'Or et de l'Yonne pour Vins AOC de Bourgogne, rue Henri Dunant, 21200 Beaune. Tel. 80 22 21 35.

Union Interprofessionnel des Vins de Beaujolais, 210 bd Vermorel, 69400 Villefranche-sur-Saône. Tel. 74 65 45 55.

4. Food

Burgundy

Burgundians are still the biggest trenchermen in France. They hold to their traditional motto, 'Better a good meal than fine clothes', as they did during the Renaissance when the chronicler Paladin said that 'Burgundians dress most modestly, yet their bellies are lined with velvet because of their great food'. Of course, the Dukes and their courts who lived in sumptuous palaces like the Ducal Palace in Dijon, dressed as magnificently as they ate, but they were devoted to show and extravagance, even when bankrupt.

The true Burgundian cooking of today was not born in the great medieval kitchens that you can see in the Dijon palace, with huge open fireplaces for roasting joints on three sides and a high central stool where the master chef stood with a great heavy soup spoon to taste each dish and to lambaste tardy underlings. Even today's more sophisticated Burgundian dishes sprang from the kitchens of the farmers and the vignerons. It is farmhouse cooking polished to greatness. The countryside, of course, has given Burgundians their appetite. Madame de Sévigné, the witty, sharp-tongued commentator on life at Louis XIV's court, said of Burgundy: 'You only have to breathe the air to grow fat.'

There are modern young chefs in Burgundy who have lightened their dishes to fashionable extremes and who even fell for Nouvelle Cuisine, but they cook mostly for food faddists. Burgundians themselves would not thank you for a few slivers of carrot and a couple of baby potatoes to accompany the main dish.

Although the people of Champagne are not such solid eaters, they are more interested in pleasing their palate than admiring décor on a dish. They mother their wine until it is exquisite but their traditional dish is coarse-cut chitterling sausage, *andouillette*, which even has a heroic mention in Champagne's history. Hungry soldiers who invaded Troyes in the 16th century ate so many *andouillettes* that they slept content while relieving forces were fetched to save the city.

Dijon is the gourmand capital of France and exports specialities all over the world—including snails in parsley butter, unsurpassed Dijon mustard, superb ham and game products of the Morvan forest, all types of sausages, canned and bottled *coq au Chambertin* and *cassissines*—sweetmeats laced with blackcurrant liqueur, crème de cassis.

Each November Dijon invites customers to a Gastronomic Fair to taste and

Fruit and vegetable market in Dijon, the gourmand capital of France

buy. And you cannot get away *without* tasting. Arthur lost count of the number of slices he tasted of *jambon persillé*, that delicious ham with parsley in white wine jelly, and of dried, cured or smoked ham. Sausages ranged from the large pork *judru*, made from pigs fed on forest acorns, flavoured with *marc* and matured for six months, to the air-dried *rosette du Morvan*. Other delights included *boudin* (black sausage), *andouillettes* with different mustards and *bresli* (thinly sliced, cured and air-dried beef). Arthur was also fed with *gougère*, the cheese choux-pastry rings, which he loves, with snails in garlic and parsley butter, which he can easily forego, and, with *pain d'épices*, spiced honey gingerbread, a speciality of Dijon, which Genghis

Khan gave to his warriors as part of their rations. He tried at least a dozen of Burgundy's flavoursome cheeses, too.

That evening he dined in the *Toison d'Or*, a restaurant in a charming mansion of a 14th century Mayor of Dijon, which is now open to the public but is also the headquarters of the Compagnie Bourguignonne des Oenophiles, an illustrious brotherhood of wine lovers. There, in a delightful old room, the chef Daniel Broyer offers a choice of his own specialities and old dishes of Burgundy. Arthur chose a real farmhouse favourite *oeufs en meurette* as a starter (eggs poached with onions in young red wine), followed by one of the famous local dishes, *râble de lièvre à la Piron*, named after the Dijonnais satirist and bon vivant of Louis XIV's reign whose jokes about Beaune led to riots in the wine town. His dish is saddle of hare marinaded in the wine spirit Marc de Bourgogne, cooked in its marinade and the juice made into a lovely creamy peppery sauce. Arthur finished with spicy St Florentin cheese and a dessert rich in crème de cassis. He showed no signs of having over-indulged. The reason, he claimed, was that the ingredients were all fresh, simply but deliciously cooked, and there were none of the complicated concoctions of unnatural mixtures which can bedevil some of the 'inventive' dishes of modern chefs.

Some great old dishes of Burgundy, such as *boeuf à la bourguignonne* and *coq au vin*, bring sneers from food snobs. A few years ago the Gault-Millau guide sneered at Dijon's *Porte Guillaume* restaurant at the *Nord hotel* as 'one of the ultimate bastions of *coq au vin* and *persillé* essentially for use by tourists'. The result was that Burgundians filled the restaurant, delighted to find the genuine dish, as served by the Fanchot family for four generations. It is said in Burgundy that the coq should be old enough to have chased a lot of hens in its life. It must be *flambé* in a glass of *marc*, and cooked with thyme in real Burgundy wine. There is a snob version—*coq au Chambertin*—but the wine used is too young to drink, anyway.

Chicken dishes are popular, among them *poulet Gaston Gérard* (chicken in sauce of cheese, white wine and mustard), named after the Mayor of Dijon, who started the Gastronomic Fair.

Burgundy's most famous dish, *boeuf à la bourguignonne*, has had many atrocities committed in its name. Even in Dijon we have been served stringy, gristly beef with a cheap wine sauce poured over it. The real thing is made of a good cut of best beef (often entrecôte), marinaded then simmered slowly with onion in good Burgundy wine. Most chefs add strips of fried belly of pork. The *Porte Guillaume* restaurant serves a good version. Apart from its main card, the restaurant has a menu with a choice of old Burgundian dishes. It also has a wine cave serving wines by the glass or bottle with Burgundian snacks and a fine wine list.

Pork is still produced in many villages of Burgundy and most pigs are kept in the old style in a sty or on a hillside. The pork is mostly made into sausages, ham or other forms of charcuterie. *Tourte* (pork pâté baked in pastry) can be delicious. Most fresh or smoked sausages are served hot, but *saucissons rosettes du Morvan* make a fine cold snack with wine.

Charolais Beef

All France believes that Charolais beef from those rotund, short-necked creamy white contented-looking cattle is the best beef in the world. Certainly, it can be very good in the hands of the right butcher and chef, especially when grilled over vine cuttings, which gives it a very special flavour. We think Scottish home-produced Angus has a finer flavour, and Canadian prairie beef can be fuller flavoured and just as tender. Yet Charolais cattle have spread to the whole of Europe and places far beyond, such as Argentina, the US, Canada and Australia. Mostly they are crossed with local or other breeds. Even at the great Perth sales in Scotland, to which the world's breeders and producers have flocked for generations, the number of Charolais or Charolais-crossbreed cattle now well outnumber the local Angus.

Many chefs and gastronomes believe rather cynically that the popularity of Charolais cattle is not unconnected with the fact that they are so fleshy that they are profitable to the producer and butcher. Glyn Christian wrote in his book *Edible France* 'The appeal is more to the breeder and producer than the eater, for the flavour of the huge amounts of flesh each animal produces is pretty inferior'. That's fighting talk in the Nivernais, where the breed was developed in the 18th century after straying from Charollais, and the Auxois where they have been fattened since the 19th century. They are mainly slaughtered at three years old, by which time they have reached around 700kg (1640lb). Many are still sold at weekly markets or fairs, including markets at Charolles and nearby Paray-le-Monial and at St Christophe-en-Brionnais. The biggest markets are now held at Sancoins in Cher (Loire). The most interesting cattle-selling events are the Fêtes du Charolais en Bourgogne at Saulieu, the first weekend after 15 August. An agricultural technical fair is held on Saturday morning. On Sunday the 400 prize Charolais cattle of Auxois appear. And from Saturday night to Sunday night, amid stalls selling all the delicacies and crafts of the Auxois, there is feasting on grilled Charolais steaks, Saulieu cheeses and good Burgundy wines.

Another old dish ruined by cheap ingredients is *saupiquet,* a gourmet dish when we were young but now usually a cheap dish on cheap menus. It used to be made with the best Morvan ham, sliced and served in a creamy, slightly sharp sauce made of cream, wine and wine vinegar. Despite the French national obsession with shooting anything that moves (*la chasse*) and the invasion of summer walkers, Morvan forests are still fairly rich in game—wild boar (*sanglier*), *marcassin* (young wild pig), venison, hare, pheasant and pigeon. Rabbit is covered in mustard and baked (*lapin rôti*) or served with a cream mustard sauce (*lapin à la moutarde*).

To start an argument among freshwater fishermen, ask what goes into the old peasant fish stew *pôchouse* (sometimes called *poch* or *pauchouse*). Most agree on eel, white wine, onion and garlic. The gourmet version used to include burbot (freshwater *lotte*) but that has become scarcer and is more likely to be served as a separate dish, probably poached in red wine (*meurette*). Some insist *pôchouse* must contain only carp and pike, some like tench, while Doubs river fishermen insist on perch. In 1949 at Verdun-sur-le-Doubs they created a Confrérie des Chevaliers de la Pôchouse—a brotherhood of the Knights of the Pôchouse. At *Hostellerie Bourguignonne* in Verdun the Lauriot family have been cooking for generations a true *pôchouse* of fish fresh caught in the Saône river.

The snail of Burgundy, *escargot de Bourgogne*, used to grow fatter and juicier than any in France (or so the Burgundians claimed) feeding in the vineyards but most have been the victims of agricultural fertilisers, weedkillers and the destruction of protective hedgerows. So now 95 per cent of snails eaten in France are imported, some already frozen and badly prepared. Even *escargots de Bourgogne* are likely to have been imported live from Germany, Eastern Europe, Greece, Turkey or south-east Asia, fattened and prepared in Dijon, then cooked with a very garlicky butter. Though the Romans loved snails, they had become a poor man's dish by late last century, when the gourmets took to them, as they have to such peasant dishes as stuffed goose neck, *andouillette* and *ris de veau* (sweetbreads).

You will still find old dishes served in the Nivernais and Morvan, including a thin clear Soupe Nivernaise of cabbage, turnips, carrots and leeks with butter but no meat stock, *rapée* (grated potato cake with one egg per potato, fried in butter) and a delicious *saupiquet* made with thickly sliced Morvan ham de-salted by soaking in milk, then cooked with shallots, juniper berries, strong beef stock, a good dry white wine (even Pouilly-Fumé) and the sauce thickened with cream.

The old vendange soup-stew (*potée*), made in huge containers to keep the grape-pickers from starvation, comprised huge joints of beef and bacon with vegetables but, traditionally, no herbs.

In the Saône valley and Bresse, farmers' wives still make Gaudes—a maize-flour porridge, served hot with cream, or cold so thick that it can be sliced. The *pain d'épices*, made in Dijon with honey, was a recipe brought back by Crusaders from the Turks. A touch of anis is sometimes added. The loaves are usually enormous and hunks are cut off to eat with Montrachet goats' cheese as a lunch snack.

Burgundians eat a lot of cows' milk Gruyère-type cheese from over the border in Franche-Comté, and they themselves produce a lot of goats' milk cheese.

The best local cheese I have tasted is Cîteaux, made by Trappist monks at the abbey 14km east of Nuits-St-Georges. It is rich, soft on the palate and extremely rare. St Florentin, a spicy, soft cows' milk cheese washed in brine,

The cheeses of Burgundy displayed in a Dijon fromagerie

Fromage Fort

The very strong version of Chevroton de Mâcon cheese, kept through the winter until it is dark brown and rank, is called in the vineyards *boutons de culottes* (fly buttons). It is grated, mixed with butter, *marc* or leek water, and herbs, sealed in a pot and given an occasional stir. It smells disgusting and it can literally blow its top. In many vineyard villages it is still a favourite snack, spread on bread or toast with a little onion or garlic. Other very strong cheeses, like Epoisses, are used, too.

Try it if you get a chance—just for the experience. We cannot promise that you will like it.

is delicious with a glass or two of Côte de Beaune or Côte de Nuits. Colette, the writer, described buying the farmhouse version, called Soumaintrain, wrapped in beet leaves, but now they use vine leaves.

Epoisses, matured in humid caves for three months, then washed with *marc* every day for two or three weeks, is Burgundy's most famouse cheese. It was invented by 15th century monks in the village of Epoisses in the Auxois, near a charming medieval and Renaissance château beloved of the witty writer Madame de Sévigné, and became over centuries one of Burgundy's great exports. Napoleon loved it and Brillat-Savarin, the diplomat and philosopher who became France's great gastronome, called it 'King of cheeses'. But through German occupation and the need for quickly produced food in two World Wars, it almost died out. Then a farmer Robert Barthaut and his wife revived the old farm-method of production and regularly since then their cheese has won the gold medal for traditional cheese at the Paris Concours Agricole. It takes two litres to make a 250g round of this creamy luxury, which has a strange but attractive and strong smell and taste, smoky in winter when kept in ashes. The Berthaut family now keep Fromagerie de la Perrière, place Champ-de-Foire, Epoisses. Arthur loves the cheese with a glass of one of his favourite wines, Savigny-lès-Beaune, but likes even better its more modern cousin, L'Ami de Chambertin, washed in young Gevrey-Chambertin wine, made by Jean Gaugny of Laiterie de la Côte Brochon, Gevrey-Chambertin. Epoisses is also used for Fromage Fort which is a waste of a lovely cheese.

The goats' cheese Chevroton de Mâcon is also used for Fromage Fort, but when fresh and creamy is often eaten with sugar.

The most widely eaten cows' milk cheese is made commercially in Dijon—Roucy. Sold in square boxes, it is flavoursome but unassuming. Charollais, made from cows' or goats' milk, or a mixture, is hard and nutty—another one used for Fromage Fort.

Around Beaune, keep a good lookout for a lovely, fresh goats' milk cheese flavoured with garlic and herbs called Claquebitou. You are most likely to get it from farms. Look for notices on farm gates.

Two good goats' cheeses from Nièvre are Lormes (near Clamecy) in a cone shape and Dornecy, from local dairies and farms near Vézelay. Vézelay itself produces a soft, gentle goats' cheese in a cone shape.

Gougère, the cheese pastry made traditionally in a ring shape but often now in one-portion squares, is sometimes served as a cheese course but usually as a snack with a glass of red wine or as a bar snack. Tonnerre is proud of its *gougère*.

Burgundy's gâteaux and desserts are often packed with blackcurrants or served with a sauce made from cassis liqueur. *Poire belle Dijonnaise* is delicious—pear poached in red wine, served with a raspberry sauce, cassis, cream and roasted almonds.

Champagne

The Champagne may have 'borrowed' many recipes from its neighbours, including Nord, Ile de France, Alsace and Lorraine, but its chefs have added that certain Champagne flair which possibly grew from their stylish wine. A few tips from neighbours, their own superb ingredients and such delights as smoked ham and venison of Ardennes help to make this a delightful region in which to eat. Within our lifetime the Champagne used to favour heavier northern dishes, especially puddings, but that was when people walked instead of going everywhere by car and did not rely on machines to do all their heavy work. On special occasions you can still buy little goose pies and a flat bacon, pork and veal pie from the Ardennes called *la palette à la viande*. The shops of Reims still sell the traditional New Year's Eve veal pies which used to be sold in the streets. You can still buy bread in traditional 2.5–5.5kg (6–12lb) loaves called *miches* or michettes (900g, just under 2lb), which workers ate for lunch, filled with bacon or simply studded with garlic cloves.

In winter *la soupe du boeuf* is still a mainstay—a beef *potée* with plenty of different vegetables. *La potée Champenoise* (the vendange soup-stew), served after the last cart or truck loaded with grapes leaves the vineyard, suitably garlanded with vines and autumn leaves, should traditionally contain five meats, including bacon and pork, plus sausages. Pork is still the main ingredient of Champagne dishes, including, of course, *sanglier*, the wild boar of Ardennes-Français. *Andouillettes* are made all over the region, although the *andouillettes* of Troyes are most famous (see above). In fact, Troyes makes them from mutton as well as pork. *Langues fumées* (smoked lambs' tongues) is another Troyes speciality. Rethel is renowned for *boudin blanc*, soft pork sausage served grilled, fried or in a sauce. The nationally popular *jambon d'Ardennes* is smoked ham, cut in very thin slices, but the cured hams of Reims are often baked in puff pastry and served as a snack or part of a main meal.

Pork chops with herbs are a very popular family dish. Fried bacon pieces are served in salads, especially with endive, cos lettuce or *pissenlits* (dandelion—see box, p 58).

Wild boar of Ardennes is delicious when marinaded on the bone in white wine with shallot, garlic, parsley, thyme, bay and pepper, then gently pot-roasted. The French Ardennes is seeking to ensure that products using its

'Wet-the-Bed'

The French name 'pissenlits' shows that the French once shared our legend about the dangers of taking dandelions into your house. But that has not stopped them. Dandelion leaves are picked to serve in salads in May when the leaves are tender but very bitter. But one of the traditional dandelion dishes (*pissenlits au lard*) is served hot. Take 225–250g (9–10oz) small wild dandelion leaves, 125g (5oz) potatoes, 125g (5oz) lean green streaky bacon, 1 shallot, 1 medium onion, 2 tablespoons (2 x 15ml spoon) wine vinegar, salt, pepper. Wash dandelion, discarding discoloured leaves, cut each plant into halves or quarters. Boil potatoes and mash. Cut bacon into 15mm (½ in pieces, sauté in a very little butter, until crisp. Put the dandelion into a thick pan, add finely chopped shallot and onion and mashed potato. Heat very gently, to soften the dandelion without cooking it. Pour the vinegar over the bacon and let it just bubble. Add to dandelion and potato, mixing well. Add pepper (and salt unless bacon is salty). Serve.

name are authentic by issuing a badge showing a boar's head for approved products, and any customers can complain to a Councillor if they think the product is inferior. Ardennes ham has to be dried in correct conditions for at least ten days.

Pigs' trotters would seem a bit out of place in a region producing such aristocratic wine. A visitor might expect to be served the fashionable lightweight dishes of modern cuisine, such as *ris de veau* (calf sweetbreads), thin slices of nearly raw duck's breast (*magret de canard*), loup de mer (sea bass), *lotte* (monkfish) or *sandre* (a delicate river fish). But pigs' trotters are still a favourite regional delicacy. A renowned dish is *pieds Sainte-Menehould* (pronounced 'menou'), in which the trotters are simmered very slowly in wine with herbs for about 24hr, until even the bones can be chopped, wrapped in breadcrumbs, then grilled in butter. Even the greatest chefs of Champagne, including the incomparable Gérard Boyer of Reims, offer their customers pigs' trotters, although they do use rather superior stuffings (see box, p 80).

Champagne once had a national reputation for freshwater fish and today it is the one region where they can make *quenelles de brochet* (pike pasta—a boring fish in a tiny dumpling) taste almost enticing. Even then, we need a Nantua sauce—the rich cream crayfish sauce from Ain. *Cervelas de brochet*, a sausage of pike, usually mixed with potato, seems to have more flavour.

The excellent old French tradition of serving seasonal dishes as a separate course is kept up in country districts. These may include cabbage, small fresh green beans, field mushrooms and asparagus. In Aube leeks (or pumpkins) are made into tarts with cream, as they are in Flemish areas of the North (Flamiche de l'Aube) and the Aube has an excellent starter or snack called *gougères de Riceys*—a hot pastry filled with cauliflower cheese.

Like the Bresse chicken, Chaource cheese has an official Appellation d'Origine Contrôlée to make sure that no cheap imitations soil our palates. Incidentally it now shares this AOC honour, originally intended for wines, with walnuts from Grenoble, Chasselas grapes, certain olives, lentils from Puy, two types of potato and even some Golden Delicious apples, which, as they say in Kent, are neither golden nor delicious, and came originally from the US anyway. The cheese comes from the Chaource area, 30km (19 miles) from Troyes, should be made from the milk of three types of cows—Brune des Alpes, Frisonne and Tachetée de l'Est—and should have a 50 per cent fat content. The white crust is slightly pink, the texture is fine and creamy and it tastes slightly of wild mushrooms and nuts. It is at its best in summer and autumn, but so are most Champagne cheeses.

Chaumont produces a cows' milk cheese with a strong spicy flavour, shaped in a truncated cone. It is rather similar to the tangy Langres cheese, which comes in flat discs, has a strong smell and can be eaten earlier, from spring through to autumn. An Emmenthal cheese is also produced in Haute Marne, around Balesnes village. From Ervy-le-Châtel, near Troyes, comes a very pleasant, smooth, flowery cheese, sold in truncated cones from spring to autumn. An enjoyable soft cheese tasting of fruit and nuts is Les Riceys, made in a small corner of l'Aube from skimmed milk, dried in humid caves and coated in ashes. Ardennes produces a similar cheese from near Rocroi (*cendré de Rocroy* or *des Ardennes*).

The best known cheese outside Champagne is the commercial Carré de l'Est, dismissed by some gourmets as being of little interest, yet consumed in great quantities by families not only in Champagne and Lorraine but in many countries of Europe. It is mild and rather bland, rather like a milder Brie, and usually appears in square boxes (hence 'carré').

The Champagne region has its share of Michelin-starred and gastronomic restaurants but it is especially rich in truly good smaller family restaurants. Some are in little wine villages. Popular with Epernay people, especially at lunchtime, is *Le Caveau* at Cumières on the north side of the river Marne, made from an old Champagne cave which became too small. One of our favourite inns is *Auberge St Vincent* in the small but important wine village of Ambonnay on the Montagne de Reims circuit. A Logis de France, it is the village bar, the meeting place, and centre for local receptions and celebrations. Its excellent meals lure food lovers from Reims, Epernay, Châlons—and Britain. It was discovered by the Hearn family of Inntravel in York. Patron Jean-Claude Pelletier has researched old recipes to produce a true *Cuisine du Terroir*. His dishes include *petits gris* (tiny grey local snails), lambs' tongues preserved in ratafia (an apéritif of local grape juice and *marc*), lamb cooked in honey, pike in *beurre rose* (butter, shallots and red wine) and a fine old dish found rarely these days—*boudin blanc* (soft white sausage) made with rabbit. His cooking is polished, his portions good. And the next village is Bouzy, where they make the red, still wine of Champagne and where the true champagne is strong in bouquet, taste and alcohol.

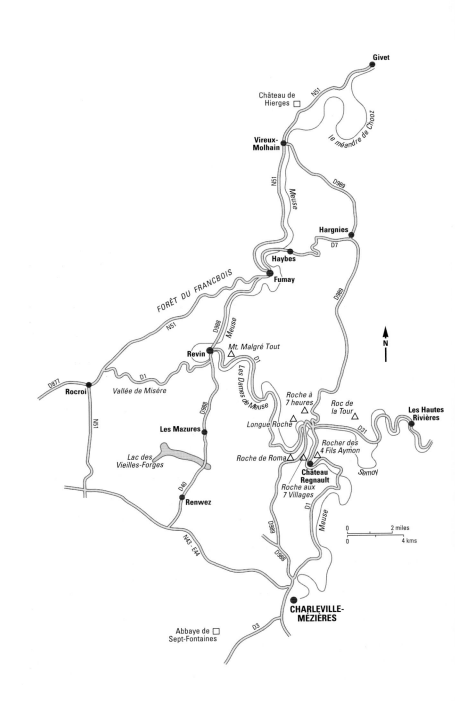

Givet

Château de
Hierges ☐

N51

le méandre de Chooz

Vireux-
Molhain

N51

Meuse

D969

Hargnies

D7

Haybes

Fumay

FORÊT DU FRANCBOIS

N51

D988

Meuse

D989

N

Revin

Mt. Malgré Tout

D1

D877

D1

Rocroi

Vallée de Misére

Les Dames de Meuse

Roche à
7 heures

Roc de
la Tour

Les Hautes
Rivières

N51

D988

Les Mazures

Longue Roche

D31

Rocher des
4 Fils Aymon

Lac des
Vieilles-Forges

Roche de Roma

Château
Regnault

Semoy

D40

Roche aux
7 Villages

Renwez

D1

Meuse

0   2 miles

0   4 kms

N43 - E44

D989

D988

CHARLEVILLE-
MÉZIÈRES

Abbaye de ☐
Sept-Fontaines

D3

5. The French Ardennes

We had had enough of big trucks on the old N43. We seemed to have been following them since Calais. So when we came to a crossroads hamlet called Mon Idée, it seemed a good idea to turn left on the D877. Charleville and Strasbourg could wait. That was how, 20 years ago when we were driving routes for Travellers' France, we found the lonely, beautiful, strange land of the French Ardennes, a quiet, little-known hideout for walkers, cyclists, horse-riders, waterway cruisers and canoeists and car drivers who like to wander, stopping to see views, to walk up hills just to see what is on the other side, to follow mysterious lanes and to get lost.

We came first to the old fortified town of **Rocroi**, its walls and forts still looking as if the Hapsburg Empire's German and Spanish armies were on the march towards it. We walked its **ramparts** planned by Vauban himself and saw in the **museum** how Le Grand Condé, then an unknown but already self-confident army commander of 21 years of age, rashly gambled on using his reserves to defeat utterly the 'invincible' Spanish infantry.

The N51 road passes through the oak and larch forest of Francbois to **Fumay**, capital of the old slate industry in a loop of the Meuse river, with 17th century narrow, tortuously winding streets and a modern town producing telephone cables and *boudin blanc* (white sausage), the latter so renowned that a sausage festival is held in July. The **museum** tells the story of the slate industry and rough life of its workers. Just up river at the attractive little resort of **Haybes** (called Haybes-la-Jolie—the 'pretty'), you can see the white sausages being made at the connoisseurs' favourite Boucherie-Charcuterie Roffidal. They use filet of pork, onion, milk, salt and spices, with no colouring or preservatives. Locals say that a fresh *boudin blanc* never stays uneaten for long enough to need preserving. In season the logis opposite the church, Le Saint Hubert, serves game from the surrounding forest, which is almost as famous. There are so many beautiful or spectacular views across the Meuse valley that tours to see them are organised locally.

At **Vireux-Molhain**, a road leads to the ancient **Collegiate Church of Molhain**, with outstanding Italian interior decoration and 14th–16th century statues. Shortly after another little road leads to the ruins of **Château de**

Hierges on the Belgian border. Built in the 11th century, the château was altered to make it more comfortable as a house in the 16th century Renaissance period. According to a famous Ardennes legend, in this château once lived three valiants, Heribrand, Geoffroy and Vauthier, with their three beautiful young wives, Hodierne, Berthe and Iges. The knights heard the call to join the Crusades to free Jerusalem from the Moslems and put their Christian duty before their nuptial pleasure. For seven months the castle was silent, the young women remained cheerless but faithful. Then, on a terrible stormy night, three young knights sought shelter. As food, drink, music and laughter flowed, the three girls put their duty of hospitality to strangers above faithfulness to their husbands. Jerusalem fell to the Crusaders that night, but all three husbands were killed. Next morning three ravens perched on the castle turrets, each carrying the heart of a dead knight. God turned the three wives into three rocky hills. You can see them, covered in dark trees, never seeing sunlight, above the river and the D1, south of Revin—**Les Dames de Meuse**. With typical irony, legend says that they had given their virtue not to knights but to three poachers in disguise.

The N51 continues to a huge loop in the Meuse (le Méandre de Chooz), with an underground canal joining the gap in the horseshoe. A minor road leads to two nuclear energy plants—Controles Nucléaires des Ardennes. 'Chooz A' was shut down in 1990 after operating for 25 years and 'Chooz B' is expected to be in operation in 1996. Three-quarters of France's electricity comes from nuclear stations. (Group visits can be arranged well ahead. Individuals can visit on Saturday afternoons in July or August. Tel. 24 42 20 96. There is usually a waiting list. The visit takes three hours.)

Givet, the frontier town at the tip of France's wedge into Belgium, is dominated by the ruins of **Charlemont**. This castle was built by Charles V in 1555, to keep the French out of his territory in Belgium, but was later strengthened by Vauban, the greatest military architect, to act as a defence against the Hapsburg German Spanish Empire. It is now used for army training but part of it can be visited in July and August.

Givet is a lovely old town on the Meuse and the 11th century **Tour Grégoire** gives a fine panoramic view over the town, the valley and the Meuse as it flows into Belgium. There is now a bridge across the river from this tower, but local people say that before Waterloo Napoleon had his men and horses ferried across to the tower, while he ate and slept at the old auberge *Maison Baudoin*, where you can still get a good meal.

The 14th century **Tour Victoire** was part of a château belonging to the Counts of Marck.

The interesting **art and craft museum** has moved to a bigger building on Quai de Fours beside the river (Centre Européen des Métiers d'Art). Artists and artisans show their work in metal and wood and can hire a workshop to show visitors how they use their skills. Making of chocolates, cheese, sausages and cider are among the crafts (open 10.00–12.00, 14.30–18.00, except Monday morning).

The river Meuse looping round Monthermé

On 11 November Givet holds an Onion Fair. That day, you are advised to take a big handkerchief to dry your tears.

From Givet railway station you can catch a train to Dinant in Belgium, pulled by a classic steam engine. It runs on Saturday and Sunday in June and September, on Friday, Saturday and Sunday in July and August. About 1.5km over the Belgian border from Vireux-Molhain is a station at Treignes from which you can catch a steam train to Marienbourg in Belgium and which has sheds where old steam locos are repaired and put on show when completed.

Returning, cross the Meuse onto the D989 at Vireux. You are entering the great **Forêt des Ardennes** which covers almost the entire massif. Drive on to Hargnies where the hilly, snaking D7 road right gives some fine views on the way to rejoining the N51 at Haybes or Fumay. Here the D988 follows the Meuse to **Revin**, set in a spectacular double loop of the river where it almost makes a complete circle. Inside the northern loop is the old part of the town surrounding an 18th century church, and the modern part of the town with factories is in the south loop.

Overlooking the town is **Mont Malgré Tout**, a name used by George Sand as the title for a novel in 1869. You must park your car and walk up a pathway to a height of 229m for a view of the town, the meandering river to the Dames de Meuse rocks of the legend and the Vallée de Misère westward towards Rocroi. There is another observation platform, **La Faligeotte**, with views over town and river, which can be reached by car on the D1 at the north-east of the town. Beside the road is a memorial to the local Resistance fighters who were killed in World War II—les Manises. A little road continues for 6.5km (4 miles), from where a sign points you along a short walk to a **Calvary** marking the spot where 106 of the Manises maquis were massacred. The plateau here (Hautes Buttes) is a popular winter area for ski de fond (cross-country skiing).

Westward from Revin, the D1 takes you along the Misère valley to **Rocroi**, passing the old **forge of St Nicholas**, a leftover from the days when iron foundries and forges dotted the Ardennes woods, supplying much of the metal for France's armament industry. The forges were in production until the end of World War II. After the forge you reach the man-made lake and dam providing the hydro-electric power for Revin. The road snakes and climbs through wild, poor countryside.

South from Revin a right fork at Les Mazures leads to a bigger man-made lake, **Lac des Vieilles-Forges**, in a quiet setting among hills covered in oaks, pines and birches, but a little paradise in summer for quieter watersports—sailing, windsurfing, canoeing and fishing, with pleasant beaches for sunbathing. (Information from Base des Loisirs, tel. 24 40 17 20.) There is a 2-star campsite with 300 pitches (tel. 24 40 17 31). About 1.5km (1 mile) south, on the Renwez road, is an unusual semi-open-air **museum of forestry**, showing the history of wood production for domestic and industrial burning and for construction of houses and furniture, some shown by means of figures of foresters made of logs, some with old machines. The woods have two other traditional crops—mushrooms and myrtle. Film shows and exhibitions are held, and competitions of lumberjacks for felling and discharging timber. **Renwez**, 1.5km south, holds three fairs—the Ham Fair (September), the Galette au Sucre et Gâteau (sweet pancake and cake) Fair (June) and the Apple Festival (October). The village has an imposing 16th century church and, 1.5km south-east, the ruined 11th century castle of Montcornet.

The most spectacular road from Revin is the D1, following the Meuse round its loops to Monthermé, the favourite touring centre for visitors. Looping below Mont Malgré Tout, the road runs across the Meuse from the three dark rocks of the unfaithful wives, Les Dames de Meuse, round another loop to **Roches de Laifour**, another wild viewpoint which looks across the river to Les Dames.

At **Monthermé** the rivers Meuse and Semoy meet in a great horse-shoe shaped loop which has been called the most spectacular in France. Certainly, many of these great meanders of the Meuse river make those of the beautiful Dordogne look rather tame. The main town is within the loop, ending in forest which looks impenetrable. Its main street, lined with old houses, leads to **St Léger church**, built between 12th and 15th centuries with local stone. On the outside of the loop along one bank has grown a more modern town and a few factories in the suburb of Laval-Dieu. There are only 27 hotel beds in Monthermé, all in two logis, but visitors stay in private houses, in the three campsites, in gîtes spread around the countryside nearby, or in the river cruisers which they hire. Within 5km (3 miles) of Monthermé are five hilltop sites with superb views. But to reach some you must leave your car and walk up a steep path.

This is true of **Roc de la Tour**, and it is not surprising, for legend says that

Horses of the Ardennes

When Duke Aymon of Ardennes took his four sons to the Court of the Emperor Charlemagne in Paris to be trained as knights, the magnificent horse Bayart went with them. The emperor was very impressed by the valour of the four boys, especially the eldest, Renault, who became a friend of Charlemagne's nephew Berthelais. But these two quarrelled over a game of chess and Renault struck Berthelais dead with a chessboard.

All four boys fled, carried by Bayart and chased by Charlemagne's troops. They hid in the fortress-Château Regnault beside the Meuse river in Ardennes. Charlemagne's troops laid siege to the castle, but Aymon's sons knew a secret passage into the forest and hunted game each night for food. Alas, a defender betrayed them and opened the gates to Charlemagne's men. Though they fought fiercely, the four sons were overwhelmed; so they quickly mounted Bayart, who jumped a great loop of the Meuse in one bound to carry them to safety. Here the story becomes muddled.

The four rocks called Quatre Fils Aymon beside the Meuse south of Monthermé are said to be the four sons turned to stone by the devil, and there is a splendid stone sculptured monument to them and Bayart on the hillside. But in the most famous chanson de geste, one of the stories sung by troubadours in the Middle Ages, the brothers (and of course the Wonder Horse Bayart) turn up in many later adventures, their travels ranging from Gascony and Brittany to Jerusalem and Cologne.

The friendly, patient horses like underslung Shires which you see now pulling carts laden with logs, machinery or especially tourists during the summer, have very different talents. They certainly can't leap legendary distances, but they can pull incredibly big loads and they can 'turn on a franc piece', as the owner of one team told us. For centuries, the great iron and steel foundries of the Ardennes could not operate without them and they made forestry very much easier. A team could manoeuvre and twist round the most difficult and steep pathways, pulling great oak trees or a huge load of logs, and they could carry the iron ore to the foundries and the completed iron and steel over the mountainsides to the main roads long before trucks were strong enough to do it. Some teams were working until the 1950s. When the foundries closed after World War II, they were still useful in the forests and mountains.

We have seen them recently in summer pulling loads of tourists. We could swear that they wore a slightly smug smile at having such a light load.

the Devil himself put the 'tower' there. You take the D31 road eastward from Monthermé for 3km (2 miles), leave your car and take a pathway left for a 20 min walk. The quartz rock, surrounded by birch trees, gives you impressive views over the Semoy river valley. A man who wanted to please his young wife offered his soul to the Devil in return for a beautiful castle, to be built between sunset and cockcrow. As the sun went down the earth opened and hundreds of minor devils rushed out and started to build like fury. But, as is the way of cocks, even in Kent, where we live, this one had a restless night and started to crow at 3.00 am. The little devils hurried back to hell and the Devil himself angrily kicked what had been built of the castle into the river Semoy below. Alas, one rock killed the girl for whom the castle was being built and another, intended for a tower, refused to move. Now it is used by rock climbers for practice.

Roche à Sept Heures is only just over 1.5km along the D989 Hargnies road north, then a tarmac track. From the spur of rock, you have a plunging view down to Monthermé and the Meuse horseshoe. Beyond you can see Château Regnault and Rocher des Quatre Fils Aymon (see box, p 65).

Beyond Roche à Sept Heures, a tarmac track leads to a car park. A half-hour stroll takes you to **Longue Roche**. Take the path to the top for extensive and quite wild views over the Meuse valley—more impressive than Sept Heures.

Three kilometres (2 miles) south of Monthermé on the D989, the road climbs to reveal a view over the valley. Stairs up the peak of **Roche aux Sept Villages** show you the Meuse twisting past seven villages between Monthermé and Deville. After this site, a road leads to another called **Roche de Roma** with a slightly inferior view of the same stretch of the Meuse.

The river Semoy is narrower, often shallower and just as sinuous as the Meuse. The lanes climbing up to the riverside hamlets are narrower and less frequented and river traffic is confined to kayak canoes and little flat-bottomed fishermen's rowing boats. Although the Meuse is a paradise for fishermen, the best they can expect to catch is the pike (*brochet*) while the Semoy fishermen still catch delicious trout. The little lanes are often a rough climb from the river into deep, wild forest, hardly penetrable off the tracks. The few people living there have a lonely life. The cult of the goddess Diana and Druidism survived here for centuries after they had died elsewhere and the legends of the Ardennes are themselves a survival among the forest people.

The nearest thing to a town is the big riverside village of **Les Hautes-Rivières**, near the Belgian border. You have only to climb to the river bridge to see the Semoy flowing in Belgium, under a different name—the Semois. Until the EEC became well established, a supermarket in Hautes-Rivières did a good trade in selling wine, spirits and food at French prices to Belgian tourists going home.

Only recently, when we could find no bed in Monthermé, did we discover *l'Auberge en Ardennes* in Hautes-Rivières, recommended to us as 'a traditional no-nonsense relais with good family cooking'. It was more than that. It was a truly rustic old family-run country inn of the type which have almost died out in France, replaced by 'smarter' places with colourful plastic furniture and juke-boxes to brighten the lives of the young. The old auberge had a rough garden down to the river and bedroom views over river and forest. We were perplexed by old pictures of the inn calling it a farm. After all, it was in the main street.

Mme Sandrine Lallouette, the friendly patronne, explained that her family had kept a farm for generations until the 1930s. It doubled as an inn to accommodate visitors coming to do business with the forges and iron foundries which prospered in the Ardennes for centuries, and with the wood suppliers of the forests. The dining room where we ate a real family-cooked country meal used to be the cow sheds. But the main farm business has been breeding those powerful, low slung horses, which we had seen in the forests—used until they were superseded by lorries. The family kept them on the hill pastures nearby and hired them out in teams (see box, p 65).

The Ardennes seen from the roads, rather than the river, looks like a different country from the river Meuse. In summer, it is usually a placid river taking its time to wander round its loops and big meanders, and the traffic is sparse, so that whether you canoe from one campsite to another or hire a pleasure cruiser to 'camp' aboard, piloting your craft is easy and locks are easy to operate. The lazy way is to take a trip aboard a bateau-mouche and sit with a cool drink in your hand watching the changing scene of dark forest-clad hills, the great rocks and crags, the little forest ravines running red with iron, green pastures of the southern Ardennes and the villages with their little old quays left from the days when the Meuse was their lifeline. A beautiful relaxing voyage—very different from taking a bateau-mouche on the Seine through Paris. Monthermé is the major centre for bateau-mouche trips on the Meuse. They start from **Quai de Paquis** and run daily in July and August, on Sunday from early April until the end of October. The main centre for hiring self-drive cruisers is **Pont à Bar**, between Sedan and Charleville.

The most interesting road from Monthermé to Charleville-Mézières is the smallest and most winding, the D1, which passes Château Regnault and, on a hilltop, **Rocher des Quatre Fils Aymon**, marking the spot where, according to the most famous of Ardennes legends, the wonder-horse Bayart jumped clean across the wide meander of the Meuse carrying four brothers escaping from Charlemagne's army (see box, p 65).

Before entering Charleville, the road skirts the industrial suburb of **Nouzonville**, where the Meuse meets the little river Goutelle. Along its banks are still metallurgic factories, descendants of the old iron forges and foundries which were worked here for centuries. Nail-making became a local industry in the 15th century when Charles the Rash, Duke of Burgundy, introduced craftsmen from Liège, part of his big empire.

You arrive at **CHARLEVILLE-MÉZIÈRES** on Quai Arthur Rimbaud alongside the Meuse. Rimbaud, the rebel poet born in 1854 in Charleville, buried there in 1891, wrote all his poetry by the age of 20. Yet he still influences modern French literature and is studied in schools (see box, p 71).

Until 1606 Charleville was a village called Arches, standing across the

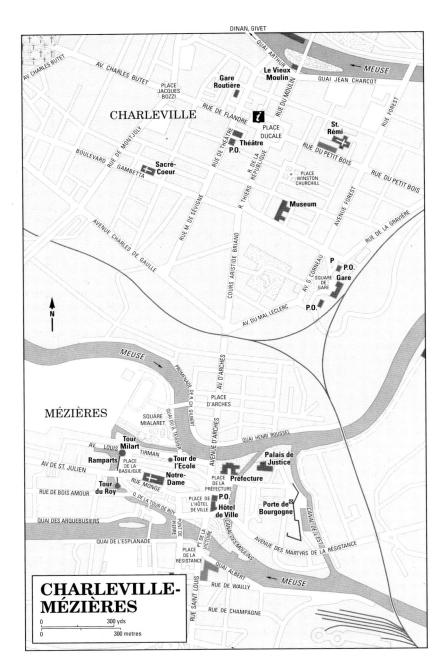

DINAN, GIVET

QUAI ARTHUR

MEUSE

AV. CHARLES BUTET

AV. CHARLES BUTET

PLACE
JACQUES
BOZZI

Gare
Routière

Le Vieux
Moulin

QUAI JEAN CHARCOT

RUE DU MOULIN

RUE FOREST

CHARLEVILLE

RUE DE FLANDRE

i

PLACE
DUCALE

St.
Rémi

RUE DE MONTJOLY

RUE DE THÉÂTRE

Théâtre
P.O.

RUE DU PETIT BOIS

BOULEVARD GAMBETTA

RUE DE GAMBETTA

Sacré-
Coeur

R. DE LA
RÉPUBLIQUE

PLACE
WINSTON
CHURCHILL

RUE DU PETIT BOIS

RUE M. DE SÉVIGNE

R. THIERS

Museum

AVENUE FOREST

RUE DE LA GRAVIÈRE

AVENUE CHARLES DE GAULLE

COURS ARISTIDE BRIAND

R. G. CORNEAU

P
P.O.

N

SQUARE
DE
GARE

Gare

AV. DU MAL LECLERC

P.O.

MEUSE

PROMENADE DE R. CH. GILBERT

AV. D'ARCHES

PLACE
D'ARCHES

MÉZIÈRES

SQUARE
MIALARET

QUAI DU G. TEISSIER

Tour
Milart

AV. LOUIS

TIRMAN

AVENUE D'ARCHES

QUAI HENRI ROUSSEL

AV DE ST. JULIEN

Ramparts

PLACE
DE LA
BASILIQUE

Tour de
l'École

Palais de
Justice

RUE DE BOIS AMOUR

Tour
du Roy

RUE MONGE

Notre-
Dame

PLACE
DE LA
PRÉFECTURE

Préfecture

Q. DE LA TOUR DE ROY

QUAI DES ARQUEBUSIERS

PLACE DE
L'HÔTEL
DE VILLE

P.O.

Hôtel
de Ville

Porte de
Bourgogne

CANAL DE L'EST

QUAI DE L'ESPLANADE

PONT DE
PIERRE

PT DE LA
VICTOIRE

CANAL DES MOULINS

AVENUE DES MARTYRS DE LA RÉSISTANCE

PLACE
DE LA
RÉSISTANCE

QUAI ALBERT

MEUSE

RUE DE WAILLY

RUE SAINT LOUIS

RUE DE CHAMPAGNE

CHARLEVILLE-
MÉZIÈRES

0   300 yds
0   300 metres

Meuse from the important fortified town of Mézières. Charles de Gonzagne, Duke of Rethel, obtained trading concessions from Louis XIII of France which made the area prosperous, so decided to build a worthy capital, giving it his name. Later he commissioned the young architect Clément Métezeau to build a complete new town with mathematical regularity, planned around a central square, place Ducale. Clément was the brother of Louis Métezeau, designer of place des Vosges in Paris, and the **place Ducale** still remains one of the finest in Europe, despite the terrible Meuse floods of January 1995, when much of the city was flooded to a depth of 6m and the rushing water did damage some of which will take years to repair. Clément built a series of houses arcaded on the ground floor with four arches, four in the two storeys above, and four smaller dormer windows in the steep pointed roofs with 'fish-scale' tiles. The ochre brick frames of the windows blend with red bricks, and the whole effect is of elegant uniformity which cannot be destroyed even by the many colours of the cars parked by the kerbs. But the scene does burst into colour every Tuesday, Thursday and Saturday morning as market stalls are filled with fruits and vegetables.

Le Vieux Moulin, near the quayside, is the old ducal mill, which does not look like one. It was built to fit into the symmetry of the town plan and has a splendid façade in Louis XIII style with Italianate Ionic columns. Housed in part of it is the **Musée Rimbaud**, with photos and souvenirs of the poet.

Behind place Ducale in an old prison lives Charleville's most distinguished citizen, Le Grand Marionnettiste. You can see the distinguished old gentleman's head poking through a dormer window, just above a **clock**. When the hour strikes, curtains open below the clock and puppets act part of the epic legend of Les Quatre Fils Aymon (the four Aymon brothers; see box, p 65), while he recites a few sentences in his booming voice. Even when he is not putting on his show, the great puppet-master moves his head, surveying the passing scene with his dark eyes. Each Saturday at 21.15 he recites the whole legendary story, scene after scene, while his puppets act the drama. And in all weathers the audience turns up.

The Marionnettiste's house is the home of the **International Puppet Institute**, which organises every three years a World Puppet Festival. Puppets and their operators arrive from all over the world—puppets modern and traditional, funny, serious and political, pretty, handsome and downright ugly. The 10th festival was held in 1994.

A new **Ardennes museum** aims to show the story of Ardennes through collections of exhibits covering archaeology, history, wood, metal, glass, painting and sculpture. Charleville is, as it always was, a great junction of roads and trade routes into Germany and Central Europe. But it keeps its elegant calm like a highly trained diplomat.

Over the Meuse in the medieval town of **Mézières**, which was a separate town until 1966, you can still see two ancient towers, a town gateway and much of the old ramparts. The marriage of Charles IX of France with Elisabeth of Austria took place in 1570 at the Basilica of Notre Dame de l'Espérance,

The puppet master's clock in action at Charleville-Mézières

Rimbaud

Considering that Arthur Rimbaud, enfant terrible of French poetry, wrote very insulting poems and letters about Charleville, his home town has been very kind to him. It has set up a little museum with photos, copies of his poems and other souvenirs in one of its most distinguished buildings, Vieux Moulin, bestriding the Meuse. It must have been difficult to find enough material for a museum collection, since he 'retired' from literature in 1873 when he was 19 years of age, burning all his manuscripts, and was dead at 37. But portraits show an angelic face with a look of bored disdain which tell us something about him. The people of Charleville have also changed the name of quai de Madeleine, where he lived, to quai Rimbaud, and put up a monument to him in the station square.

Rimbaud published his first book of poems at 16. At 19 he wrote a prose volume *Une Saison en Enfer* (A Season in Hell), in which he tried to show by symbolism his wish to break from the past. The critics were unkind about it. He never wrote another work. He took to wandering.

Rimbaud's father was an army captain, who was rarely at home and in 1860 finally abandoned his wife and her three children. She brought them up strictly. At the Collège de Charleville, Arthur won prize after prize and his professor of literature introduced him to contemporary poetry. After his first book was published, he ran away to Paris with a ticket good only as far as St Quentin, was arrested and spent two days in prison. Back in Charleville, between drinking and idling, he wrote *Le Bateau Ivre* (The Drunken Boat), probably his best work. The language is eccentric but brilliantly evocative. He was invited to Paris by the poet Verlaine, ten years his senior, already established as one of the 'art for art's sake' poets, and press officer of the Communards, the extreme left-wing group who temporarily seized power in Paris in 1871 but lost it because the rest of France was not interested.

Verlaine and Rimbaud started a stormy relationship. They debauched, drank and quarrelled their way around London and Paris. But somehow in 1872 Rimbaud wrote his major work *Les Illuminations*, poems in prose and verse written as if in sudden fits of inspiration and sensation, using childhood memories, dreams and mysticism to show his dislike of worldly materialism. In Brussels, in 1873, during what must have been a particularly violent quarrel, Verlaine shot and wounded Rimbaud. As a consequence, Verlaine went to prison for two years.

After his 'retirement', Rimbaud worked for a while in an office in Reading. Then he became a nomad. He joined the Dutch Colonial

CHAMPAGNE & BURGUNDY

Army in Batavia (now called Djarkarta) but deserted, worked in Cyprus as foreman on the building site of the governor-general's palace, joined a German circus troupe bound for Sweden and in British-controlled Aden worked with a coffee company, which sent him to Harer in Ethiopia, where he lived with a local girl, explored parts of the country unknown to Europeans and even turned gunrunner, very unsuccessfully.

He brushed aside impatiently any references to his previous life or his writing. When Verlaine had his book *Les Illuminations* published in 1886 and it was a success, he completely ignored it. The publishers described it as 'by the late Arthur Rimbaud' and Verlaine pocketed the proceeds. Rimbaud did return occasionally to his mother's farm at Roche. In April 1891, his leg became badly infected and he sailed for Marseilles, where it was amputated. He went to Roche to recover, but the leg got worse, so he returned to Marseilles, where he died on 10 November 1891. He was buried in the cemetery at Charleville.

He is honoured in Charleville these days by the very people he despised—the bourgeoisie. They use his name or the title of his best-known poem *Le Bateau Ivre* for bars, cafés and shops, and his story as bait for tourists. His poems are compulsory reading for school-children. They have inspired many moderns—Tennessee Williams, Jim Morrison, William Burroughs and even Bob Dylan. He might be summed up in his own phrase, used now as the title of a student magazine *Je est un Autre* (I is someone else).

'restored' over centuries but ending in full Flamboyant Gothic style with interesting stained glass.

In World War I the Germans had their headquarters for the Somme Front in Mézières, and the Kaiser himself stayed there.

Eight kilometres (5 miles) south-west of Charleville in the charming Fagnon valley is the old *Abbaye de Sept-Fontaines*, built in the 18th century. It is now a high quality hotel with a nine-hole golf course and a game forest nearby. In World War I, the Germans turned it into a casino where Kaiser Wilhelm II gambled. Then it was owned by Yvonne de Gaulle, wife of the General, who stayed there. The rooms have bathrooms, television and mini-bar. The monks in their cells would surely have wondered whether it was heaven or temptation.

Some 24km (15 miles) south-east along the river is the ancient and historic town of Sedan with the biggest fortress in Europe.

6. *Charleville to Reims*

Forty years ago, Reims was a dream city to most Britons. They hoped to go there once in their lifetime. Faster ferries, the Channel Tunnel, but above all the modern network of French motorways have changed all that. Reims is one of the major targets for weekends and organised short breaks. So the idea of driving there via Charleville is pure wanderlust. But that is the way to see France—connoisseurs' France—and we would certainly not regret having gone that way often.

The fastest way out of Charleville towards Rethel and Reims is by the N51, but the most attractive is by the little D3. The first 19km (12 miles) to **Launois-sur-Vence** is especially pleasant, and Launois itself is interesting. It is a 17th century staging post where horses were changed and it still has a genuine old **Relais de Diligence** with attractive old stalls. An antique and secondhand dealers' fair, famous all over France, is held on the second Sunday of every month except August. You can buy anything from very old books to fresh local sausages. Launois specialises in festivals from vintage car rallies to flower shows.

If you are not in a great hurry, it is worth taking the D27 north-west for 11km (7 miles) to **Signy-l'Abbaye**, a pleasant little town beside two forests of oaks, beeches, ash and maple, with small driveable roads and marked walking and cycling tracks. It is a good centre for a weekend, staying at the 2-star logis, *Auberge de l'Abbaye* (in the same family for a century and well known for its regional dishes). The little Vaux river divides the two forests, re-emerging after a stretch underground in the middle of Signy-l'Abbaye at Gouffre de Gibergeon.

A charming, quite short wanderer's route to Rethel is to take the D2 forest road from Signy to **Lalobbe**, a village renowned for its cider. Then turn left onto D102 to the fascinating village of **Wasigny**, where the 16th–17th century château has a prime site by the river Vaux. Most of the village is of old half-timbered houses, some superb, and there is a fine wooden covered market. The bent beams which make the old houses look so delightful did not show originally—they were covered with daub of mud and sand which has washed away over centuries.

The D8 takes you to **Novion-Porcien** on the main road to Rethel. Novion has a **museum of Three Wars**, showing military items from the Franco-Prussian War and World Wars I and II. The section on the Battle of the Ardennes is interesting—so are the vehicles. Only recently have historians

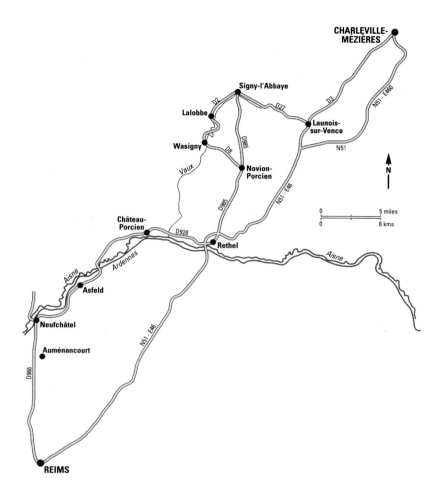

realised the true importance of this last great effort in France by the Germans in World War II.

Rethel is a pleasant town on the banks of the Aisne river and Ardennes canal but has a number of eccentricities. It looks modern because 85 per cent of it is. The French 2nd and 14th Infantry divisions defended the Aisne crossing so stoutly in 1940 that German artillery, tanks and bombers knocked down most of the town to dislodge them. Local people seem proudest of the fact that Louis Hachette, the publisher whose name is still on dictionaries, guide books and textbooks which are found all over the world, was born there in 1800. Paul Verlaine, the 'art for art's sake' 19th century poet, gets less attention because he only taught Literature and English at the College of Notre-Dame.

On a hill opposite the château is the strange but dominant **Church of St Nicolas**, much restored after damage in 1940. It is two churches in one, with two naves. One part of the church started life in the 12th–13th centuries as the chapel of Benedictine monks attached to the abbey of St Remi at Reims. The other half was built in the 14th–15th centuries as the local parish church, and has a splendid Gothic-Flamboyant doorway. A heavy square tower was added in the 17th century.

An important cattle market is held in Rethel, but it is known nationally for Boudin Blanc de Rethel, white sausage of pork and onion, which is delicious. Taste it in *Au Sanglier des Ardennes*, a family-run logis which has arisen like a phoenix from destruction in two wars and is renowned for boudin.

The smaller winding D926 road following the Aisne from Rethel to Reims, is slower and 9.5km (6 miles) longer than the N51 but much more interesting. The little port where the Roman road from Reims to Cologne crossed the Aisne river was called Portus, then Portien and is now **Château-Porcien**. It remained an important crossing for centuries and the local people built fortified houses for protection against wandering bands of soldiers who ravaged the countryside. Many of the houses are still there, reminders of this area's warlike past. Even churches doubled as fortresses. But not the **village church** at **Asfeld**, just past the village of Balham on the D926. It is a remarkable extravaganza in Baroque. Jean-Antoine de Mesmes, brother of the local count, had travelled widely in Europe, studying and admiring Versailles, St Peter's and other 'modern' buildings and when in 1680 the village (then called Avaux) needed a new church he determined to give it a truly memorable building. He called in a Dominican father, François Romain, to plan it with him. The result is more like a cathedral than a village church. It is a synthesis of domes, rotundas and curves, with hardly a right-angle, built not in stone but in local brick. It is said to be in the shape of a viola, but you would need to fly low over it to be sure of that. As you look at it in surprise, wonder or admiration, just imagine the effect it had on 17th century villagers—and the arguments it caused.

The road joins the D966 at Neufchâtel-sur-Aisne and proceeds to Aumenancourt, near where it leaves Ardennes for the département of Aube, renumbered RD366. Shortly afterwards you reach **REIMS**. Reims is a French national ikon. When it was attacked in World War I, Parisians stopped strangers in the street, crying 'Reims is burning' and they shed tears together.

Today Reims is a puzzling place. Other cities can be a mixture of old and new but few others have them blended to the point of bewilderment. It is such a hurried, harried commercial city, with traffic jams, Paris-style driving and a desperate shortage of car parking, yet it is also a tranquil city of lovely ancient churches and is built on mile upon mile of secretive tunnels and caverns lined with precious nectar called Champagne. It can come as a shock to find that the wonderful 13th century bourgeois **Le Vergeur** house with a 16th century Renaissance wing, now used as a museum of Old Reims, is a

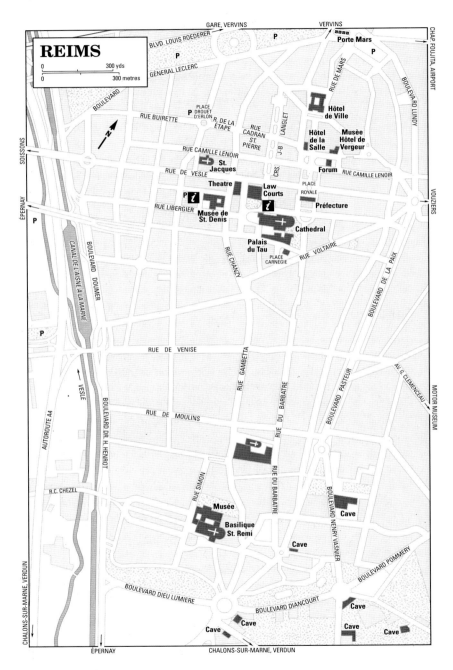

GARE, VERVINS

VERVINS

CHAP. FOUJITA, AIRPORT

REIMS

BLVD. LOUIS ROEDERER

P

Porte Mars

0   300 yds
0   300 metres

P

P

GÉNERAL LECLERC

RUE DE MARS

BOULEVARD LUNDY

BOULEVARD

SOISSONS

RUE BUIRETTE

PLACE DROUET D'ERLON

P

R. DE LA ÉTAPE

RUE CADRAN ST PIERRE

LANGLET

Hôtel de Ville

Hôtel de la Salle

Musée Hôtel de Vergeur

RUE CAMILLE LENOIR

St. Jacques

J-B

Forum

RUE CAMILLE LENOIR

RUE DE VESLE

CRS

Theatre

Law Courts

PLACE ROYALE

VOUZIERS

ÉPERNAY

P

RUE LIBERGIER

P *i*

i

Musée de St. Denis

Préfecture

Cathedral

Palais du Tau

PLACE CARNEGIE

RUE VOLTAIRE

BOULEVARD DE LA PAIX

RUE CHANZY

BOULEVARD DOUMER

CANAL DE L'AISNE À LA MARNE

P

RUE DE VENISE

RUE GAMBETTA

BOULEVARD PASTEUR

AV. G. CLÉMENCEAU

MOTOR MUSEUM

VESLE

BOULEVARD DR. H. HENROT

RUE DE MOULINS

RUE DU BARBATRE

AUTOROUTE A4

R.C. CHEZEL

RUE SIMON

Musée

Basilique St. Remi

Cave

Cave

BOULEVARD HENRY VASNIER

BOULEVARD POMMERY

CHALONS-SUR-MARNE, VERDUN

BOULEVARD DIEU LUMIERE

BOULEVARD DIANCOURT

Cave

Cave

Cave

Cave

Cave

ÉPERNAY

CHALONS-SUR-MARNE, VERDUN

76

complete reconstruction skilfully using old parts which survived from the original, a victim of the terrifying martyrdom of Reims in World War I, when the city was part of the front line, bombarded until 85 per cent of the houses were destroyed.

It is an even bigger shock to find that so many of the sculptures on the **Cathedral of Notre Dame**, perhaps the finest expression of Gothic art in the world, are casts or copies, replacing not only stone damaged beyond repair by four years of shelling in World War I but stone worn away by weather, so that sculptured features have been obliterated. You can see the worn originals next door in the Bishops' Palace—**Palais du Tau**—itself much rebuilt. But you have only to stand and drink in the perfection and beauty of this extravagant religious offering to know that these restorations not only don't matter but were wise. And no upstart architect has dared to alter or add to the original plan of the building started in 1211 and not completed for another two centuries. No one has added spires, or extra towers, or widened the nave. Those sorts of additions have been the curse of French restorations.

In Périgueux, Abadie, who later built Sacré Coeur in Paris, 'restored' St Front's cathedral by adding 17 turrets, replaced Romanesque carvings with 19th century work and scrapped a Romanesque refectory to make the cathedral more 'geometric'. Imagine what he might have done to Reims!

The great west façade is truly breathtaking. Above three deep-set doorways are 13th century sculptures, including a row of 63 unidentified kings, each about 3m tall and weighing 6 tonnes each, and the superlative rose-window, crowned by two great sculptured towers. Above the left doorway is the famous **Ange au Sourire** (the smiling angel) whose smile is said to be sexy. Strange, because St Nicaise next to her has been scalped by vandals.

The time to be inside the cathedral is in low season, when there are few visitors and no guides talking in different languages to groups. Then you can study the 17 tapestries of the 16th century, which are used so effectively to temper the sobriety of the stone. You have time to stand and drink in the sheer beauty of the colourful glass **windows**—the 13th century rose-window, the other 13th century windows cared for and restored by the Simon family over generations, the modern abstracts by Brigitte Simon-Marque and the superb, dominantly blue windows by Marc Chagall which are some of the finest of this painter's work. It is a pity that Chagall did not produce more work in glass. Strangely, one of his very few collections is in a little village church in Tudeley, near Tonbridge in Kent. He designed them as a memorial to a beautiful girl we knew, heiress daughter of one of his English friends. She was drowned at the age of 20 in a sailing accident.

The cathedral was built to mark the site of a baptism which took place here way back in AD 498. The Romans had returned to defend their city against invaders. The northern tribes were invading Belgium and Champagne and the main defender was Clovis, King of the Franks. St Remi, Bishop of Reims, converted him to Christianity and baptised him, which must have done a great deal to influence, if not dictate, the future history of Europe. It certainly added to the importance of Reims. French kings were crowned in the old Abbey of St Remi, built in the 11th century at the place where St Remi was buried, and the tradition was continued when the new cathedral was finished. Unwillingly, Joan of Arc's 'gentil dauphin' was crowned Charles VII here in 1429, with Joan holding her banner over his head. Joan had led him to Reims through English-held territory.

St Remi Basilica, built mostly in the 12th century, is an enormous old Benedictine abbey church with two towers and a great, high Romanesque nave, from which is suspended a gilt crown with 96 lights, once candles, one for each year of St Remi's life. The cathedral was built over a church which replaced a little chapel where St Remi was buried in AD 533. His grave is now covered with an enormous tomb built in 1840 which incorporates 16th century statues depicting Remi's baptism of Clovis. In a rather sombre but peaceful setting, the Renaissance Gothic choir screen gives elegant and light relief. Alongside is the **Abbey of St Rémi**, remarkably restored after tremendous damage while acting as a hospital in World War I. It houses the city's museum of history and archaeology. This includes a military section with a remarkable collection of old arms (épées, sabres, muskets and all sorts of pistols) showing the development of arms from the 16th to the 19th century.

The city's arts museum (**Musée St Denis**) is in an enormous 18th century abbey in rue de Chanzy, with rooms so big that exhibits can look rather lost. The paintings of local dignitaries are rather dull, but the tapestries are very interesting, including the inevitable life of St Rémi; so are the portrait drawings by the two Germans, Cranach father and son. The French paintings, mostly landscapes of the 19th century and early 20th century, are excellent. Good pictures by Géricault and Delacroix are followed by landscapes by the artists who worked at Barbizan in the 1850s, including 25 landscapes by Jean Corot. The best Impressionist paintings are Monet's landscapes Belle Ile and Ravines of the Creuse and Pissaro's Avenue de l'Opéra. Nearly all the modern masters are represented—Renoir, Bonington, Matisse (an early work), Gauguin (two excellent still-life paintings), Millet, Monet, Sisley, Dufy, Boudin, Picasso and others.

The **motor museum**, in avenue Georges Clemenceau, is little publicised, perhaps because it is shut in winter, but is certainly one of the best in France. Exhibits range from early De Dion Bouton cars to recent racing cars, including a magnificent collection of the ostentatiously luxurious Hispano Suiza cars of 1929–35, family saloons of the 1920s and 1930s and an odd vehicle used by General de Gaulle in World War II.

The Romans started the prosperity of Reims. When Caesar was conquering Gaul around 50 BC he made this settlement of the Gallic tribe called the Remes the capital of the Province of Belgica; so roads were built to it and it became a centre of trade as well as administration and the army. Three souvenirs remain of the Roman occupation—above ground is **Porte de Mars**, the biggest triumphal arch in the Roman Empire when it was built in the 3rd century AD and in the 18th century incorporated into the city's defence ramparts. Now it is damaged and dirty but still impressive. Half above ground is the arcaded **Cryptoporticus**, in what is suitably called place du Forum, for

The Baptism of Clovis by St Remi, a stained glass window in Reims Cathedral by Marc Chagall

it is believed to have been part of the Gallo-Roman forum. Below ground are the big **caves**, made by Roman slaves digging 18m (60ft) down to extract chalk for building houses.

After the Romans left, these caves were gradually shut down until, at the end of the 18th century, Claude Ruinart, owner of the oldest Champagne house, bought 250, dug them deeper to 30m (100ft), linked them with galleries and used them as places to mature and store his Champagne. Conferences, meetings, big dinners and dances are held in one of the caves. Mme Pommery, who became the owner of Pommery Champagne house after she was widowed last century, persuaded Ruinart to sell some of its chalk pits and she had them made into ornate wine caves. Between the galleries she had archways carved in various styles, from Classic Greek and Roman to Gothic, and named them after the cities which drink the most Pommery Champagne—Paris, London, New York, Rome and so on. Then she made a superb great stairway of 116 steps and commissioned an artist to carve bacchanalian scenes in bas-relief in the chalk. The effect is dazzling. It is one of the most rewarding caves to visit. And as a bonus you will see a cask holding 100,000 bottles, beautifully sculpted in 1903 by Galle. Above your head is the old Pommery mansion *Les Crayères*, where Gerard Boyer now cooks his superlative meals, set in an English-style park of 7 ha (17 acres).

Information on visiting Champagne caves is in Chapter 3.

Chefs of Champagne

Though they do adopt a light modern touch, the renowned chefs of Champagne have not abandoned regional traditions. In Reims, the great Gérard Boyer has cooked for some years now in the sumptuous surroundings of *Château les Crayères*, the old Pommery wine family residence in a park on the edge of the city. He cooks flawlessly, but without pretension. He even uses his superb foie-gras as a stuffing for pigs trotters, which brings inflated goose-liver down to earth. His duck dishes reach heavenly heights and his dessert trolley would tempt a fasting saint. He adds that final touch to the simplest dishes. 'There is never a false note,' says Marc de Champérard, our favourite French critic.

At the delightful *Aux Armes de Champagne* at L'Epine, the inventive young chef Patrick Michelon, who deserves more than his one Michelin star, uses fresh black truffles to stuff trotters and borrows oeufs meurettes (eggs poached in red wine) from Burgundy to serve with what he calls his 'pike hamburger'.

At Montchenot, between Reims and Epernay, Dominique Giraudeau of the *Grand Cerf* stuffs his pigs' trotters with *ris de veau* sweetbreads and mushrooms—preferably the subtly flavoured *morilles* when in season in springtime.

A local legend claims that the Porte de Mars triumphal arch was built at the expense of Reims people in gratitude to the Roman Emperor Probus. Two centuries earlier, another Emperor had decreed that Gaul's vines should be dug up to protect Rome's wine exports. Probus cancelled the decree and let the people of Gaul make wine again. When Henry VII of England invaded France in 1495 the French military ordered the vignerons near Reims to pull up their vines for fear that the British would cook them and eat them or fill up moats with them, in order to scale the city walls.

Henry VIII owned Champagne vineyards, ensuring that he was supplied by his own presses and wine-makers. His merchant in Ay bought fine wines for the English court. The house of Bollinger had not been founded in Ay at that time, or Henry would have known what to order.

7. Reims to Epernay

The two great Champagne wine towns of Reims and Epernay are 24km (15 miles) apart by the direct route N51. They are quite different, both convinced that they are the true capital of Champagne wine, and are secretly not very friendly. Much of the direct route by the N51 is boring and often crowded. Those of us who are addicted to wine tend to drive a few kilometres down it to the turn-off for Rilly-la-Montagne, then take the horseshoe drive through the wine villages of La Montagne de Reims to Epernay (see Chapter 3). This is not only a great wine-tasting route but passes through the attractive hilly scenery of the Montagne de Reims.

The roads and villages west of the N51 are usually neglected. One route is by the N31 west from Reims for a short distance, then left on the little D27 to **Gueux**, a suburb of Reims which was once a mecca for motor-racing enthusiasts. You can still see the grandstands used around 50 years ago and more, when the Reims Grand Prix was fought out between Alfa Romeos, Maseratis, Mercedes and Bugattis, the sports cars raced in the Reims 12-hour race. Even the French Grand Prix was held here.

Cross the A4 motorway to Vrigny, where you see the first vines. The little roads are attractive through Coulommes-la-Montagne, a *village fleuri* (flowered village) of Marne, to Pargny-lès-Reims. The D26 follows the side of Petite Montagne, already passing vineyards, to **Ville-Dommange**, a village that once had such big ideas that in the 12th century it planned a church of huge dimensions. Alas, this was never finished, though they went on building until the 15th century.

A little road diverts to the tiny **chapel of St Lie** in a small wood on a hill. This was once a place of pilgrimage. From the pathway around it are long views of the Reims plain, the Tardenois woods to the west and the skyline of the Montagne de Reims. **Sacy** on the D26 has a less ambitious 12th century church which was finished, and at least its nave is very long and its spire is long and elegant, so that it stands out for miles from its terrace overlooking the village. **Ecueil**, the next village, hides its church in a wood among vineyards. Chamery and Sermiers follow, with roads and tracks leading off through vineyards and a big forest. At Montchenot you reach the N51 and the *Grand Cerf* restaurant (see box, p 80). Across the N51, the renowned village wine route begins at Villers-Allerand, through which the great Roman road once ran to Barbary (the frontier of the Empire defended against the Barbarians). It is lost now among vineyards.

Rilly-la-Montagne is a pleasant little town for a stroll. It has a large wine

Vineyards near Ville-Dommange, with Sacy in the distance

cooperative and the cave of H. Germain et Fils (38 rue de Reims, tel. 26 03 40 19), one of those excellent producers not yet well enough known in Britain, except among connoisseurs. Even the **church stalls** are decorated with 16th century sculptures of vineyard life. The town nestles under Mont Joli and is a good centre for discovering this mountain and the forest. **Chigny-les-Roses**, in the forest's shade, lengthened its name when a lovely rose garden was planted here in the early 20th century. On a hill above Verzenay, which lies in the heart of the valley between two headlands, stands a historic windmill, known as the **Mill of Heidsieck Monopole**, the Champagne house that now owns it. In World War I, it was an important artillery look-out post. In the next village, **Verzy**, where two early saints once built a large Benedictine monastery, England's Edward III set up headquarters while planning an attack on Reims, which failed, and in 1918 General Gouraud set up his headquarters in the **Observatory of Mount Sinai** for the final French offensive. You can reach Mount Sinai along a network of paths for ramblers or cyclists. There is a splendid view of Reims and the plateau from the top. Opposite the observatory is a strange and intriguing wood of twisted beech trees with knotted and deformed trunks, called Faux de Verzy.

Cross the A4 motorway at Verzy and just off the N44 at Sept-Saulx is one of those true old French inns becoming rare these days, *Le Cheval Blanc*, alongside the river Vesle. Decked in greenery and flower boxes, with comfortable bedrooms, it has been in the Robert family since 1870. The meals are a delight to us—traditional, using fresh seasonal ingredients, but never dull. Tradition probably cost the Cheval Blanc its Michelin star a few years ago. That is Michelin's loss—not ours.

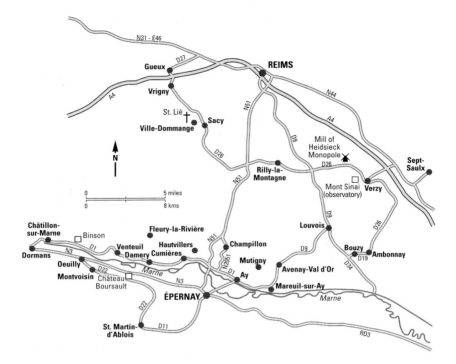

The road from Verzy dives down to **Ambonnay**, village of fine wines and outstanding cooking at *Auberge St Vincent* (see p 231) and through vineyards marked with the names of great Champagne houses to **Bouzy**, the village of red still Bouzy wine and of some of the very best Champagne made. The best of the big Champagne houses may use magicians to blend a wine from grapes of various areas, but most of them include Bouzy grapes. We have found the single village wines, like the powerful Carte d'Or of Herbert Beaufort of Bouzy, intense and rich in bouquet and body, to be just as rewarding as all but the most expensive.

A road joins Ambonnay and Bouzy to the river Marne and the Marne canal at two interesting villages, Condé-sur-Marne and Tours-sur-Marne (see Chapter 9), but the Montagne de Reims road leads to **Louvois**. Here one of Louis XIV's war ministers, François le Telier, had a **château** designed by Mansart, who designed much of Versailles including the Grand Trianon. The vast, luxurious château was similar to Versailles and, as at Versailles, the gardens were designed by Le Nôtre, the great French landscape gardener who also laid out St James's Park in London. Le Telier became Marquis of Louvois. On his death the château was bought for 'Mesdames', the daughters of Louis XV, but it was partly knocked down between 1805 and 1812 and these parts were later rebuilt. Still in a vast park, it has the original gates, moat and outbuildings. It is a private house, but you can see it through railings. The 12th century **village church** was repaired quite recently. Louvois was originally called Loupvoie because hungry wolves used to come out of the great forest of the mountain and take this voie (route) to Val d'Or.

The route down to the valley now follows the small river Livre through Fontaine-sur-Ay to **Avenay-Val d'Or**, where it is well worth taking the tiny road up to Mutigny for one of the best views around the Montagne. Return to Avenay, where there is a 13th–16th century **church** with a beautiful Flamboyant façade and containing a 16th century organ and paintings of a local Benedictine abbey built in AD 600 and destroyed in the Revolution. Continue to the Marne river and canal at the pleasant village of **Mareuil-sur-Ay**, a resort of fishermen, canoeists and walkers and motorists who just want to picnic or rest on the banks. The château is private but alongside its garden are paths and picnic areas. Built in the 17th century with a rather severe façade, the château was owned by Marshal Lannes, the son of a stable keeper who became one of Napoleon's most successful commanders, winning the battle of Montebello for which he was made Duke of Montebello. He played an important part in victories at Marengo, Austerlitz and Jena before being killed at the battle of Aspern in 1809. His son, the Duke of Montebello, developed the excellent local vineyards and still has a good Champagne named after him.

The little Marne-side town of **Ay** is the third most important Champagne wine town, after Epernay and Reims. It was already well known for its wine in the Gallo-Roman period, and the house of Gosset's founder was registered as a vigneron in 1584. Henri IV called himself 'Sire of Ay' and a half-timbered house behind St Bricés Gothic church is said to be where his wine-press was kept. Much of the old town was destroyed in the two World Wars.

EPERNAY is almost entirely a wine town. From the centre, **place de la République**, the wide main N3 road towards Châlons-sur-Marne is called **avenue de Champagne**, and so it should be, for it is lined with many of the greatest Champagne houses, from Moët et Chandon at one end to Mercier at the other. There are 103km (64 miles) of galleries beneath these buildings lined with millions of bottles. But first comes the handsome and very elegant **town hall**, which looks like a huge white private mansion set in a park, which it was from 1858 to 1919. In front of it at No. 7 is the **tourist office** (tel. 26 55 33 00), where you can get a map of the town and a list of Champagne caves which welcome visitors, with or without previous notice. The town hall gardens, designed in the 19th century by the Bühler brothers, are very pleasant. Almost opposite are the great **caves of Moët et Chandon**, the top selling Champagne. They are the best and easiest to visit, with a highly organised tour by electric train and clear, informative help from a guide. The cave galleries are 28km (17H miles) long and lined by 75 million bottles. The small **museum of wine** (including Napoleon's hat left after a visit) is interesting.

85

Visits: Monday–Friday 09.30–11.30; 14.00–16.45. Saturdays also 1 April–31 October. Tel. 26 54 71 11. Quite rightly, a statue of Dom Pérignon, the monk who discovered the secret of the bubbles, stands outside.

The other big cave which encourages visits is Mercier at No. 70 at the other end of the avenue de Champagne. Mercier belongs to the same consortium as Moët et Chandon, which includes also Ruinart, Hennessy cognac, Rozès port, vineyards in California and Christian Dior perfume. You tour the **Mercier caves** (18km/11 miles of galleries) in a mini-train, with time to study the great Mercier barrel which will hold 200,000 bottles. Sculpted with wine scenes by Naviet, it was made for the Paris Exposition of 1889. It was taken from Epernay to Paris on a cart pulled by 24 horses. The journey took 20 days. Walls had to be knocked down and bridges strengthened to let it pass. Some Mercier galleries are so wide that a car rally was held in them in the 1950s. Visits: all week 09.30–11.30; 14.00–16.30. Shut Tuesday, Wednesday in December, January, February (tel. 26 54 75 26). Mercier also has a fascinating and historic **museum** of 35 wine presses. Visits are only by arrangement, as it has limited space.

Nearly opposite Moët, at No. 13, is the Château-Perrier, originally the house of the Perrier family, the big wine négociant, now containing three museums in one. The regional **museum of prehistory and archaeology** has a wide range of discoveries from the Stone Age 3000 BC to the 8th century AD. The fine **arts museum** is rather disappointing, though the French 17th–19th century paintings and the pottery from Rouen and Nevers are quite interesting. Inevitably, the best of the three is devoted to vineyards, vignerons and wine, with old bottles, presses and vineyard workers' clothes from the past. The museum is closed on Tuesdays and from December to February.

A surprising museum is at No. 63b avenue de Champagne—**Le Jardin des Papillons**. In a huge greenhouse, among tropical plants and flowers, pools and cascades, magnificent butterflies from all over the world fly in freedom. Each day, new butterflies are born and you can see them stretching their wings and flying. It is open every day from 1 May until late September (tel. 26 55 15 33).

One of the most rewarding visits in the Champagne wine region is to the **tower and caves de Castellane** at 57 rue de Verdun, backing on to the Jardin des Papillons. You can visit the wine caves (9.5km/6 miles of galleries). De Castellane also owns the Maxim brand of wine. Adjoining the caves is a tower with 239 steps to the top, but with a splendid view over Epernay and vineyards when you get there and plenty to see on the way up. The walls show dioramas of the process of wine-making from the vineyards onwards and a history of the de Castellane family, with a collection of wine posters, labels and bottles. Boni de Castellane was a renowned collector, who married the American multi-millionairess Anna Gould. De Castellane is open from Easter to 1 November daily, by appointment in other months (tel. 26 55 15 33).

Epernay is a prosperous, calm, almost self-satisfied town. The great mansions left by earlier wine-makers and négociants have been converted rather than knocked down and replaced by tall modern blocks. Yet Epernay has not had a placid history. In 1432 the English threw out most of the population and banned them. Then came the plague. In 1544 François I ordered the town to be burned. When he was the Protestant Commander Henri of Navarre, Henri IV besieged it. The Marne has drowned the town with floods. The Bavarians occupied it 1814–15 after Napleon's first débacle, the Prussians in 1870–71. Bombardments in World War I caused terrible destruction and the Germans occupied the town 1940–44, doing their best to drink it dry. General Patton's Army liberated it.

Bottles of champagne in riddling racks in Marc Herbrart's cellar, Mareuil

A nice lazy way of exploring the **Marne** is by the pleasure cruiser *Coche d'Eau*, which sails daily. It has a restaurant, bar, dance area and promenade deck. It runs daily April–October from Magenta, the industrial suburb of Epernay (tel. 26 72 68 27). You can also take cruiser trips on the Marne from Cumières, 5km (3 miles) west on the D1, with lunch or dinner and entertainment (1 May–30 September—Croisières Vallée, tel. 26 54 49 51). Champagne Decouverte, 3 place Chocatelle (tel. 26 88 55 00) runs mini-bus trips through the vineyards.

Before driving to Cumières and following the Marne westward, it is worth going north on the little road N2051 through Dizy to Champillon, where you can park and see the most beautiful view over the Marne valley. The hotel here, the Royal Champagne, is one of the best and most interesting in Champagne. Its bedrooms are in little bungalows with superb views from their terraces. It has a Michelin star for cooking and is duly expensive. The wine list is dreamlike—not surprisingly, for the hotel is owned by Moët et Chandon. So is the cave of the former abbey in **Hautvillers**, the village about 3km (2 miles) west over the N51—the very cave where Dom Pérignon looked after the wine from the time he finished his noviciate until he died in 1715. They will tell you in Hautvillers that when he had mastered fermentation and produced his nectar with controlled effervescence he shouted 'Brothers, come quickly! I am drinking stars'. Alas, only a very few people can be shown round the abbey where he lived and the museum devoted to his life. You must try to persuade Moët et Chandon at Epernay that you are worthy of this honour. But anyway, Hautvillers is one of the most attractive of wine villages, conscious of its importance, its well-kept old stone houses announcing their names in hand-forged iron along narrow streets. You can see the Romanesque parish church inside which Pérignon is buried. It contains some large painted tableaux including the life of St Helen and three saints founding the abbey in AD 660.

Cumières is just south in a loop of the Marne, with narrow streets leading to old quays, popular with fishermen. People of Epernay come here to relax and to eat in *Le Caveau*, in an old wine cellar opposite the wine cooperative. The hillsides behind produce a much-praised red wine.

A pleasant short walk by the river takes you to **Damery**, with an imposing 13th century church, floodlit at night. A long avenue of plane trees leads to the village and a bridge crosses the Marne with a good view of the village from the other side. Three kilometres (2 miles) inland from Damery is **Fleury-la-Rivière**, which gets its flowery name from the roses still planted at the edge of each row of vines—a method used in many French vineyards until recently for spotting the first signs of disease, which attacked the roses first. A traditional 'Crowning of the Rose Queen' takes place annually. A young girl is chosen from the loveliest in the region. The D1 road from Damery through Venteuil is very attractive. At **Venteuil**, a village of narrow streets, is a viewpoint with views overlooking Boursault château among greenery across the Marne.

Past the 12th century **Binson Priory** you reach **Châtillon-sur-Marne**, which has ensured a certain fame by building a huge **statue of Pope Urban II**, who came from around here and who preached the First Crusade in 1095, so persuading Christian zealots, fiery adventurers and seekers after loot to march to the Holy Land and start a bloody argument, which in one form or another still persists. The statue is 18m (60ft) high and has an internal staircase to the Pope's arm. You can see 22 villages marked on an orientation table.

The D1 leads to **Dormans**, a pleasant little town on the banks of the Marne, which is gaining popularity as an activity resort, mostly for walking, fishing, golf and watersports—sailing (Centre Nautique, tel. 26 58 82 33), water skiing (Ski Nautique, tel. 26 09 30 27), kayak canoeing (tel. 26 58 81 03). It suffered severely during the last German push on the Marne in 1918, and was mostly rebuilt. The 17th century **castle** with two 14th century towers has survived but is not open to the public. The old **church** has been restored, as has an old windmill. In a huge, attractive park is a two-storey memorial of the two battles of the Marne of World War I, which was built by order of the Allied Commander-in-Chief Marshal Foch. (Open Saturday afternoon and Sunday, May–November. Weekdays July, August.) There are two wine coop-eratives in the town, a good restaurant (*La Table Sourdet*, 6 rue Dr. Moret, tel. 26 58 88 82), an hotel restaurant (*Le Champenois*, tel. 26 58 20 44), and a municipal campsite (*Camping Sous Le Clocher*, tel. 26 58 21 79).

Returning to Epernay by the bigger road, the N3, along the south side of the Marne, you climb towards vine-covered slopes and, on the edge of woods, come to a group of wine-producing hamlets: Cerseuil, Leuvrigny, Festigny, Le Mesnil le Huttier and Le Chène-la-Reine (on D423). The Maison Champenoise of Oeuilly and Montvoisin has an **éco-museum** presenting the life of wine-producers since the 18th century (open weekends in summer). Then you reach **Château Boursault**, the massive Renaissance-style castle built for the Veuve Cliquot in 1845. She held receptions there, attended by the great. So did her granddaughter, the Duchess of Uzes. Mlle Ponsardin married the wine-producer Cliquot in 1799 and was only 27 when she became a widow. The Napoleonic Wars were at their height, the thoughts of most French families were turning to other things than Champagne and Napoleon's Continental System, banning trade with Britain and the British Empire, was operating, doing no good to France's Champagne business at all. So she personally went east as far as Moscow to sell her wines. Once Napoleon had gone they soon became known all over the Champagne-drinking world, especially in England, and smart young men still order 'another bottle of the widow' in wine bars all over Britain. One sparkling widow we knew in Kent was so addicted to Veuve Cliquot that she changed the name of her house to Cliquot Cottage.

Continue along the attractive little D22 to Vauciennes then turn right past a series of ponds where water lilies grow and fishermen patiently ruminate, until you reach **St Martin d'Ablois**, surrounded by hills, with Epernay forest to the north. From there, the D11 leads you to Epernay through Vinay Moussy, a small place where little bridges over the river Sourdon link the main road to the sidestreets, and finally **Pierry**, where the present Mairie was the home of the 18th century author Cazotte (Diable Amoureux), whom the Revolutionaries sent to the guillotine in 1792.

To the south is the heart of the Côtes de Blancs, where the grapes grown are mostly Chardonnay and much Blanc de Blancs Champagne is made.

8. Epernay to Troyes, Sézanne and Burgundy

Côtes des Blancs, to the south of Epernay, is like a sea of vines. Its harvest is of white Chardonnay grapes, producing such a fine wine that almost every big, distinguished Champagne house owns vineyards here. Not until you get to Vertus do you see hillsides of black grapes. If you return to Epernay then go to Pierry and take the little roads to Chavot and Courcourt, you reach Mont Felix, where only the 12th century church is left of a castle and village. After Monthelon, the road runs down to Mancy by a picturesque route through the vines. Make your way round to **Cuis** on the D10, a little village with a Romanesque church at the bottom of its cliffs and views over the Montagne vineyards. We are very glad that we discovered this village a few years ago. It has an excellent wine cooperative and the caves of De Blémond, whose wines have a light richness which is almost unique. The premier cru Grande Réserve is delicious.

Cramant has made a world reputation for its Blanc de Cramant. Its vines spread along a hillside and in case you should miss it, the village announces itself with a giant Champagne bottle. This is the heart of the Côtes de Blancs and it was fitting that **Avize**, a lively little town, should train here wine-growers of the future at its renowned agricultural college. May it last at least as long as the 12th century church has done already.

After the two wine villages of Oger and Le Mesnil-sur-Oger, which has beautiful floral displays in season, fork right off the road onto a lane which winds through the vines on the hillside to **Vertus**, a pretty place to stop a while. In the 13th century Thibaud IV, Count of Champagne, who became King of Navarre, had a castle there and it became a very important commercial centre. It was dotted with fountains and surrounded by city walls which are now circular boulevards lined with elderly chestnut trees. It is a pleasant village, quite lively but relaxing. **St Martin's church** is lovely. The crypt is built on wooden piles sunk in the underground river which feeds St Martin's well. The church itself was heavily reconstructed after damage in 1940.

The poet Eustache Deschamps, born in Vertus in 1345, was a prolific writer considering that he was also a soldier and a magistrate, undertook diplomatic missions in Italy and Hungary and held positions at Court in Paris

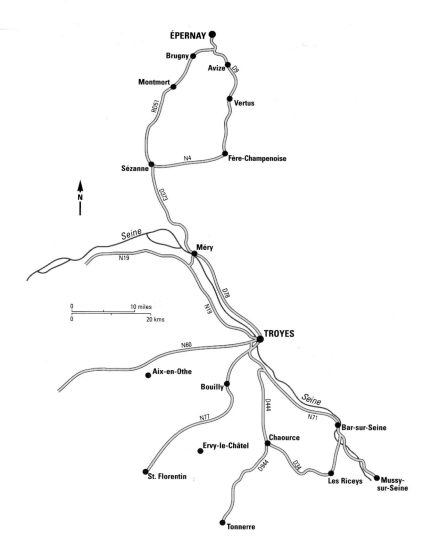

and important posts in Champagne. He composed 1175 lyrics, a satire on women called *Miroir de Mariage* and a pile of poems. His works, published in 1878, ran to 11 volumes.

Opposite the next village, **Bergères-lès-Vertus**, is **Mont Aimé**, last peak of the Côtes de Blancs. The hill was occupied in prehistoric days and constantly fortified by the Gauls, the Romans and the Counts of Champagne. A few remains of the Counts' feudal castle can be found among the greenery. It was called after Blanche de Navarre, the wife of Count Thibaud III of Champagne, who was widowed while expecting her first child. She placed the boy for his safety in the care of King Philippe Auguste of France, in return for a number of châteaux. The boy, Count Thibaud IV of Champagne, became King of Navarre and the most successful Count of Champagne.

After the defeat of Napoleon at Waterloo in 1815, Czar Alexander of Russia, who liked shows of pomp and power, held a review of 300,000 Russian, Prussian and Austrian troops at the foot of Mont Aimé. One wonders how he managed to feed them in a France made almost destitute by Napoleon's Wars.

South from Mont Aimé is the Marais de St Gond and the chalk plateau where the bloodiest fighting took place in 1914 during the first Battle of the Marne. General Foch, later Commander-in-Chief of the Allied Forces, made a determined stand with his French Army against the attacks of Von Bülow's German Army, including the Prussian Guard, who courageously approached through the Marais peat bogs, now partly drained for meadows and growing sweetcorn. Many megaliths still stand here. The Germans took the important little town of **Fère-Champenoise**, at the meeting of roads to Epernay, Troyes, Châlons-sur-Marne and Sézanne, but Foch held them and so defended the Seine and approaches to Paris. His Moroccan troops, then French 'Colonials', defeated the Germans with great slaughter in a violent battle in the park of a château at the little hamlet of Mondement. A huge commemorative monument in red cement stands 18m (60ft high) in the hamlet and from its terrace are long views over St Gond marshes.

Sézanne, south-west of Epernay, is a charming little provincial town grown from a medieval city at the foot of the Brie hills. Ancient houses in narrow streets still surround the impressive 16th century church, but the old ramparts, flattened after the Revolution, have become a delightful promenade from which you can see the now tranquil countryside of orchards, woods and vineyards. It is lined with chestnut trees and leads to the ruins of the château of which two towers remain. Sézanne has always been proud of its *andouillettes* (sausages).

From Epernay, the RD51, the direct route to Sézanne, passes two castles. **Brugny**, overlooking Cubry valley, is a Champagne wine village. The cooperative is near the château which was originally from the 13th century. Its walls and towers are from the 16th, but some of it was rebuilt in the 18th. A little road to the right leads to the D11, and **St Martin d'Ablois**, which has a medieval château, rebuilt in 1760 and now a retirement home. Jean-Baptiste Isabey (1767–1855), the portrait and miniature painter, lived there. He painted pictures of the leading Revolutionaries and later became official painter to Napoleon and the 19th century Bourbon royals—a sort of Vicar of Bray of painting.

The RD51 continues through forests to the valley of the Surmelin amid very pleasant country. The **château** at **Montmort-Lucy** is delightful to visit. Surrounded by a park, with its own vegetable garden, it was originally built in the 12th century and although it was much altered in the 16th century, it has kept its medieval look, with four pointed round towers, ramparts and moats more than 7.5m (25ft) deep. One entrance is across a drawbridge, the other by a circular ramp from the outer courtyard, built originally for horses, like the entrance at Château d'Amboise on the Loire.

The château was bought by a mathematician, Pierre Rémond de Montfort, in 1704. He was known for a treatise dealing with a mathematical problem which generations have tried to solve. His descendants still live in the château. From its lawns General von Bülow announced the German retreat in 1914. Visits are welcome in afternoons from 15 July–15 Sept (tel. 26 59 10 04 for the times).

The RD373 from Sézanne crosses the river Aube at Anglure, taking you from Marne to the Aube département shortly afterwards, and then (as the D373) to the river Seine at Méry-sur-Seine.

From Méry little roads through riverside villages follow both banks of the Seine to Troyes. Or you can take the bigger N19, passing the **Château of Barberey** on the edge of the city. Built in pure Louis XIII style in brick and stone in 1626, it has a big French-style formal park around it.

Luck has smiled on **TROYES** through the centuries and today it is a prosperous, attractive town, rich commercially and rich, too, in fine old houses from medieval to Renaissance, beautiful old churches and museums with excellent works of art.

Its first stroke of luck came in AD 451, when Attila the Hun, who was sweeping through Gaul, pillaging, wrecking and burning everything before him, and who had just burned down Reims, was persuaded by Loup, Bishop of Troyes, to leave the city alone. He went to Attila and offered himself as a hostage. Attila was so impressed that he left Troyes in peace.

Troyes was capital of the Champagne in the Middle Ages and the counts enriched it. Count Henri I alone founded 13 churches and 13 hospitals. His grandson, the successful Thibaud IV, created the great Fair of Troyes, a truly international trading exposition where the money changers did great business and debts were settled by international traders for the whole year. The province of Champagne came under the rule of France when Jeanne, Countess of Champagne and Navarre, married in 1284 Philippe le Bel who became King of France the next year.

Even when a fire ravaged Troyes in 1524, many of the medieval houses and towers survived, and are still there, while the town was rich enough to replace houses destroyed with Renaissance mansions. A good example is **Hôtel des Chapelaines**, 55 rue Turenne. Built in 1530 by a rich merchant, this has a beautiful Renaissance façade. The merchant's descendants became Barons de Chapelaines. Rebuilding after the fire left the outline of Troyes as it is today—a town the shape of a Champagne cork, with the Seine running in a half-circle round the top. In the centre is the huge cathedral around which the aristocrats lived. The old houses of the merchants were in the 'body' of the cork, around the 14th century **church of St Jean**, where England's Henry V married in 1420 Catherine, daughter of the demented King Charles VI of France and his promiscuous wife Queen Isabella of Bavaria. The 'cork' is surrounded by boulevards which replaced the old city walls, dividing the city from its more modern suburbs and industrial area, and the Haute Seine canal, partly covered, divides the head and body of the 'cork'.

Around the time of the fire, Troyes became the capital of hosiery (*bonneterie*), making cotton stockings, socks, gloves, bonnets and undervests (undershirts in America). It still has about 300 factories making hosiery and garments. There is an interesting **museum of bonneterie** in the **Hôtel de Vauluisant**, a 16th century Renaissance mansion which also contains a museum of the history of Troyes and Champagne. Among exhibits tracing the history of Troyes is a panorama of sculpture and paintings of the Troyes School of the 16th century, mainly religious.

The museum is alongside **St Pantaléon church**, which has high Renaissance windows and, with its statues by the Italian Dominique Florentin, looks rather like a religious museum itself. This 16th century church was named after a local man, Hyacinthe Pantaléon, son of a shoemaker, who later became Pope Urban IV. He had started to build in 1262 the **Basilique St Urbain**, on the site of his father's old shoemaker's shop. The present façade was added in 1875–1905. The land on which most of the church was built belonged to a nunnery. Pope or no pope, the nuns made a protest march, led by their abbess. They put the workers to flight and vandalised the site. Next day the Bishop of Auxerre arrived to bless a cemetery. The abbess went up to him and slapped his face. Among sculptures in the church is a very pleasant 16th century La Virge au Raisin of a smiling Mary and child holding a bunch of grapes from which a bird is having a snack. The church is round the corner from place de la Libération.

At the end of the 16th century, during the Religious Wars, Troyes was occupied by the Catholic Leaguers, an army of extreme Catholics founded by the Duke of Guise, who instigated the massacre of Protestants on St Bartholomew's Day and was ambitious to be King of France. King Henri III was a Catholic king who nevertheless opposed the Catholic Leaguers and his troops attacked Troyes where the League had appointed the 11-year-old Claude de Guise as Governor of the town. When Henri's troops reached the suburbs, the Governor took fright and locked himself in the cathedral tower.

Troyes was famous for its *andouillettes* (sausages). The invading troops were tempted to the quarter of St Denis, where these were made. They liked the sausages so much that they ate themselves into a stupor. The Leaguers had time to bring up reinforcements, who found the royal soldiers in no fighting condition and massacred them by the hundreds. Troyes remained in League hands. Making large and small sausages and bacon products is still a major industry in Troyes.

The stained glass **windows** of Troyes first became renowned for their rich colours and artistic originality around 1480. Despite wars, carelessness and vandalism, a large number have survived, though some restoration has been second-rate—certainly not in the same class as the work on the windows at Reims. The **cathedral of St Pierre-et-St Paul** has a most interesting collection from several centuries, beginning with rather primitive designs of the 13th

La Virge au Raisin, 16th century sculpture in Basilique St Urbain, Troyes

century which nevertheless have surprising intensity of colour. The 'portraits' of popes and emperors and the series of the life of the Virgin from the early 16th century have remarkable purity of colour and tone, dominated by red.

This is a huge cathedral, built from the 13th to the 17th centuries, and is a blend of all styles of Gothic architecture. One reason why it took so long to build was ground subsidence, which also accounts for its rather squat appearance. It is 34m (113ft) long and 29m (96ft) wide but only 16.5m (54ft) high without counting the vaulting. The Renaissance tower, with double lanterns, is 38.5m (126ft) high. Even the nave was unfinished when the building was consecrated in 1429 in the presence of Charles VII. A plaque at the base of the Renaissance tower tells us that Joan of Arc was there, too.

Of the other old churches, **Ste Madelaine**, the oldest, is the most interesting for its beautiful interior stone rood-loft of three Flamboyant arches topped by a stone parapet, a masterpiece by the architect-sculptor Jean Galide, who remodelled the church from 1508, with splendid 16th century glass in the choir. Do try to see it.

The Revolutionary

Georges-Jacques Danton, the French revolutionary who set up the pitiless Revolutionary Tribunal, which sent so many to their deaths, came from a peasant family in Arcis-sur-Aube in the Champagne. He learned English, read extensively, became a lawyer in Paris and formed the Cordelia Club, which was the meeting place of the hotter revolutionaries. Tall, strong with a fierce expression and a strong voice, he thundered against the Court, its extravagance and the treatment of the poor. He became the Revolution's Minister of Justice. Even history acclaims him for his urging of 'courage, courage, courage' when the invading Prussians, having taken Verdun, were entering Champagne to march on Paris.

Danton's call for clemency for prisoners or revolutionaries who had fallen into disfavour led to his downfall. The utterly ruthless Robespierre had him arrested and charged before the Revolutionary Tribunal. For two days his brilliant oratory moved proceedings in his favour. Robespierre then invented a decree ruling that by 'insulting justice' he had no right to speak. Danton was guillotined, aged 35. He was probably the greatest of the revolutionaries.

Troyes has almost as many museums as churches. The **Musée d'Art Moderne** has some unusual exhibits, such as a collection of African art. The exhibits were all presented to the French nation by an industrialist from Troyes, Pierre Levy, and his wife. Troyes was the lucky recipient and housed the museum in the old bishops' palace next to the cathedral. There are 388 paintings, all of the end of the 19th and the early 20th centuries,

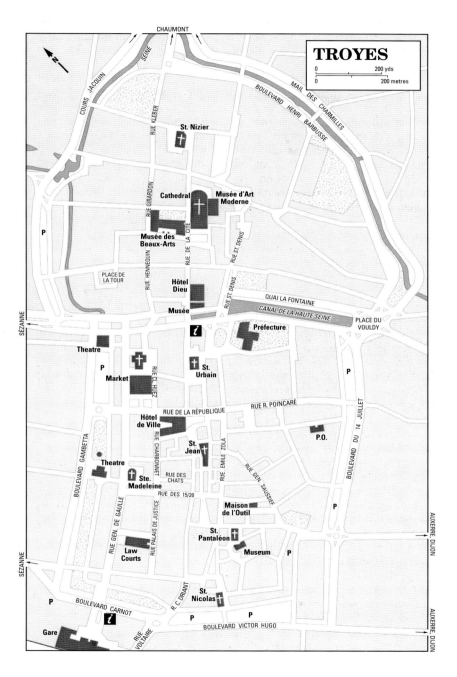

104 sculptures, as well as the African works, and ceramics, glass and crystals. It is especially rich in Fauvist paintings—literally 'wild beast' paintings, a name given in 1905 to a group of painters (including Matisse, Rouault, and Vlaminck) by critics who were overcome by the brilliant, explosive colours they used. Only Matisse continued to use such bold colours as he grew older. One of the founders, André Derain (1880–1954) is represented here by a really delightful painting of the Port of Collioure and two of London (Hyde Park and Big Ben). Derain, a close friend of Levy, unfortunately became a dull, academic painter by 1920, which cannot be said of Braque, whose Fauvist painting Paysage à l'Estaquet, shown here, uses the same bold colours. With Picasso he was co-founder of Cubism. Other outstanding exhibits are a fine double portrait by Dégas, a Fauvist work, Paysage à Chatou, by Maurice de Vlaminck (1876–1958), an eccentric who was a racing cyclist, then a violinist before taking up painting and who slapped on paint direct from the tube, paintings by Matisse, several by Picasso, and others by Dufy and Modigliani, whose love life brought him almost as much fame as his work. There are sculptures by Degas, Rodin and a rare bronze bust of a Jester by Picasso (1905).

The **Beaux-Arts museum** is on the opposite side of the cathedral in the huge modernised 17th century caves of St Loup abbey. It has archaeological exhibits, medieval sculptures and galleries of well-displayed paintings. All schools of painting from the 15th to the 19th century are represented, but the 17th century is strongest, with Rubens's Portrait of a Man Playing the Lute the most pleasant. In the 18th century section are works of Watteau and Fragonard and a fine portrait by David of Antoinette Gabrielle Charpentier, first wife of Danton, the greatest Revolutionary leader. Among 19th century exhibits is an excellent nude by Pierre-Paul Prud'hon, favourite painter of both wives of Napoleon—the Empress Josephine and Marie-Louise.

One of the most enterprising museums in North France is **Maison de l'Outil et la Penseé Ouvrière**—an exhibition of tools used by workers and tradesmen working in wood, metal, stone and leather over centuries and a large library of books about these crafts. It was collected by a workers' association called Compagnons du Devoir. They were offered an almost derelict half-timbered building in chequered brick and stone from around 1550 called Hôtel de Mauroy which had been originally given by a rich merchant as a place where poor boys could be taught a manual trade and had fallen into disuse from about 1745, when mechanisation was introduced in the hosiery industry. The Compagnons restored it scrupulously.

The **Hôtel Dieu** in rue de la Cité, with a superb monumental grill gate from 1760, contains a pharmacy which includes interesting 18th century jars and 320 wooden boxes painted with motifs (mostly of plants) showing what medicines they contain. There is also an ancient laboratory.

Troyes **Tourist Office** (16 bd Carnot, tel. 25 73 00 36) has a tour of the old medieval town which is entirely traffic-free, using narrow streets which are for pedestrians only. They supply map and guides.

Troyes' old quarter

Our favourite crossing from the Champagne into Burgundy is by way of **St Florentin**, famous for cheese and a very pleasant Burgundian town convenient for Chablis and its vineyards. The N77 from Troyes through Bouilly leads directly to St Florentin, but you might like to explore the Othe countryside, a great contrast to the Champagne plains. It is a land of green hills topped by forests, and valleys where cereals and apples grow. The cider is well worth drinking—a change from Champagne or Chablis. Its villagers made hosiery for centuries but since mechanisation they have turned almost entirely to agriculture. Tourism has been growing recently and people from the towns have been buying second homes there. The little capital, **Aix-en-Othe**, is close to the N60, running west from Troyes. Aix was a Roman spa and still has remains of its aqueduct. **St-Mards-en-Othe**, 8km (5 miles) south, was the scene of a bloody battle in June 1944 between the Germans and the Resistance.

Or take the N77 from Troyes to Bouilly, then turn right on the very attractive D72 and wind your way in a circle through a forest with the odd name of La Vente de l'Avocat along more attractive roads to rejoin the N77 at Villeneuve-au-Chamin, 3km (2 miles) from the Burgundian border. From the N77 crossroads at Villeneuve the D22 reaches in 8km (5 miles) the interesting little town of **Ervy-le-Châtel**, with a covered market, lovely 16th century church and old town gatehouse. The market, which is circular, has two storeys and is half-timbered.

Another attractive way to Burgundy from Troyes is by the D444 through the **Forêt d'Aumont** to cross the border north of Tonnerre. The route becomes delightful once you reach the forest, which is joined to the east by the forest of Rumilly. **Chaource** has very old houses, some on wooden stilts, and a church with a tomb showing the body of Christ surrounded by mourners whose faces show remarkable emotion. It is one of the greatest works of art of the 16th century school of Troyes. Chaource also, of course, gave its name to the best known cheese of Champagne (see Chapter 4), known since the 12th century. There are several fromageries in town and a Cheese Fair is held on the third Sunday in October. Chaource is also a village fleuri and looks exceptionally pretty in early May, when lilies of the valley are in bloom. The Fête de Muguet (lily of the valley) is on 1 May.

The N71 from Troyes, the old 'fast' way to Dijon before the motorway was built, hugs the banks of the river Seine over the Burgundy border and way past Châtillon-sur-Seine to the river's source.

As you leave Troyes, going south-east, the road by-passes the village of **Buchères** where, as they fled from the Americans and Free French on 24 August 1944, the German 51st SS regiment massacred 66 men, women and children and burned down the village. At Fouchères, a little road right leads in 3km (2 miles) to **Rumilly-lès-Vaudes**, which has a charming manor house with a 15th century pepper-pot tower, a red roof and arcades below a pretty wooden balcony. It must be a delightful place to live.

Bar-sur-Seine, on the Seine's left bank, is one of the most attractive villages in the area. Many houses survive from its days of importance in the 16th–17th centuries, when it was a frontier post between Champagne and Burgundy. So do a 17th century town gate, a clock tower and remains of a 12th century château of the Counts of Bar. Reaching the château by way of a street with steps, you have a fine view over the town and river. The 16th century **church**, a mixture of Gothic and Renaissance design, has interesting windows of the Troyes school, some by Dominique Florentin, an Italian who married a Troyes girl and settled there.

This is the beginning of the Aube Champagne and still wine country: you can taste at the cooperative. Local *andouillettes* are renowned, trout are a speciality. Fishing is excellent round here, especially in the little River Arcé, which meets the Seine in Bar, the Ource, 3km (2 miles) upstream, and the Laignes, which flows in from the left bank having passed through **Les Riceys**, a historic little town near the Burgundy border. Riceys is known these days as an activity centre (bathing, canoeing, fishing and tennis) and for its wine, especially the still rosé. The town has three Renaissance churches—it is an amalgamation of three villages, which were once all fortified. Ricey Bas has a museum of vintage cars in Garage Fournier.

Mussy-sur-Seine is the border village on the Seine. Its town hall was once the summer 'palace' of the Bishops of Langres. A small but interesting **Resistance museum** is open 1 May–1 October. The Resistance units from this area of Champagne put up a tremendous fight in 1944. Their headquarters were at Grancey-sur-Ource, to the north-east but in Burgundy. You can reach it, as the Resistance fighters did, by a path about 8km (5 miles) long through Bois de Réveillon.

9. *Troyes to Lac d'Orient and Châlons-sur-Marne*

The beach at **Géraudot** on **Lac d'Orient** is only 16km (10 miles) from Troyes. There you can swim, sail, sailboard, fish or go adventuring by pedalo. **Mesnil-St Père** at the southern end has a fine sandy beach, too, and a marina which is home to dozens of yachts, which take part in the lake's many regattas. There are sightseeing boats which take you round the lake. You can eat well at the auberge and stay in one of the 15 rooms. Both resorts have three campsites.

There was much local resentment when in 1965 Lac d'Orient and the reservoir to the north, Lac du Cap, were constructed in the delightful Forêt d'Orient to control the flow of the river Seine, but they have since given great pleasure to a lot of people in Troyes and smaller towns in Aube, especially to families with children and to young and active adults.

Driving round the newer, top lake, Lac du Temple, is not very rewarding, because the road swings away from the waterside in long stretches and in others the view is obstructed by defence walls, but there are pleasant lake views from around Lac d'Orient, especially alongside the bird reserve, which is fascinating when birds are migrating. The lakes are surrounded by the **Forêt d'Orient**, in which attractive drives and even more attractive walks are marked. It is a Regional Park, which covers 69,000 ha (17,500 acres) and includes 49 little towns and villages. You can get information from Maison du Parc (tel. 25 41 35 57) a converted farm at the eastern end of the little road separating the two lakes.

East of Mesnil-St-Père on the N19 you reach **Vendeuvre-sur-Barse**, a centre for exploring the Forêt d'Orient. It has a huge 16th–17th century **château**, built on the remains of a 12th century château, in a big, pleasant park which is open to the public. Each summer dozens of the local people take part in a historical Son-et-Lumière. They are all amateurs and all so enthusiastic that they draw audiences from great distances. Route D443 north takes you to **Brienne-le-Château**, a town of only 4000 people but of some fame. The founding family of Jean Brienne distinguished itself in the Crusades. One married into the family of the King of Sicily, two became King of

Boy fishing in Lac d'Orient

Jerusalem and one of these also became Emperor of Constantinople. They were called *la fleur de la noblesse de Champagne* (the flower of Champagne nobility). The last male heir was killed in 1356 at Poitiers by the English under the Black Prince.

The château was one of the last to be built before the Revolution, designed by Jean Louis Fontaine in 1770. But Brienne's true fame is based on a 9-year-old boy who started a five-year course at the military school in 1779, following in the footsteps of his elder brother. The boy was called Napoleon Bonaparte. He returned in January 1814, with his army, and gained some success over Blücher and his Prussians in one of those skirmish-battles that were fought to try to keep the Allies from Paris. He drove the Prussian-Russian army back to Bar-sur-l'Aube, but was defeated two days later at Rothière, 5km (3 miles) up the Aube from Brienne. A **museum** depicting his cadet life and his victory at Bar-sur-Aube is housed in the former military college. His report at the college said that he was excellent at military exercises and mathematics but feeble in French and Latin. (He came, of course, from a Corsican-Italian family.) His character was 'submissive'!

On St Helena, as a captive after Waterloo, he described Brienne as 'my native country' and he left the town 1,200,000 francs, partly to build a new town hall. Perhaps this was compensation for the damage his own artillery had done to the town. All Brienne ever got was 400,000 francs paid out by Napoleon III in 1854.

Nowadays Brienne is a centre for growing cabbages and is renowned for its sauerkraut, called *choucroute de Champagne*.

North of Brienne by the D6 is a clump of attractive villages which were

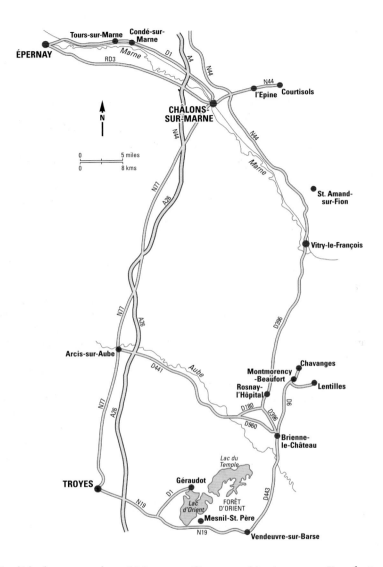

English for more than 100 years. One was **Montmorency-Beaufort**. Its owner, Blanche of Artois, was widowed in 1274 when the last Count of Champagne, Henri III, died. Blanche married the Duke of Lancaster. Their grand-daughter, Blanche of Lancaster, married her cousin John of Gaunt, son of England's Edward III. The most attractive of the villages, **Chavanges**, has St George as its patron and its annual fête is on his day. **Lentilles**, to the east, has a delightful 16th century church, with chestnut wood tiling on its gable, bell tower and its unusual porch, which is capped by a statue of St James.

Rosnay l'Hôpital, 8km (5 miles) north of Brienne on the D396, is another charming village, on the banks of the little river Voire, which abounds in fish. Its church was consecrated by Thomas à Becket, Archbishop of Canterbury, when he was in exile at Pontigny in Northern Burgundy, some five years before he returned to England, only to be murdered on the steps of the cathedral.

By taking the D441, which follows the Aube north-west, you reach the A26 motorway, which continues to Calais. On the way it can take you to Châlons-sur-Marne, the administrative capital of the Champagne. By driving over the A26 you reach **Arcis-sur-Aube** and the N77 Troyes–Châlons road. Arcis, in the heart of grain-country, was the home town of Georges-Jacques Danton (see box, p 96), perhaps the greatest French Revolutionary leader. He was born there in 1759 at No. 62 rue de Paris and during the height of the Revolution he retired there for short breaks of peace and quiet at a house by the river Aube.

The **town hall** is in a 17th century château where Napoleon slept the night before one of his last battles. Just outside Arcis, Napoleon's 20,000 strong army took on an Allied army of 90,000 men, led by the Austrian Prince Schwarzenberg. Schwarzenberg and an Austrian contingent had marched with Napoleon on his disastrous Moscow campaign. But more recently he had defeated Napoleon at Dresden and Leipzig and had just retaken Troyes. Napoleon rushed across the Marne to intercept him. Napoleon's outnumbered army held up Schwarzenberg for some hours before it retreated, but Schwarzenberg and the Prussian Blücher were left free to march on Paris and Talleyrand signed France's surrender.

The route to Châlons-sur-Marne passes a military camp (set up originally by Napoleon III) before crossing into Marne département nearby.

CHÂLONS-SUR-MARNE, as administrative capital of the Champagne-Ardennes region, does not compare with Reims for exciting discoveries and grandeur, but it has a very pleasant, bourgeois calm, with dignified old town houses and restored half-timbered houses. Two small arms of the Marne, called the Nau and Mau, are canalised through the centre of the town, while the main river skirts it. You can take pleasant walks by the waterside and over bridges, particularly through Le Jard, a park already known in the Middle Ages. Here in 1147, in front of Louis VII and the Pope Eugène III, St Bernard preached the Second Crusade. The gardens were designed in the 18th century. **Le Grand Jard**, stretching from the river Marne to avenue Général-Leclerc, is a big esplanade under chestnut trees with a network of paths. A bridge crosses the canal to Le Jardin Anglais, laid out in 1817. Beyond avenue Leclerc is **Le Petit Jard**, a charming garden in Napoleon III style with remains of the old city walls and tower of a château. It is bordered by the Nau canal. Boat trips on the river and canals give an interesting perspective of Châlons.

The 13th century **Cathedral of St Etienne** was not improved by a Classical front added in 1634, but it has some really excellent glass, showing the development of this art from the 12th to the 16th century, plus some interesting more modern windows, especially one in red and gold from 1938, showing local history. The cathedral survived not only many wars but also the indignity of being used as stables and a store for fodder in the Revolution. Even its high altar of 1686 by Hardouin Mansart, who designed much of Versailles, has survived. It was modelled on the high altar of St Peter's in Rome.

The **church of Notre-Dame-en-Vaux** is the most imposing building. Founded in the 7th century, reconstructed in the 12th century, it was damaged in the Revolution, especially its cloisters. They were rebuilt this century and excavations revealed more than 50 carved Norman columns from the 12th century. A carillon of 56 bells of the church still plays ancient tunes.

The Romans built up Châlons as a garrison town for one of their front-line legions and it still is one, thanks to Napoleon III. Someone has called it 'the French Aldershot'. Napoleon III used to stay in Châlons with the Prefect and invited top brass from the military and foreign dignitaries to great fêtes. Then he built the great military camp at Mourmelon and liked to watch or join in the military manoeuvres and to test new weapons. He never lost the delusion that he should follow in the footsteps (and successes) of his uncle. Even his very young son, the Prince Imperial, was allowed to join in as a sort of mascot of the soldiers. Napoleon was last seen at the camp on 17 August 1870. He was there to form a new army, to be commanded by Marshal MacMahon, to fight the Prussians in the Ardennes. His dreams of a successful invasion of Germany had just been dashed in Alsace. By 1 September MacMahon and this new army had suffered a crushing defeat at Sedan. The Emperor himself and 83,000 troops were captured. The Prince Imperial escaped to England. On 4 September Napoleon III was no longer Emperor. In March 1871 he and the ex-Empress Eugénie were living beside Chislehurst Common in Kent. The ex-Prince Imperial was a cadet at Woolwich Artillery Academy. He was killed in the Zulu War of 1879, fighting as a British Officer.

But the camp at Châlons stayed open and inevitably the town was attacked in both World Wars. The Germans bombarded Châlons in 1914, 1918 and heavily in 1940. Not only the churches survived—so did the Champagne wine houses, including Joseph Perrier, 69 ave de Paris (tel. 26 68 29 51), whose house is 18th century, its caves dug by the Romans, and whose wines were drunk by Queen Victoria and Edward VII. Telephone for a visit; ask for the secretary. English is spoken. But it is shut in August.

Standing like a great sentinel on the edge of the little village of **L'Epine**, 6.5km (4 miles) east of Châlons, is the vast **basilica of Notre Dame**, described truthfully as a jewel of late Gothic art rising out of a sea of wheat. Designed in about 1400 by Guichard Antoine, it grew over the next two centuries, so that now it has a Flamboyant-Gothic façade, a richly sculptured entrance, and gargoyles which would have frightened the most hardened sinner in the Middle Ages. The evil spirits are so sinister that they seem to spring at you from the stone in which they are carved. Alas, during restoration last century, those regarded as too obscene were 'eliminated'. Let us hope that they returned to haunt the prudes who showed such callous disregard for an artist's warning to sinners. The transepts are flanked by turrets and five chapels radiate to form the apse. The west side is capped by two spires of delicate fret-work. The inside is typical of elegant Gothic purity, with touches of Renaissance décor.

The story of the church is one well known in France. Shepherds found a statue of Mary in a burning thorn bush and this was taken to be a signal to build a church. L'Epine was an important place of pilgrimage in earlier centuries and to this day pilgrims make for it in July. Paul Claudel (1868–1955), the French Catholic poet, dramatist and essayist who was noto-rious for his violent anti-Protestant feelings, called the church a burning brazier and a bush of flowering roses in his drama *L'Annonce Fait à Marie*. It looks superb illuminated at night.

A more worldly shrine which lures pilgrims from many countries most of the year to L'Epine is opposite the church—the restaurant of the very comfort-able hotel *Aux Armes de Champagne*, where a meal cooked by Patrick Michelon leaves you smiling with contentment, so pleasing to the palate and stomach without too much slimming of your bank balance. The choice of Champagne wines is a delight, the service very politely informal, the welcome and organisation of Jean-Paul and Denise Pérardel a lesson to many hoteliers. M. Pérardel finds time, too, to run a wine business offering a bril-liant choice of good wines from most of France, with a new shop in Calais for the British, a shop in Beaune for everybody and a cave round the corner from the hotel with a choice which tempts many visiting wine lovers to drive away with their cars laden to the point of law-breaking. In 1907 the Pérardel family started a café on the site. Over three generations with much hard work they turned it into a 3-star hotel, with a Michelin star, 2 toques and 16/20 from Gault-Millau, and three stars from our favourite Champérard guide. Jean-Paul Pérardel has also found time to be Mayor of L'Epine.

Take the road to the right of the basilica and you are soon in **Courtisols**, said to be a typical village of the Champagne countryside. It is 6.5km (4 miles) long. Of the two routes from Châlons to Epernay, the little D1 alongside the river Marne and Marne Rhin canal is more interesting to us than the bigger D3, and passes within 4km (2½ miles) of the wine villages of Ambonnay and Bouzy, then through the wine town of Ay.

At **Tours-sur-Marne** the river and canal lie side by side and since commer-cial traffic died back young people have discovered that it is an excellent place for canoeing, especially for learning to handle a canoe. It is a peaceful spot now, with benches by the water, and has a very pleasant *Logis Auberge La Touraine Champenoise*, 100 years old, run by the same family for three generations, which offers colourful window boxes, old-style comfort, good regional cooking and a nice choice of Champagne, including good village wines.

Condé-sur-Marne, 5km (3 miles) east, was once a very important place for transport. Here the Marne river, Aisne canal and Marne canal all meet.

The N44 road from Reims to Châlons-sur-Marne runs close to the Aisne-Marne canal and later near to the Marne river to reach Vitry-le-François, capital of the Perthois. Some 9.5km (6 miles) before you reach it, a small road left takes you to **St Amand-sur-Fion**, another typical Champagne farming village with many old half-timbered farmhouses and barns surviving. On the bank of the little river is an unusual **church** dating from the 12th, 13th and 14th centuries. There is a Son-et-Lumière in mid-summer.

Poor **Vitry-le-François** suffered for centuries from war damage. But it survived as a prosperous town on the fertile Perthois plain, strategically placed for transport and trade on the right bank of the river Marne where it meets the river Saulx. In its town centre the Marne-Rhin and Marne-Saône canals meet the Canal Latéral of the Marne. Vitry is only 9.5km (6 miles) from **Lac du Der-Chantecoq**, one of the biggest artificial lakes in Europe, a superb centre for sailing, swimming, water-skiing, fishing, horse-riding and a magnificent place for bird-watching (see Chapter 10).

The original **Vitry-le-Perthois** is now a hamlet 3km (2 miles) north-east. In 1142 Louis VII burned down the church, killing 1300 townspeople who had taken refuge inside. That was one reason why he went on the Second Crusade. St Bernard had pricked his conscience. The little town was called Vitry-le-Brûlé (the Burned). Then in 1420 Jean de Luxembourg sacked it and in 1544 Charles V rased it.

The flamboyant François I had it rebuilt on the present site as a fortress town, on a geometric plan round a great square, place d'Armes, by an engineer from Bologna, Jerome Marini. François I would not ever have built a fort which was not a pleasing work of art and the centre of Vitry-le-François is a very pleasant town. It is not, in fact, very old. The Germans destroyed about 90 per cent of it in 1940 by air and artillery attacks and it has been rebuilt to Marini's plan.

As you enter from Châlons, you are faced with a great **triumphal arch**, raised to the glory of Louis XIV in 1748. It was taken down in 1938 and raised in its present position in 1984. The big church of Notre Dame dominates place d'Armes.

10. Sedan to Chaumont and Langres

It would seem perverse to drive through Champagne on the eastern side, missing Reims, Epernay and their vineyards. That is a route for Germans coming through Lorraine and making for Burgundy and most of them use the motorways that descend on Metz. But it is an explorer's land with a wealth of interesting sights.

Haute-Marne, the south-eastern département of Champagne, has been called 'desolate'. It isn't. It is blessedly short of big buildings and apartment blocks. It is rich in forests with tracks for walkers, cyclists and horse-riders, in rivers, streams, waterfalls and little lakes, in sheep pastures and meadows, and active farming villages. If that is desolation, Europe could do with more of it.

The woodlands are full of wildlife. The rivers Marne, Meuse and Aube all spring to life in Haute-Marne. And Haute-Marne shares with the département of Marne the huge man-made lake of Der-Chantecoq, which is a playground for watersporters and a beach resort for families.

Sedan, on the bank of the Meuse upstream from Charleville-Mézières, is in a beautiful wooded setting, which makes its monster-fort look even more formidable. Begun in 1424, the fortress was strengthened and extended over centuries until now it covers 35,000sq m on seven different levels. The last building was in Renaissance style, and it is now a museum of military science, from the crossbow to the cannon. Three Marshals of France were born in the castle, many French kings stayed there and it was for a while a safe haven for persecuted Protestants.

In the 15th century the Lord of Sedan, Jean de la Marck, built a new defensive wall, enclosing two suburbs of Sedan and so making the castle a fortified town. The defences proved useful in 1495, when Jean's grandson Robert II was defending Sedan against an attack by Archduke Maximilien, and later in 1521, when Robert was attacked by the powerful Hapsburg Emperor Charles V.

The fort became a Protestant stronghold when Henri de la Tour d'Auvergne of the great Protestant family married Charlotte de la Marck. He later married Elisabeth de Nassau, and their son Henri de la Tour d'Auvergne, born in the Sedan fortress in 1611, became one of the greatest soldiers in the history of France. He was made Marshal-General of France and Vicomte de Turenne. Late in his life he became a Catholic. Louis XIV and Cardinal Mazarin, his chief minister, took refuge in the fortress during the Fronde uprising of disgruntled nobles. The Sedan town councillors were imprisoned there during the Revolution for helping La Fayette to escape to Belgium, before they were taken to Paris to be guillotined. Napoleon visited Sedan in 1803 and stole the great collection of arms and armour to take to Paris.

In the Franco-Prussian War in 1870, General MacMahon, Napoleon III's Commander-in-Chief, brought the new army he had formed in Châlons-sur-Marne (see Chapter 9) to Sedan but was comprehensively beaten by the Prussians. Apart from 3000 men killed, and 14,000 wounded, 83,000 French were taken prisoner, including the Emperor Napoleon III himself and MacMahon. They were imprisoned in Sedan fortress before being sent to Wilhelmshöhe.

It was the end of Napoleon III's dream of crossing the Rhine and conquering as his ancestor had done about 70 years before. It was also the end of his rule over France. He retired to Chislehurst Common in Kent.

Visits to the **fortress** are well organised—all guided, or they might lose a few visitors in the maze of the stone corridors, low dark passageways and rooms. One big tower was built around a smaller one, so that there is a wide, low corridor between the walls. There is an 'oubliette' of course—a well into which the Lords would lower someone who had displeased them and leave them forgotten, crouching on a slimy, cold ledge with a sheer drop into the water below. Each day a loaf of bread and a pitcher of water was lowered for the prisoners to fight over. Incredibly there were men who survived this for years, to be released when someone very important started to ask questions about them, or when the castle was captured by someone more humane. The fortress is open daily for visits (afternoons only in winter). There are even torchlight tours at night—by flaming torch. And there are a bar and restaurant.

In 1940, during the 'blitzkrieg' breakthrough of German armour, supported by the Luftwaffe, the invading Nazis destroyed much of Sedan town, but did very little damage to the old fortress. Much of the town had been built in the 17th–18th centuries. In rebuilding, the architects chose a more modern look. You can see much of the town from the ramparts of the fortress.

Although he was not there, Emile Zola wrote such a true description of the French defeat in his novel *La Débacle* that he was accused by the army, the church and the politicians of 'demoralising' the French nation.

Sedan still makes its traditional black cloth, called sedan, but these days it specialises in metallurgy and chemicals.

Bazeilles is almost a part of Sedan now. Its château, built in 1750 by a very rich local textile manufacturer, is a perfect example of Louis XV architecture, with lovers' bowers, a dovecote, an unusual orangery and park. Once known

The massive Porte des Princes of the fortress at Sedan

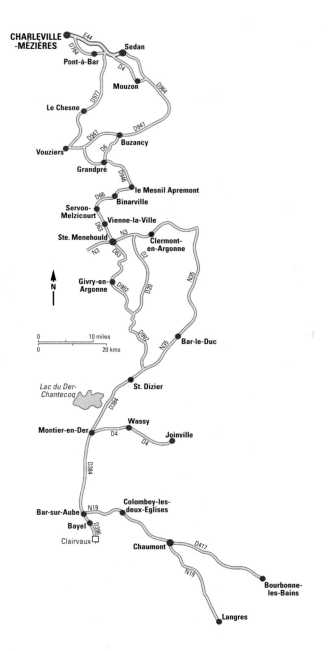

as a meeting place for statesmen, diplomats, royals and writers, it is now a luxury hotel, with bedrooms in a side building, all opening onto the château and park.

The orangery, like an upturned boat, is a restaurant under separate management, with a Michelin star. Its rough stone dining room has a huge fireplace and beamed ceiling.

Thirteen kilometres (8 miles) west of Sedan by the D764, where the Ardennes canal meets the Meuse, is **Pont-à-Bar**, a base for hired cruisers called Périchettes—little flat-bottomed barges. You can hire boats for two to 12 people for two days to two weeks, sailing down the Meuse through Charleville and Givet to Dinant or Namur in Belgium, to Monthermé and Revin, or for two days to Monthermé and back. Or you can sail east along Canal de l'Est through Sedan and Mouzon as far as Verdun. More adventurously, you can start going down the Canal des Ardennes and join the network to Reims and Epernay and back. That takes a fortnight, covers 362km (225 miles) and takes you through 146 locks; Ardennes is hilly! (Information Ardennes Nautisme, 1 rue de la Rochefoucauld, BP78, 08202 Sedan, tel. 24 27 05 15).

Mouzon, 18km (11 miles) from Sedan by the attractive little D4, which hugs the Meuse, was for centuries a frontier town between the Kingdom of France and the Germanic Empire. Old buildings still exist, including a magnificent Gothic **church**, similar to the superb 13th century church in Laon, with a wonderfully rich carved door. Mouzon suffered three great sieges. The fortified walls were demolished in 1671 but the 15th century Gate of Burgundy survives. The gate tower houses a museum, mostly of Gallo-Roman remains. We were intrigued by the felt museum (**Musée de Feutre**) where you can watch wool turned into felt perfect enough for any championship snooker table.

Travelling south from Sedan, you are soon in quiet, sparsely populated country, even if you follow the D977 main road. Forêt du Mont Dieu can still be so quiet that it is almost eerie, especially if you sit in silence among the remains of the ancient **abbey** in a rather sombre valley, just east of D977. Odon, abbot of St Remi in Reims, went on a pilgrimage in 1130 to the Grande Chartreuse in the Dauphiné (the place where monks sworn to silence collect the hillside herbs to make the strong green and yellow Chartreuse liqueur which makes us, at least, rather talkative). Odon set up a Chartreuse here in the Ardennes where the monks of the order of St Bruno took the vow of silence. Odon did not join them. Later, in the Revolution, it became a prison. Now the young people, dressed in clothes far removed from monkish habits, walk chatting happily along its marked pathways of GR14—one of those Grande Randonnée long-distance footpaths which are a challenge and a blessing to walkers in France.

The D977 livens up around **Le Chesne**, a pleasant market town on the Canal des Ardennes. You can see one of the interesting fortified churches of the Bar valley here. A small road north leads to Lac de Bairon, where you can sail, canoe, windsurf or laze on the beach. Of its 140 hectares, 100 are open for watersports, while the remainder are a reserve for birds. (Leisure base, tel. 24 30 13 18.) There is a campsite. The scenery, for 9.5km (6 miles) to the south-west of le Chesne, alongside the Canal des Ardennes on D25 to Semuy on the Aisne river, is delightful. The canal has 27 locks on this little stretch— giving some idea of the hilliness of this country.

The river Aisne zigzags crazily between Semuy and Vouziers as it takes evasive action from rocks, hills and obstacles, and it is small wonder that a canal was built alongside in the days when transport by water was so vital. The small town of **Vouziers**, a centre for basketwork, is proud of its magnificent Renaissance church door and of being the birthplace in 1823 of the philosopher Hippolyte Taine. He believed that you could apply the same precise scientific rules to the behaviour, moral qualities and artistic excellence of people as you can to the body and biological facts; that the same laws apply to the mechanism of the spirit as to the mechanism of the body. His most famous work was *The Origin of Contemporary France* (1875–94), which attacked the French Revolutionaries and their motives. He even made a critical analysis of La Fontaine's *Fables*.

There are very attractive roads eastwards through the Forêt de la Croix-aux-Bois. This was the way the US army advanced in October 1918, winning a tough battle at Grandpré (on the D946) before taking Buzancy on 2 November 1918. The US troops continued their advance to the Meuse opposite Sedan and had taken the important Meuse crossing at Stenay, which had been the HQ of the German Crown Prince at the Armistice on 11 November 1918. They threw in 22 divisions, numbering 630,000 men, and their casualties were 119,000. **Buzancy**, an ancient fortress, has a 13th–16th century church and the Château de la Cour, home of General Alfred Chanzy, one of the few generals of Napoleon III's army to resist the Prussians with notable success.

Some 9.5km (6 miles) north-east of Buzancy in the Forêt de Belval is the Parc de Vision, a wildlife park where animals can be seen living as they have lived here for 1500 years. There are wild boar, red roe and fallow deer, stags, does and bucks, wild sheep, elk, moose, bison and bears, in 1133 ha of woods, plains and ponds. An 8.5km (5 mile) car track goes through the park and there are footpaths with observation posts.

The D946 from Vouziers is a delightful road. From Buzancy you can pick it up at Grandpré by taking the D6 south. At Le Mesnil Apremont take the D442 right, then through Binarville onto the D66 to Servon Melzicourt, the D666 to Vienne-la-Ville and the D63 to Ste Menehould. You are now in Marne, not Ardennes. This lovely countryside is on the edge of the Forest of Argonne, a forest massif, with deep gorges and many ponds, which is shared between Champagne and Lorraine. Victor Hugo and Alexandre Dumas wrote of its beauty and it is spectacular walking country, using Ste Menehould as a base.

Now that the A4 motorway passes within 2km of **Ste Menehould** on its way to Châlons, the peaceful town has more visitors, some arriving, no doubt, to pay respects to the monk Dom Pérignon, the father of Champagne wine,

Sailing lessons on Lac du Der-Chantecoq

who was born there, others to taste the town's renowned dish, pigs' trotters (see Chapter 4). Though there is not a lot to see, Menehould is one of those French towns where you can wander round and feel contented and in no hurry to leave. The old town, called the château, is on a rocky height above the river Aisne. The 13th century **church** has a 15th century organ. The **Maison de Poste** has been restored. Here on 21 June 1791, J.B. Drouet, son of the postmaster, recognised the man sitting in a *berline* having its horses changed. He had seen the man's image on an écu coin. It was Louis XVI, fleeing with his wife Marie-Antoinette, their two children and the King's sister Elizabeth. They drove off, followed by six dragoon guards. He told the National Guard, who stopped the dragoons from riding away, then he galloped by pathways through the forest to Varennes in Lorraine to give the alarm. The Royal Family was arrested and returned to Paris. It was said that Louis XVI was travelling to Metz to meet the Marquis de Bouille, who had a force of soldiers waiting. The plan was to get Austrian military help to march on Paris and put the King back on the throne. Marie-Antoinette, of course, was an Austrian princess.

The **castle of Braux-Sainte Cohière**, 5km (3 miles) west of Ste Menehould, was home of the light infantry from the time of Henri IV and Louis XIII. Surrounded by moats, it is an unusual military building. During the Battle of Valmy, when two days after the French Republic was declared, the young, inexperienced soldiers of the Revolution (the Sans Culottes) defeated the Prussians, it was the headquarters of General de Dumouriez. Among many festivals held here is a midsummer Festival of Valmy, an audio-visual show illustrating the history and curiosities of the area. Each Christmas the traditional Champagne Shepherd's Mass is held.

At **Clermont-en-Argonne**, 16km (10 miles) east of Ste Menehould, is a ridge where in World War II, two artillery batteries were firing at the Germans. One was commanded by a French Commandant named Lebrun, the other by a US Lieutenant named Truman. Later Albert Lebrun was President of France until forced to hand over to Pétain in 1940. Harry S. Truman became President of the United States (1945–52). West from Clermont you can follow the D2 and the D20 southward through the forest but you are not quite in Champagne. You are just over the border in Lorraine. The RD382 through Givry is less attractive. Unless you take a very round-about route by tiny roads, you will need to go through Revigny-sur-Ornain in Lorraine or drive well west through Vitry-le-François (see Chapter 9) to reach St Dizier.

If you take the little D63 from Ste Menehould, you find some pleasant villages such as **Verrières**, with old wooden houses and an attractive brick church. Follow little roads to Villiers-en-Argonne, Ante, Bournonville on the edge of a big pool. Then the D270 takes you to La Neuville-aux-Bois. It is a shady route, with lily of the valley in bloom in May. **Givry-en-Argonne** is a 'green' holiday resort for fresh air and action enthusiasts, with bathing, canoeing, sailing, pedalos and fishing on its bog pools. But we find the attractive forest route over the border the best way to reach St Dizier.

St Dizier is a large industrial city in Haute-Marne. In the new industrial section, where high-rise buildings abound, the low modern church of **Ste Thérèse au Vert Bois** has been built to contrast with them. Foundries have existed here since the Middle Ages, and now steel is one of the main industries.

South of St Dizier are pleasant walks through the Forest of Val, but its great advantage is that **Lac du Der-Chantecoq**, the biggest man-made lake in Europe, is only 9.5km (6 miles) south-west. The lake, created in 1974, to control the flow of the Marne and the Seine, covers 4798 ha, half in Marne and half in Haute-Marne. It has three pleasure ports—Giffaumont, Nemours and Nuisement—six beaches with lifeguards, a port (Chantecoq) for motor boats and water-skiing and around the lake facilities for sailing, canoeing, pedalos, fishing for trout and perch, horse-riding and bird-watching. In season motor-boat trips round the lake leave from Giffaumont (tel. 26 41 62 80). There are fine old half-timbered buildings in several of the villages, and some churches that were moved and rebuilt when the area was flooded. A **museum village** in the old style has been set up at Ste Marie-du-Lac.

At Argentolle on the west side and Reservoir de Champaubert on the east are reserves for ducks, herons and migrating birds, including cormorants and cranes. In March an estimated 25,000 cranes stay to rest a while on their flight to northern Scandinavia, to spend the summer there, following a winter vacation in Africa.

Information about the lake is given by the Maison du Lac, Giffaumont-Champaubert Tourist Office, 51290 St Remy-en-Bouzemont (tel. 26 72 62 80). There are five campsites round the lake and four hotel-restaurants nearby: *Cheval Blanc du Lac*, 51290 Giffaumont (tel. 26 72 62 65); *Cheval Blanc*, Ceffonds (tel. 25 04 20 46), about 1km south-west of Montier-en-Der; *Hotel de la Cloche*, 52290 Eclaron (tel. 25 04 11 17); *La Bocagère*, 51290 Ste Marie-du-Lac (tel. 26 72 37 40).

The D384 from St Dizier bridges a corner of the lake and runs through part of the Forêt du Der on its way to **Montier-en-Der**. This is cattle-breeding country, so it is not entirely surprising that there should be a stud for horses, part of the National Stud. Horse race meetings of four days are held in June, July and August. Montier started in AD 673 as a monastery in the forest. Although raided and devastated several times in the Hundred Years War, it was very rich by the 15th century and owned 21 surrounding villages. Dissolved during the Revolution, its **abbey church** became the parish church and was much restored and rebuilt in the 19th century with several unusual architectural features, especially in the choir. In 1940 it was burned, with half of the town, in a German attack, but it has all been exceptionally well rebuilt, making Montier a very pleasant airy town. Its stud (Haras) was originally in the remains of the abbey but these were replaced by a more modern building.

East of Montier is the historic little town of **Wassy**, where the murder of Protestant families at prayer on 1 March 1562 by the Duke of Guise and his men raised the fury and fear of Protestants all over France and lit the fuse for the terrible Religious Wars.

François de Guise had been staying at his mother's château in Joinville and turned aside to visit Wassy, which was owned by his family. The Protestant families were holding their Sunday service in a big barn. Guise claimed that their singing was interrupting his prayers and sent his soldiers to stop the service. Someone threw a stone and hit Guise in the face. His soldiers massacred the families—23 people were killed and 130 badly wounded. The Catholics called it an incident, the Protestants, a massacre.

Guise had gained the town when the child Mary Stuart (Mary, Queen of Scots), who had owned Wassy, returned to Scotland, following the death of her sickly young husband, King François II. The English had owned it during the Hundred Years War. Today it has foundries, breeds cattle and produces famous almond meringues called caisses de Wassy.

Joinville, east of Wassy, is also a historic town. Its first Sire was Johen de Joinville (1224–1319) who was companion and chronicler of Louis IX and went with him on Crusades. Louis was canonised after his death and as St Louis was patron saint of France until Joan of Arc took over in 1920. When he was 85, Jehan wrote the Life of Louis, which is still of great historic interest.

The medieval château came into the hands of the Guise family, who became local lords. There, in the Religious Wars, Henri de Guise, younger brother of François, and the leader of his extremist Catholic League, signed a treaty with Philip II of Spain under the title Ligue de Bien Public (League of Public Good). Not many of the public thought much good of it when it introduced Spanish soldiers into France and was infiltrated by thugs, crooks, looters and other main-chancers. It was fighting soon against the Catholic King of France Henri III. Guise had ambitions to be King of France, and was acting as a spy for the Spanish. Philip of Spain's contribution to the Public Good was to build the Armada to invade and destroy Protestant England. After its comprehensive defeat by the English and Dutch navies, Guise had lost his powerful ally and Henri III had him assassinated.

The old château was bought by Philippe, Duke of Orléans, brother of Louis XV and friend of England's Prince Regent (later King George IV). He was a great gambler and drinker. He joined the Revolution, changed his name to Philippe Egalité (Equality) and became Deputy for Paris in the Revolutionary Convention. He had already knocked down a wing of his château at Fère-en-Tardenois to show how 'equal' he was. He sold the château at Joinville on condition that it was pulled down completely. Unfortunately for him his son Louis-Philippe, fighting in the Republican forces, deserted to the Austrians. So Philippe Egalité was guillotined.

In 1830 his son returned to France as King Louis Philippe, 'the Citizen King'. The citizens, however, lost patience with him and he escaped to England as Mr Smith and lived in Surbiton. His third son, the Prince of Joinville, served in the French navy, then went to America to serve on McClellan's staff in the Virginian Campaign in the American Civil War. Though exiled from France, he returned incognito in 1870 to fight the

Rue St Didier in Langres

Prussians. Afterwards, he was elected to the National Assembly and died in Paris in 1900.

A château built in the 16th century, **Château de Grand Jardin**, stands as you would expect in gardens and is richly decorated with sculptures, but was not improved by a flight of stairs added in the 19th century. Joinville is on the river Marne and the Marne-Saône canal.

From Montier the D384 runs down to **Bar-sur-Aube**, most southerly centre of Champagne wine. Bar is a pleasing, busy little town on the right bank of the Aube river, with a canal almost enclosing it on the other three sides. There are nice walks on the wooded slopes.

The 12th century **church of St Pierre** in rue Nationale is worth seeing. Outside are strange 15th century wooden balconies. Inside, the floor is well below street level. There are good statues and the organ came from the old nunnery at Remiremont, over the border in Vosges, a very snobbish institution of 50 noble canonesses (Dames de Remiremont) who were admitted only if they could give proof of 200 years of unblemished noble ancestry. They were given the title of Countess and several times took to the field in battle! Not surprisingly, they were suppressed during the Revolution.

In the Middle Ages, one of the six great trade fairs which made Champagne prosperous was held here. Now, as Bar is the centre of the southern Champagne wine area, its major fair is Foire aux Vins de Champagne on the second Sunday in September, filling the centre streets with stalls, temporary bars and café tables. Two cooperatives in Bar-sur-Aube offer tastings and Bernard Robert Voigny makes quality wine. Follow the D4 to Meurville, the D44 south and the D70 north to reach several little wine villages—Urville, where Drappier produce a good Champagne, Arconville (Bernard Goucher is recommended) and Baroville (Château Barfontare).

The little town of **Bayel**, 8km (5 miles) from Bar down the D396, has produced hand-made crystal glass since 1666. The factory was set up by a Venetian named Mazzolay. The local sand and silicon proved excellent for glass-making and the chance to save money on expensive imports delighted the Chief Minister Colbert, fighting to balance France's budget against the wild extravagances of Louis XIV and his Court. About 8km (5 miles) further down the D396 are the remains of one of the most influential and richest abbeys in Europe, **Clairvaux**. It was started in 1124 at the request of the austere St Bernard by Etienne (Stephen) Harding, the English abbot of Cîteaux and was under the strict rules of the Cistercian Order, so when Napoleon turned it into a prison, life did not get very much harder for the new inmates. Now the prisoners are in a more modern building behind the abbey's old outer walls. There are some attractive walks through the surrounding Forêt de Clairvaux.

Sixteen kilometres (10 miles) east from Bar-sur-Aube along N19 at **Colombey-les-Deux-Eglises** stands a huge **memorial** in pink granite—a 44m high double cross of Lorraine. Here, in his house La Boisserie, just outside the village, sheltered by trees, General de Gaulle spent the quieter moments of the last 25 years of his life. He bought the house in 1933. In 1940 he escaped to England and during the German occupation the house was wrecked—a wall knocked down, part of the roof burned. De Gaulle moved back in May 1946. He died in November 1970, while playing patience, and is buried simply in the village cemetery by the church. His son Philippe owns the house. You can visit his salon with pictures of his family, his library and dining room. National and international pilgrims still visit De Gaulle's grave. But we wonder what acid remark he would have made about the souvenir shops lining the village road selling De Gaulle cuckoo-clocks, corkscrews, snail-eating tongs, T-shirts, bellows and snowstorms in glass cases falling on his memorial.

Some 27km (17 miles) down the N19 is **Chaumont**, an old town with some fine old houses with staircase towers, villas with sculpted doorways and, around its town hall square, picturesque narrow streets. It is remembered mostly for its superb **railway viaduct** over La Suize valley, a magnificent work of 19th century engineering art. Its 50 arches are in three stages, 343m long and 29.5m above the valley. It carries the Paris–Basle line.

Chaumont was the resident city of the Counts of Champagne in the 13th century. The **tower of Hautefeuille** remains of the Counts' château. Although it has only 30,000 people, Chaumont is the prefecture town of Haute-Marne. Here in 1814, after Napoleon had refused their peace proposals, Austria, Russia, Prussia and Britain decided to continue fighting him.

Each June the town holds an unusual international meeting for graphic arts (posters, exhibitions, auctions and contests).

The river Marne and the Marne-Saône canal sweep round the town's eastern side and one reason why it remained important was that its canal port served the towns and villages of the great Haute-Marne plateau. Now the A5 motorway passes within 13km (8 miles) and meets the A31 after 18km (11 miles), giving Chaumont a through-route to Paris, Calais, Metz and through Burgundy to the south.

Bourbonne-les-Bains, east of Chaumont by the D417, has been a spa since Gallo-Roman days, dedicated originally to the Celtic god Borvo, meaning hot fountain. The present thermal establishment, built in 1980 and equipped with the most modern techniques, is still called Centre Borvo. In the 18th century the army used it for treatment of wounded soldiers and in 1812 Napoleon bought it—no doubt at his own price! It offers a wide range of treatments, mostly for mending of broken bones and treatment of arthritis. The town is well known locally for the sport of moto cross, which might well supply the spa with extra customers.

LANGRES is one of the oldest towns in France and one of the most blessed. For centuries it was a walled, fortified town and the **ramparts** remain, encircling the town for 4km (2½ miles). The views from them over the Marne valley are intensely satisfying and the walk of just under 3km (2 miles) is certainly worth the effort. You pass seven surviving towers with look-out platforms, furnished these days with panoramic tables, and there are still six old gates into town. Though it dates from before the Roman occupation, Langres keeps up to date with history. The road which turns off the N19 past place Bel

Air to enter the town is called rue 8 Mai 1945. At the far end of **place Bel Air** is the tourist office, where you can get a map of the town with two walks around it, one following the ramparts, the other encompassing the most interesting sites of the centre. The routes are marked in the streets with arrows in enamelled stoneware.

For hundreds of years Langres was an archbishopric and **St Mammès cathedral** was built in the 12th century. It is a fine illustration of the change from Romanesque to early Gothic, but the west façade was reconstructed in the 18th century and restored in the 19th. Langres has a few medieval and many attractive Renaissance houses, but it is by no means just a 'museum' town. For centuries it has been proud of its culture and entertainments—fêtes and festivals. Les Rendez-Vous de Juillet is a renowned theatrical spectacle, with Son-et-Lumière and drama, played each year through July in a different historic background in the town. La Ronde des Hallebardiers is a moving spectacle, a jolly walk round the ramparts and old parts of the town led by 16th century-clad Hallebardiers (armed guards), all participants becoming a member of the cast.

The country surrounding Langres makes it a very attractive holiday centre. Immediately to the east are two large lakes—Charmes and La Liez. A little further west is Lac La Mouche and southward Lac La Vingeanne. Lac Liez is especially popular for bathing, sailing, canoeing and sailboards, though all the lakes are open for watersports and fishing. Walks and drives through the Forêt d'Arc and the woods and forests around Auberive are very pleasant. Boar and deer are often to be seen.

The sources of the Marne, Meuse and Aube rivers are all fairly near to Langres. The source of the Aube, signposted in the forest just south of the D428 Langres–Auberive route, attracts picnickers. The source of the Marne is along a pathway off the little D290 5km (3 miles) south of Langres. Parking is provided. The river rises in a little cave guarded by an iron door. Nearby is another cave where the chief of the local Lingon tribe, Sabinus, hid for nine years after his defeat by Julius Caesar's Roman army. He was discovered, taken with his wife to Rome, and killed.

Langres was once a fortified frontier town of Burgundy. It is only 66km (42 miles) from Dijon.

11. Sens to Auxerre

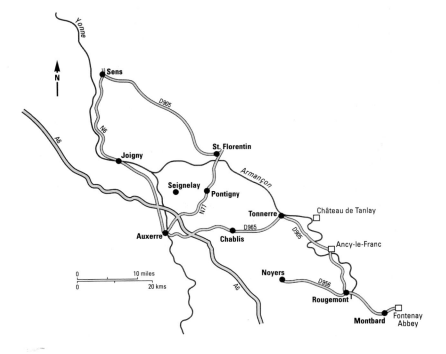

A few years ago, the old N6 was a beloved curse to everyone driving to the south of France. We knew every mile of it. We hated it for its endless stream of trucks. If you overtook a dozen, there were 12 more a mile up the road. We loved it for its auberges and Relais Routiers where we could quench our thirsts, assuage our hunger and take our eyes off the road. We all had our favourites, which we 'knew' to be the best even if we had not tried the others. We could pick up the road south of Paris around Fontainebleau and keep on it to Auxerre, right through Burgundy to Beaune, only abandoning it after Lyon. We even spotted that village shops had closed and new ones opened.

Now visitors hurry along the motorway, missing the truck-jams but missing, too, many treasures like the once powerful old town of Sens, among orchards and cereal crops in the north-east corner of Yonne. We forget sometimes that **SENS** is in Burgundy for it is a mere 119km (74 miles) from Paris. To add to our confusion, it was once in Champagne. But it has had great moments of power. The Senones, a Gallic tribe, marched to Rome in 390 BC and captured it. They might well have destroyed it but for the honking of the holy geese in the Capitol, which woke the Romans from slumber. The Gallic invaders only agreed to go home after being paid a ransom in gold that left Rome poor for a long time.

The Romans, of course, got their own back, in gold, according to legend, when they conquered Sens on their way through Gaul. But they made it capital of a Gallo-Roman province called Senonia and gave it such strong ramparts that they were not destroyed entirely until the 19th century, when they were replaced by the oval of leafy boulevards that now surrounds the town. For 700 years, until the 16th century, the Church gave Sens power. The archbishop was called Primate of the Gauls and of Germania and had authority over Auxerre, Troyes. Chartres and Orléans, as well as Paris. Power waned when Paris became an archbishopric in 1622.

Though battered in wars, the **cathedral of St Etienne** is oddly beautiful. It was built over five centuries and inevitably is a fusion of styles. The great west façade is lopsided, with one tower uncompleted above roof height while the other soars to 46m (150ft), topped by a Renaissance bell tower housing two massive bells weighing just over 14 and 16 tonnes. The original tower fell down in the 13th century because yet another medieval architect was too ambitious. Thirty years earlier it might have hit the Crusader King Louis IX (St Louis, patron saint of France until ousted by St Joan in 1920). He was married to Marguerite of Provence in St Etienne's in 1234.

Thomas à Becket, murdered Archbishop of Canterbury, features in four of the magnificent **windows** ranging from the 12th to the 17th century. They show Thomas and his former friend Henry II striving to be reconciled, Becket's return to England from happy exile in Sens, his welcome and his tragic murder by four over-zealous knights who had taken too literally the despairing cry of an exasperated Henry II, 'Will no one rid me of this poxy priest?'.

Experts in church architecture see similarities between Sens and Canterbury cathedrals. The original head mason at Sens was William of Sens (Guillaume de Sens). After fire destroyed parts of Canterbury in 1140, William rebuilt it. Unfortunately he fell from scaffolding and died from his injuries.

In one of the richest collections of church treasures in France, among priceless ivories and tapestries, are part of Becket's vestments. But strangely, one of the finest pieces is a 12th century Islamic casket. To wander the pedestrianised **Grande Rue** and its side-streets is delightful, if only for their half-timbered houses.

Because of motorways, much of the département of Yonne has become one of France's hidden treasures. Though Auxerre and Chablis are hardly hidden from visitors, there are small towns and villages of quiet charm known only to wanderers untroubled by time or to tourists lucky enough to get lost. The Yonne is a river of beauty and character, but perverse in its eccentric flow. It rises in Burgundy, in the Morvan, and reaches its zenith at Auxerre, but remains a power through the land until it joins the Seine at Montereau, 40km (25 miles) after Sens and 88km (55 miles) before Paris. True Burgundians say that at Montereau the Yonne really swallows the Seine and that the river which then flows through Paris to the sea is the Yonne. That reminds us that but for a few flukes of medieval history, Burgundy would have swallowed France.

Up river from Sens, the Yonne meanders into **Joigny**, a very attractive and busy little commercial town, built in brown stone and tiles on terraces above the river. It is something of a phoenix. Destroyed by fire in 1530 during the Wars of Religion, it was hit by the Luftwaffe in 1940 and many old houses were destroyed in a terrible gas explosion in 1981. Each time it has been restored. It is a joy to wander aimlessly round the steep narrow streets of the old town, to discover little squares and to find out what happens beyond the hilltops. Traffic is much better on the N6 now that the A6 motorway has taken away the trucks, the coaches and the tourists who are in a hurry.

This was a thriving wine area until phylloxera struck last century. The little Côte St Jacques vineyard, part of a medieval winery, is operating, and a few others have re-opened recently, producing a *vin gris. A la Côte St Jacques* is the name of Joigny's distinguished restaurant, where Michel Lorain and his son have gained three stars from Michelin—rather surprising, for Michel prides himself on Burgundian dishes and they are not in fashion these days. Meal prices are *very* high; the hotel is most attractive.

There is a lovely view of the river and town from the six-arched 18th century bridge. **St Thibault church**, a mixture of Gothic and Renaissance, has a very graceful bell tower above its 17th century tower. Inside is a delightful smiling 14th century Virgin in stone. Strange how the Virgin was shown smiling through most of the early medieval period, but became more thoughtful and sad around 1400.

The people of Joigny had the happy name of *Joviniens* until 1483. Then they rebelled against their Lord, Count Guy de la Tremoille, captured his castle and killed him with mallets (*mailles*) used in the vineyards. Since then they have been known as *Maillotins!*

AUXERRE is a gem of a town, not only for its lifestyle, its looks, its setting, its interest and atmosphere but because every road, big or small, that leads out of it takes you to somewhere delightful. As a touring base, few towns in France are better. Even the pronunciation of its name, osserre, is soft and seductive, inviting you to return. It is strictly a Burgundian town, more interested in what happens in Dijon than in Paris.

Terraced up a hillside from an ancient port on the Yonne, and at the head of the Nivernais canal, its tree-shaded boulevards made from the old city walls still encircle busy narrow streets. Auxerre looks superb from across the river, with the Gothic spires of its churches rising above old roof tops. On a sunny day, with the cathedral, the spires and the fine arched bridge reflected in the river and the blue sky as a backcloth, this is one of the most pleasant

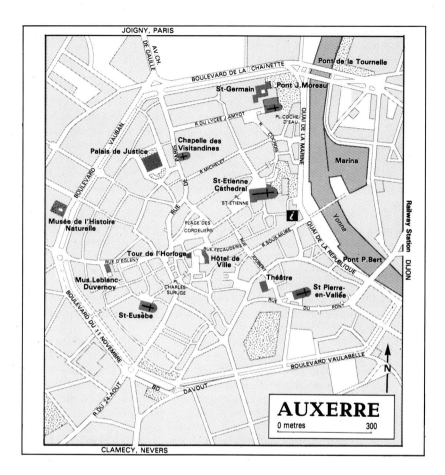

Map labels:
JOIGNY, PARIS
AV. CH. DE GAULLE
BOULEVARD DE LA CHAINETTE
Pont de la Tournelle
St-Germain
Pont J. Moreau
R. DU LYCÉE J. AMYOT
PL. COCHE D'EAU
QUAI DE LA MARINE
R. COCHOIS
VAUBAN
Chapelle des Visitandines
Palais de Justice
R. MICHELET
RUE DE PARIS
Marina
BOULEVARD
St-Etienne Cathedral
PL. ST-ÉTIENNE
Yonne
Musée de l'Histoire Naturelle
PLACE DES CORDELIERS
RUE FÉCAUDERIE
R. SOUS-MURS
QUAI DE LA RÉPUBLIQUE
Railway Station
DIJON
Tour de l'Horloge
RUE D'EGLENY
Hôtel de Ville
RUE JOUBERT
Pont P. Bert
Mus. Leblanc-Duvernoy
PL. CHARLES-SURUGE
Théâtre
St Pierre-en-Vallée
RUE DU PONT
BOULEVARD DU 11 NOVEMBRE
St-Eusèbe
BOULEVARD VAULABELLE
N
BD. DAVOUT
R. DU 24-AOUT

AUXERRE
0 metres   300

CLAMECY, NEVERS

scenes in Burgundy. Renaissance houses, and some earlier, line attractive streets and narrow lanes which lead to small squares. Along the old quays are pleasant riverside walks under the trees.

But Auxerre is not a sleepy town. Even the canal is busy. The canal head has been converted into a pleasure-boat harbour, a leading centre of inland waterway holidays. Pleasure boats run dinner cruises. In warmer weather the squares, and especially the attractive pedestrianised centre, are lively with people drinking and dining at outside tables. And in the football season, you have only to be in Auxerre when the famous football team are playing at home to find the town full of life—especially if they are playing Paris or, as in 1994, Arsenal in the semi-final of the European Cup Winners' Cup.

Auxerre: the quayside with the Abbey of St Germain dominating the skyline

It was the port which made Auxerre so prosperous, and the wine the boats carried—not only the local wine produced liberally until the phylloxera struck, but wine from south of the area.

The importance of churches in Auxerre can be traced to the 5th century when a local man, Germanus, became bishop. As St Germain, he is now one of the most popular of French saints. A lawyer from a rich Gallo-Roman family, he was practising in Rome when he was sent back to Auxerre as military adviser. When converted to Christianity, he gave up sharing his wife's bed, slept on bare planks, wore a hair shirt and lived on three meals of coarse bread a week. A very dedicated man. It must have been uncomfortable to be a Christian then. He tracked down heretics zealously, even as far as England. He was a brilliant bureaucrat, which might account for his popularity with the French.

He has a church in Paris named after him, opposite the east side of the Louvre, called St Germain l'Auxerrois, to avoid muddle with another Burgundian, St Germain-des-Prés, a Paris bishop. A Benedictine abbey called **St Germain** was founded in Auxerre in the 6th century by Queen Clotilde, wife of Clovis, first Christian king of the Franks. Within 100 years it had 600 monks and 2000 students. The abbey church and cloisters remain, with a fine 14th century **belfry**, 29m (96ft high), now standing separate from the church owing to demolitions. The crypt is really two crypts, one built on top of the other, to fool pillaging Norsemen. RAF prisoners of war used the technique in escape tunnelling to fool German guards.

The superb Gothic **cathedral of St Etienne** was originally Romanesque, but in 1215 the Bishop decided that it was too old-fashioned. The 'new' church was not finished until 1560. The result was certainly outstanding—pure Flamboyant style, a bit lopsided but with exquisite tracery on the façade and vivid 13th–14th century glass rivalling that of Chartres. The rose-windows are lovely, the high choir windows of Christ in Majesty have unique grandeur. A fresco of a man on horseback attended by angels, in shades of ochre, was painted in 1100.

Joan of Arc prayed here when she passed through dressed as a boy in 1429 on her way to Chinon to persuade the Dauphin to give her an army. She returned with 12,000 men on her way to Reims, taking the Dauphin to be crowned King Charles VII. A window shows her at the head of her troops. Ironically it was in this cathedral that the English and Burgundians met in 1423 before advancing to beat the French and Scots at Cravant. The Burgundian commander Claude de Beauvoir, Baron Chestelux, was able to return Cravant to its owner, the Bishop of Auxerre. As a reward, de Beauvoir and his descendants in perpetuity were created hereditary lay canons with the right of attending services in full armour, booted, spurred, wearing their swords over their surplices and carrying their falcons on their wrists.

There are fine views over the town from the cathedral tower. **Place l'Hôtel-de-Ville**, lined with half-timbered houses, contains a painted statue of a poet much loved in France, Marie Noël, who died in 1967. Her poems were often set to music. Nearby is a favourite corner of Auxerre, **Tour de l'Horloge**, originally a 15th century tower in the defence walls. The belfry and clock tower, with a 17th century clock, were added by a Duke of Burgundy. One face of the clock shows the time, the other the movement of the sun and moon. In this square on 17 March 1815, Napoleon, having escaped from Elba and marching towards Paris with a small army, met his old commander Marshal Ney and his troops. After Napoleon's defeat and internment in Elba, Ney, one of his most successful commanders, was loaded with favours by Louis XVIII and given command of a royal army. When Napoleon landed from Elba, Ney marched with a big force to meet him, swearing that he would 'bring him back to Paris in a cage'. But when they met, Ney embraced Napoleon and joined him, giving him the army he needed. Ney commanded the Centre at Waterloo. After the monarchy returned, he was shot. Beside the clock tower is a vaulted passage with a plaque recalling Cadet Roussel (1743–1807), a local man who was the blighted hero of a very well-known French song.

The N6 Joigny–Auxerre follows the Yonne, passing close to **Seignelay**, a pleasant little town spreading down a hillside overlooking the little river Serein. For a while it was a barony. Colbert, appointed Chief Minister by Louis XIV to make France solvent, longed for a title, although he was busily trying to break the power of the aristocrats and make them condescend to pay taxes. So he bought the château at Seignelay, which was a barony, and had it raised to the status of Marquisate. Thus he became a marquis. That was the way the rich French middle class bought titles and became blue-blooded overnight.

The route we prefer to Auxerre is through **St Florentin**, a town with a pleasant atmosphere, fine views, and a church with richly coloured windows from the heyday of Troyes glass-making of the 16th century. St Florentin makes two delicious cheeses—St Florentin and Soumaintrain, both strong and spicy. Its restaurant *Grande Chaumière* offers the kind of meal that is becoming rare—very good cooking indeed of classic regional dishes. Five kilometres (3 miles) north by the D30 and D129 is *Moulin des Pommerats*, a delightful little mill turned hotel-restaurant run until recently by Paul Rémaux d'Equainville, a Frenchman who was a wartime Wing-Commander in an RAF squadron. Alas, Paul has retired, but his successor is a very good cook. He cooked for President Mitterand at the Elysées Palace.

At **Pontigny**, on the N77 to Auxerre, is a fine 13th century **bridge** on which it was said that three bishops (of Auxerre, Sens and Langres), three Counts (of Auxerre, Champagne and Tonnerre) and an abbot (of Pontigny itself) could dine together while each remained on his own land. It was here that in 1114 Stephen Harding, English abbot of Cîteaux, St Bernard, founder of the Cistercian Order, and 11 monks arrived to build a daughter-abbey to Cîteaux. Its position at the meeting of the lands of different counts and bishops gave it independence. It became in the Middle Ages a bolthole for leading English churchmen fleeing the wrath of kings in the battle between the English crown and Rome. Thomas à Becket, Archbishop of Canterbury, came in 1164 for two years before returning to his death at Canterbury. Stephen Langton was appointed Archbishop of Canterbury in 1207 by his friend from Paris University, Pope Innocent III, but King John of England refused to accept him, so he lived in Pontigny for six years until John let him in. He supported the English barons against the King and was first witness on the Magna Carta document. Edmund Rich of Abingdon, appointed by the Pope to preach the Sixth Crusade in England, became Archbishop of Canterbury in 1234 but fell out with King Henry III and even threatened him with excommunication from the church. St Edmé, as he became, spent the last year of his life at Pontigny and was buried behind the high altar.

The D965 eastward from Auxerre to Chablis is attractive once you have passed under the A6 motorway. Although **Chablis** itself is hardly beautiful, with new ugly filing-cabinet apartments on the fringe, we can forgive it anything for its wine. It is a loveable old place once you know it, with old shops of individuality, attractive stone alleys and plenty of chances to taste wine. The little river Serein, in which Pontigny monks used to fish, passes through the vineyards and skirts the town, with a nice walk under old trees called Promenade du Patis.

St Martin church, founded by monks from Tours fleeing from Norsemen raiders in the 11th century, has a Romanesque doorway with dove and serpent motifs. In medieval times, the patron saint of travellers was not St Christopher but St Martin, who had deprived the Devil of a sackful of souls by jumping a huge ravine on his donkey, so travellers attached horseshoes to the porch of St Martin's Romanesque doorway praying to the saint to protect their precious mounts.

The Pontigny monks first planted the vineyards of Chablis. They kept their wine in the stone building called Petit Pontigny in rue de Chiché, now used for the happy, wine-flowing meetings of the renowned wine brotherhood

Piliers Chablisiens (Pillars of Chablis). When Arthur was made a member in 1991, a rare honour for a foreigner, we ate a seven-course banquet with three different Chablis wines with every course, except the red meat, with which we drank Vosne-Romanée and Gevrey-Chambertin. At 'half-time', the young growers of Chablis brought bottles of their own wines and insisted that we should taste these, too!

Restaurants in Chablis are used to handling parties of day visitors. We still have affection for the old *Hôtel l'Etoile* (tel. 86 42 10 50), a shadow of its former glory when Jean Cocteau among others used it, but still offering traditional Burgundian dishes on good value menus. For gourmets with full wallets, the arrival ten years ago of young Michel Vignaud was a great day. Even before he opened his little hotel-restaurant *Hostellerie des Clos* (tel. 86 42 10 63) in an 18th century Romanesque chapel of an old Hôtel-Dieu, Michelin gave him a star on his previous reputation. He is a modern cook, but keeps many classical traditions. We have learned to be suspicious of 'brilliant', highly advertised young chefs, whose roots seem to be in the cookery school rather than in the kitchen of a master-chef. Vignaud's meals are tasty and satisfying.

Chablis has spent centuries fighting the weather. Now it is fighting competition from quaffable Chardonnay wines from south-west France and some very good Chardonnays among the many now produced in Australia and New Zealand. But likeable as these may be, they are *not* Chablis, especially premier cru or grand cru. These are inimitable and inevitably rather pricey. Unfortunately Chablis cannot copyright its name. And the Burgundians do get mad when they see low grade wines called Chablis in California. President Nixon, being shown round the cellars of our favourite Simonnet-Febvre, in the same family for 150 years, said 'We have a good Chablis in California. Have you ever tried it?'

'Only when I bet that I could give up drinking wine for a month', said a forthright Burgundian.

Tonnerre is a pleasant but rather sleepy town, terraced up the steep banks of the Armançon river and Canal de Bourgogne. It was deteriorating until recently because the young were being lured to Paris to seek more money or just to find jobs. Then suddenly in 1989 Mitterand 'planted' a mayor upon it—Henri Nallet, then Minister of Justice, once Minister of Finance. Though an 'absentee' mayor, he woke up Tonnerre and its economy, gaining it Government subsidies and setting up new companies and trades. He encouraged the replanting of vines—Chardonnay especially, but also Pinot Noir. However, Monté de Tonnerre, one of the best premier cru wine areas of nearby Chablis, is not to be confused with Tonnerre's own vineyards.

Tonnerre still has a medieval atmosphere in its narrow streets and old quarter below the 11th century **St Pierre church**. The 13th century **Ancien Hôpital** has a tall roof covering a huge area and an impressive ward 80m (262ft) long and 18m (59ft) wide, with a remarkable oak roof. The sick lay in beds in alcoves along the walls, placed so that they could see an altar, as in the Hospice de Beaune built 150 years later. The hospital was founded by the

One of the beautiful rooms in Château de Tanlay (see p 132)

enlightened Margaret of Burgundy, sister-in-law of Louis IX (St Louis). Married to Charles d'Anjou, she led a luxurious life in Loire valley châteaux until widowed at 36, when, as Comtesse de Tonnerre, she devoted her life to her subjects, even washing their wounds. Her tomb is here. So is the tomb of the Duke of Louvois (1628–1716), one of Louis XIV's war ministers, who acquired the nearby château of Ancy-le-Franc in 1684. A big green marble sarcophagus is missing from the tomb. Napoleon stole it for use as a bath tub!

A 'tub' used until recently as a public wash-house is the mysterious **Fosse Dionne**. A bubbling blue-green spring fills an 18th century stone basin, under which you can see a sharp shelf leading to caverns below. For about 200 years divers have explored the rock galleries, but narrow tunnels, strong currents and utter darkness have beaten them. Legend tells of a serpent living in the depths.

Tonnerre's most notorious citizen was Charles Eon de Beaumont, Chevalier d'Eon, born in 1728. Even his parents could not make up their minds if 'he' was a boy or a girl and at three put him in girls' clothes and called him Charlotte. He had a military education as a man and was said to be a courageous soldier (which proved nothing!). He shone at intelligence work and the French sent him (as a woman) to spy in St Petersburg, where he (or she) gained the confidence of the Tsarina Elizabeth and became her personal reader.

He was then sent in 1762 to the French Embassy in London as a French secret agent, but 11 years later Paris began to suspect that he was a double-agent, working for the British, and recalled him. Compromising documents were found and Louis XVI imposed a condition that he must always wear women's clothes. While in London he had become a subject of heavy betting about his sex at the Hell Fire Club at Medmenham Castle, a lechers' association to which belonged Lord Sandwich (the gambler who invented sandwiches to eat at the card table so that he would not have to stop playing to have supper) and John Wilkes (the politician and editor who won a great battle for freedom of press comment). The gambling members persuaded d'Eon to attend the Club to be examined by a jury of 'Ladies of Quality' to decide his sex. The jury's verdict was indecisive.

He returned to England from France in 1785 as a man and gave fencing exhibitions. He was re-examined by the Ladies of Quality, who pronounced him to be a woman. He spent the rest of his life dressed as one. He died in 1810. A post-mortem reported that he was without any doubt a man.

Nine kilometres (5½ miles) east of Tonnerre, beside the Armançon river and Canal de Bourgogne, is the unusual and beautiful **Château de Tanlay**. Its beauty is enhanced by a great moat of running water and lovely park. Bought in 1553 by Louise de Montmorency, mother of Admiral Gaspard de Coligny, the Protestant leader murdered in 1572, and his brother Odet, a bishop who turned Protestant, it was partly rebuilt by her fourth son, François d'Andelot, from 1559 until his death in 1569, but not finished until 1648. It is a rather rambling house but an elegant monument to French Renaissance architecture which in the mid-16th century broke away from the more ornate Italian style from which it had sprung.

You approach Tanlay through a wooded park and down a double avenue of elms. You reach first the Petit Château, a gatehouse which is really a small monumental château, then you cross a solid bridge over a wide moat, which leads to the Court of Honour.

The main château was finished by Michel Particelli d'Hémery (d. 1650), Superintendent of Finances, who imposed such high tax rates that he had to be removed temporarily from his job to avoid a people's revolt. He hired the Classical architect Le Muet to finish Tanlay. It was completed in six years with a workforce so big that two surgeons were employed full time to tend the sick and injured. Particelli died owing 200,000 écus, to the intense fury of his son and heir.

The château has round domed towers, steep roofs and arcades round its Court of Honour. In the park, Le Muet built a 530m-long canal, called the Grand Canal, with an ornamental water tower which feeds the 22m-wide (nearly 70ft) moat with spring water.

Inside, the apartments are sumptuously furnished and decorated, especially the long gallery and a corner tower room where there is a strong allegorical painting based on the rivalry between Catholics and Protestants at the Court of Catherine de Medici, wife of Henri II, with figures in various states of undress, including Catherine appearing naked as Juno with her peacock. Henri II's intelligent mistress, Diane de Poitiers, features becomingly as Venus and the Catholic leader François de Guise as Mars, his followers forging weapons of war. Gaspard and François de Coligny are Neptune and Hercules.

In life, François de Guise was assassinated by a Protestant, and Gaspard de Coligny was murdered in his sick bed on St Batholomew's Night, when hundreds of other Protestants were killed. Gaspard has been described as the noblest Frenchman of his time and was a national hero. He became a Protestant mainly to defeat the scheming of Spain, for whom Guise's son was a spy and collaborator. Odet de Coligny fled to England, only to be poisoned by one of his servants. Only François d'Andelot de Coligny died a natural death. It was in the tower room that the Protestant leaders met during the Religious Wars. The Dutch Royal Family, descendants of the Coligny line, still visit Tanlay, which has been owned since 1704 by the financier family Thévenin. (Guided tours 1 Apr–1 Nov, except Tue.)

A little country road south from Tanlay follows the canal and river Armançon to Ancy-le-Libre village, then **Ancy-le-Franc**, an Italian Renaissance house based on an Italian palazzo, built just before Tanlay. The **château** of Ancy-le-Franc is a family house and an extremely elegant one, with magnificent decorations inside. It was built in 1544–46, when François I, deeply influenced by Italian Renaissance building and art, had brought French Renaissance into flower, and it was designed by an Italian, Sebastiano Serlio, who had come to François's Court. Antoine de Clermont, Comte de Tonnerre, Grand Master of Waters and Forest, built it. He was the husband of Anne-Françoise de Poitiers, sister of the cultivated and intelligent Diane de

The kitchen at Château de Ancy-le-Franc

Poitiers, mistress of Henri II, and they must have loved their house. It is in that classical Renaissance style, with a quite simple, almost austere face hiding the most beautiful decoration. The huge galleried inner courtyard is a Renaissance masterpiece.

The inside was decorated by Il Primaticcio, who had come to France from Italy to help François I decorate Fontainebleau, and by his pupils, including Niccolo dell'Abbate, who was better known for his landscapes. The furniture, mostly from the 16th to the 19th century, is superb; so are the ceilings and panelling. The frescoes in the Salle des Nudités and Chambre de Diane are very interesting.

The paintings, panelling and frescoes are not only sumptuous and mostly beautiful, but often surprising. The long Gallery of the Sacrifices is named for its 19th century wall panels depicting Roman sacrifices, in great contrast to the Pharsalus Gallery with vast 16th century murals showing Julius Caesar's defeat of Pompey at Pharsalus during their fight for power in 48 BC. The fight seems to have taken place largely in the nude. The most charming room is the Flower Bedroom with delicate pictures of flowers and the goddess Diana over the fireplace.

The Marquis de Louvois, who had wanted the château since he had visited it ten years earlier, bought it in 1683 because the Count of Clermont-Tonnerre had made himself bankrupt buying Tonnerre County. Louvois commissioned Le Nôtre of Versailles fame to lay out the gardens. He had little time to visit it, but his wife lived there. Louis XIV did stay there on his way back from the 'conquest' of Franche-Comté in 1678. In 1845 the Clermont-Tonnerre family reclaimed the château, which it held until the last count died in 1981.

The chapel has some excellent panelling by a Burgundian painter of talent, André Menassier. In the outbuildings are veteran cars, including a Truffault of 1900, Renault and Dion Bouton of 1905, with about 60 carriages. (Château and Car Museum open end Mar–early Nov. Tours precisely on the hour, 10.00–18.00. Park also open.)

From Rougemont, further down the D905, the D956 going right, reaches **Noyers** (21km/13 miles), a rewarding drive. Noyers, nestling in a loop in the Serein river, is a delightful, dreamy little place, refusing to change with the times, though conscious of being classed among 'les plus beaux villages de la France'. Even its pronunciation is old-fashioned—Noyaire. But inevitably, it has its tourist 'craft' shops. Around it are ramparts and 16 round towers, and in the streets and squares are many old half-timbered and gable-ended houses, as if its defences had kept out time itself. Gaston Roupnel, the novelist, described it as 'background for a historical pageant'. Or a film, perhaps.

In the ramparts are two gates, Porte Peint and Porte Sainte-Verrotte. The latter has a statue of the Virgin in a niche in the arch and each year on 15 August (the Feast of the Assumption) local vignerons used to put a bunch of grapes in the Virgin's hand. The rue Franche was given its name, meaning free, because the residents were exempt from manorial taxes. During a depression the towns-people appealed for tax relief and the Countess of Noyers pleaded their cause with her husband. The Count said that he would exempt the houses as far down the street as she could throw a bowl, so long as she performed naked. Like Lady Godiva, she stripped—but there is no suggestion that the men of Noyers behaved as discreetly as the men of Coventry.

Wooden Renaissance houses and others with arcades line the little **place Hôtel-de-Ville**, with its 17th century town hall and there are more round **Marché-au-Blé** and other little squares, old cobbled streets and narrow passages. You will notice that many houses have front doors reached by flights of stairs. The little Serein may look quiet enough but has flooded the town in winters past.

Le Petit Train de l'Yonne runs between Noyers and Avallon on Sundays (1 May–30 Sept, 15.00–17.30, every 15 min) taking you on an old line, partly through the Serein valley.

Back on the N6, you follow canal and river to **Montbard**, once a great ironworks. The man who made the forges was Georges Louis Leclerc de Buffon (1707–88), botanist, royal gardener, scientist and industrialist. Landscaping over a ruined château (which he hated), he made Parc Buffon, containing different and unusual trees, plants and vegetables. His study is in one of the two medieval towers of the castle that he left standing (he knocked down another eight). There he wrote the 44 volumes of his *Histoire Naturelle* (Natural History). The study has been restored. So has the other remaining tower, gargoyles and all. It is 40m (131ft) high. Climb the 142 steps for good views of the town, canal and countryside.

Buffon's Grande Forge foundry is just down river. Built in 1768, it was one of the biggest in France. Until 1866 it produced tools and weapons, including cannon used against the English at Waterloo. It became a cement works in 1945, but is now being restored. Four hundred workers lived on site in 'model' housing. The houses look spartan now. Working models and recreated workshop sounds make a visit interesting.

Buffon was a brilliant scholar of his time, dedicated to progress, but he was certainly not self-effacing. He advised bright young men to read the works of the five great geniuses, 'Newton, Bacon, Leibniz, Montesquieu and myself'.

Montbard remained important until very recently for making steel tubes and pipes. Over-production of steel has caused a big slump. A branch line of the TGV fast train from Paris serves Montbard, but not many people use it for business these days. The **Beaux Arts museum** has an interesting collection of 19th and 20th century paintings and sculptures, including Picasso's portrait of Cézanne.

We find **Fontenay Abbey** (5km/3 miles north-east of Montbard) one of the most interesting religious buildings in France because it shows what a medieval monastery was really like.

The abbey was founded by St Bernard in 1118, one of the first three daughter-abbeys of Cîteaux. After the Revolution the Montgolfier family made it into a paper mill, knocking down part of it. Two of the Montgolfier sons invented the first hot-air balloon, which flew over Paris in 1782. So now you can sometimes see balloons over Fontenay. In 1906 new owners began restoring it to its original state. The monks lived under the austere Cistercian rules, as laid down by St Bernard. The abbey was expected to be self-sufficient, and it grew very quickly, soon luring 300 monks. The abbey church was built while St Bernard was still alive, because of the generosity of the Bishop of Norwich, who fled here from the wrath of the English Court during the war between King Stephen and Matilda. In Cistercian tradition, the façade disdains ornament. Inside, a night staircase leads to the monks' dormitory: they were required to pray from one to two in the morning.

The monks slept in their clothes on the floor on straw mattresses, without heating and covered by one blanket. They attended services for seven hours a day and devoted the rest to work in the gardens or intellectual studies and copying the Bible or religious manuscripts. Gradually they stopped physical labour because it interfered with their long programme of worship, and these duties passed to less-educated lay brothers and serfs. For the first 100 years of the abbey's existence, the monks lived on two meals a day of bread, made in their own bakery, water and boiled vegetables. No meat or fish was allowed and even in Clos Vougeot they were not permitted to drink the superb wine they made.

Monks and lay brothers were forbidden to talk except in the chapter house, where they discussed the abbey's business and received daily orders. They confessed publicly and were given physical punishment as penance on the spot. There is a big forge worked by a watermill. Only two fires were allowed apart from those in the forge and kitchen, one in the scriptorium, where copying was done and the other in a warming room where the monks could go to warm up when and if they were allowed a few minutes' free time.

The cloisters are superb. But how could they walk round them with their fellow monks without saying a word to each other?

One of the oddities of their meals was that the monks bred trout, which had a gastronomic reputation, and made trout pâté which was always served to kings who visited Burgundy. Yet for the first years the monks were never allowed to taste it. That is true abstinence. The trout was saved for any visitors of importance. The water in their stream and lake was so pure that it was always served on Louis XV's table. After the abbey was sold, the first trout farm in France was started in the old abbey domaines at La Fontaine de l'Orme. It stopped in World War I but was restarted in 1947. The stream flows past the forge and down a waterfall to a pond which holds 4000 fish. The hatchery is downstream towards Marmagne. You can hire a rod at the hatchery and catch your own fish.

When the Revolution came, the abbey had long since gone into terminal decline, partly from damage in the Religous Wars but mostly because kings had appointed commendatory abbots—laymen who just took the abbey's income but very often did not even visit it. This pernicious system, particularly practised under Richelieu, who collected abbeys, almost destroyed the whole monastery system.

The fascinating Château Bussy-Rabutin and the old Gaulish camp of Alise Ste Reine, where the Gauls made their last stand against Julius Caesar, 16km (10 miles) south, are described in Chapter 12.

The medieval abbey of Fontenay

12. Auxerre to Dijon

The Yonne valley south of Auxerre is a lovely land rich in fruit orchards and vines and we try to find time to ignore the N6 and follow little roads in a sort of drunkard's roll through our favourite villages. All the way to Vermenton boards invite you to *dégustation*, and although the wines are not in the Côte d'Or class they are very drinkable. The first village of **Vaux** beside the river no longer produces wine but its slopes are covered with cherries and apples, magnificent in blossom time. Vines begin at **Escolives-Ste-Camille** just south, and there, in a medieval château, Gérard and Régine Borgnat produce rosé and a white Aligoté in a medieval cellar said to be the longest in Burgundy.

Over the Yonne, the agreeable village of **St Bris-le-Vineux** is almost entirely built over a warren of medieval cellars. The ornate 13th century Gothic **church of St Prix**, rich in flying buttresses, is lit by Renaissance stained glass windows, and has a great fresco of the Tree of Jesse from 1500 and a Renaissance pulpit showing wild boar, snails, corn and wine. Old houses, some from the 14th century, some with stone gables and dovecotes, pack the town centre and even the mairie and school are in an old château. The choice of wines is wide as local growers try to bring back some of the ancient popularity of wines of Auxerre.

Irancy, 3km (2 miles) away, is surrounded by banks of cherry trees and vineyards, a setting which lures artists. The Gothic church, with Renaissance buttresses and a square bell tower is among traditional vignerons' houses with outside staircases. The wines are earthy red from Pinot Noir, with a little local César grape juice added for fruitiness—much appreciated in Burgundy.

At **Cravant**, a town of crumbling medieval towers and gates, the Yonne and Cure rivers meet. The beautiful road beside the Yonne leads to Clamecy and on to the Morvan, where the river has its source in wild mountains. The N6, in a very attractive stretch, follows the Cure to Givry, a short distance from Avallon, where we begin our crossing to Dijon. A fork onto the D951 at Givry follows the Cure to Vézelay.

The Yonne, still fast-flowing despite some control, cuts through valleys and woodlands amid dramatic landscape, often thrusting its way through narrow valleys between sheer cliffs. Like the Cure, it was used for floating logs down to Paris until the railways came. Now the Yonne is one of the favourite inland waterways for pleasure boats.

CLAMECY, a fine old town with narrow winding streets, sitting on a spur overlooking the meeting of the rivers Yonne and Beuvron, was the centre of the timber trade. In the 16th century a timber merchant from Paris, Jean

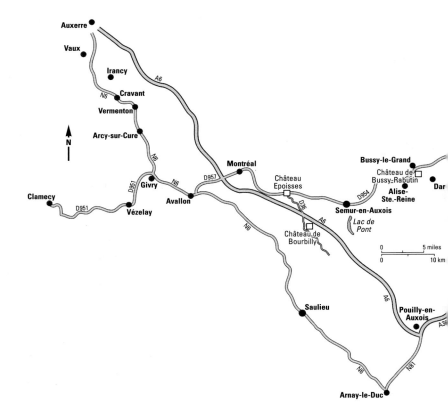

Rouvet, started running logs by water from Burgundy to Paris. When the logs were felled, they were dragged by horses or oxen to the banks of the rivers Cure and Yonne, where they were stacked and given an owner's mark. On a given date the river sluices were opened to give a rush of water and the logs were pushed in. Those from the upper Yonne floated down to Clamecy, where they were stopped by a dam, pulled ashore by men with long hooks and sorted. When the spring floods came in mid-March, the logs were trussed into rafts which were joined to make huge 'trains' of logs. These were loaded with various cargoes and directed down the Yonne into the Seine and on to Paris. I wonder how many innocent fishermen, boat and ferry men were hit and sunk by this formidable armada of rafts?

Running logs reached its peak at the beginning of the 19th century. In 1861 a large dam was built on Lac des Settons to help the process on the river Cure. But from 1834 the Nivernais canal linked Decize on the Loire to the

Yonne near Auxerre, enabling barges to get nearer to the logging camps. Then came the railways. For cheapness, the flottage lasted a while. The last logging 'train' left Clamecy in 1923; the carbon plant, the largest in France, lasted until 1983.

On the **Bethlehem bridge** is a statue to the loggers and upstream on a point overlooking the river and canal is a bust dedicated in 1849 to Jean Rouvet. The face may look familiar. The sculptor was David d'Angers and it seems that he was very busy when he got the order—so busy that he sent an old bust that was lying around his workshop. He felt certain that no one in Clamecy would have any idea what Rouvet had looked like. Some people did spot the familiar features—the bust was of Napoleon I—but by then, the sculptor had been paid.

Across the Pont de Bethlehem lies an area called **Judaea**. In 1168 Duke William IV of Nevers died of the plague at Acre on a crusade. In his will he asked to be buried at Bethlehem and he bequeathed a property at Clamecy to serve as a refuge for the Bishop of Bethlehem if Palestine fell into the hands of the Moslems. When Jerusalem fell, the Bethlehem bishop did take refuge in Clamecy. Fifty succeeding bishops did the same, ruling their non-existent see of Bethlehem from this little French town. Their little chapel (now gone) was upgraded to a cathedral. In 1801 the see of Bethlehem was abolished by the Pope, although the last bishop refused to resign. The title was revived in 1840, but is now held, for some reason, by a bishop in Valais, Switzerland. In 1927 a modern chapel called Notre Dame de Bethlehem was built on the spot where the old chapel had stood.

Clamecy has many old houses, a 12th century church and a **museum** in a mansion which belonged to the Duc de Bellegarde, with a room devoted to the log flottage, paintings by Breughel and Vernet and interesting Art Deco posters of the 1920s and 1930s, including well-known advertisements.

South from Cravant, the old N6 has one of its most attractive stretches to Givry. Soon after, Cravant vines give way to wooded slopes and the landscape hides a strange underworld of caves. The Cure itself becomes a fast-flowing trout stream, with weirs made originally to control log-running, for which

Romain Rolland

Outside the museum in Clamecy is a bust of Romain Rolland (1866–1944), writer and musical critic, who was born here. Rolland won the Nobel Prize for Literature in 1915 with his ten-volume novel *Jean-Christophe*, the hero of which is a musician—the author being a professor of music history at the Sorbonne. In World War I he became unpopular for his writings from Switzerland criticising the war, and in the 1930s and 1940s he was the mouthpiece of opposition to the Fascists and Nazis. He wrote a play on the French Revolution and many biographies, including ones on Gandhi, Tolstoy, Michelangelo and Ramakrishna, and two on Beethoven. He was an idealist biographer, always seeking to show the greatness of humanity and hope for the future. He called Clamecy 'the town of beautiful reflections and graceful hills', and there are still peaceful walks on those hillsides.

Vermenton was an important port. Now the river is loved by canoeists. Vermenton has a medieval watch tower amid some 16th century houses. Its moss-covered church is Romanesque merging with Gothic and has a handsome slender Romanesque tower.

The Cure cuts **Arcy-sur-Cure** in two, joined by a humpback bridge from which you have attractive views of the river and of **Manoir du Chastenay**. Built in 1349 and once owned by the Knights Templars, this became a resting place on the pilgrim route to the shrine of St James at Compostela in Spain. Alterations and additions are from the 16th century. It is in the hamlet of Val Ste Marie, and has a five-sided stairway tower and turret and an elegant façade, but the sculptures are weird, a jumble of symbols of Renaissance mythology, Christianity and masonic ritual, well described as an esoteric cocktail of alchemy, numerology and scriptures. Medieval scholars used 'divine' numbers to try to unlock secrets of the universe, even St Bernard believed in them, and this belief was reflected in the placing of windows in Cistercian monasteries. The manor is open daily in July and August, except Sunday mornings. The rest of the year it is open weekends except Sunday mornings.

One kilometre (½ mile) along a narrow road from the manor, great limestone cliffs on the west bank of the Cure are pierced with caves used by prehistoric man. The **Great Cave** is open, although you can visit only 1km of its 2.5km length. Chambers and galleries are filled with stalactites, stalagmites and curiously shaped concretions. There are two small lakes and convincing carvings of mammoths and bison.

From outside, a river bank pathway passes more caves which are not open to the public—a pity, because they contain wall drawings by prehistoric man of horses, mammoths and hyenas. (Guided 45 min tours of the Great Cave Mar–Nov.)

The tympanum of Ste Madeleine, Vézelay, with a view into the narthex and beyond

143

Just after Sermizelles, the D951 follows the Cure to the beautiful but strange town of **Vézelay**, beloved by painters and mystics. In a gorgeous setting on a climbing ridge, overlooking beautiful wild Morvan scenery, this tiny town of 600 people is one of the treasures of France. You do not have to be an amateur of old churches to enjoy Vézelay's historic basilica, **Ste Madeleine** (Mary Magdalene) which stands above its old houses and ramparts.

Leave your car at Champ de Foire and walk up the sloping narrow and winding old streets to the church past old houses with sculptured doorways, staircase turrets, mullioned windows and wells with fine wrought-iron wellheads. The walk may tire you—but no more than it did hundreds of thousands of pilgrims back to the Middle Ages when they were on their way to the tomb of St James at Compostela and may well have already walked more than 1000 miles. The original abbey was founded in the middle of the 9th century at nearby St Père by Girart de Roussillon, Count of Burgundy, a soldier so heroic that the stories of his exploits were told in ballads and by troubadours, including the famous Chanson de Geste. But the Norsemen destroyed the abbey, so the count rebuilt it on top of a hill to make defence easier.

Then, in the 10th century, one of the monks claimed to have brought the relics of Mary Magdalene from Provence. It was a highly improbable claim, but typical of the time and it was not only the simple people who believed it. Pilgrims poured into Vézelay and a basilica was built to accommodate them. A thousand pilgrims were killed in a fire in 1120, but the church was rebuilt and in 1146 St Bernard arrived to recruit for the Second Crusade against the Moslems in Jerusalem. He preached the crusade to Louis VII of France, Eleanor of Aquitaine who was then still Louis' wife, his family and many powerful barons who, with Louis, were so impressed that most of them volunteered to go. Louis took Eleanor with him and later accused her of going to bed with other crusaders. He divorced her on her return, whereupon she married the future King of England, Henry Plantagenet (Henry II).

When the Third Crusade set out in 1190, those great rivals King Philippe Auguste of France and King Richard the Lionheart of England, Eleanor's favourite son, joined forces at Vézelay, to fight the Saracens together, brothers in arms. When Philippe Auguste left the fight before Richard, he swore an oath that he would not lay a finger on Richard's lands before Richard returned. But of course he did, finding Richard's younger brother John a much weaker opponent and a collaborator. Richard was held in prison in Austria for ransom on his way home, and Philippe had done quite well in the takeover business by the time Richard got back to put a stop to it.

St Francis of Assisi was at Vézelay when he decided to build his first monastery of Minorite monks in France and chose a spot near the place where St Bernard preached and where Ste Croix chapel had been built.

St Louis (King Louis IX) went to Vézelay on pilgrimage several times before going on two crusades. The abbey was now extremely rich, but at the end of the 13th century other relics claimed to be the true remains of Mary Magdalene were 'discovered' at St Maximin in Provence and when Pope

Boniface VIII announced that those, and not the ones at Vézelay, were the true relics, pilgrimages began to fall of and the once-lucrative fairs and festivals lost their importance.

By 1538 secularized canons replaced the monks, under a commandatory abbot (an absentee who just took a lot of the abbey's income). In the Revolution the monastery buildings were virtually demolished. The basilica was closed. When the poet and novelist Prosper Mérimée saw it in 1834 he found the beautiful basilica falling apart. Hens were running in and out of it. He was dismayed, but luckily he was then Inspector of Historic Monuments and his report made the ministry take action. They decided to restore it but could not find an architect to take it on until in 1840 young Viollet-le-Duc, aged 27, offered to restore it. The work took 19 years. Then he restored Notre Dame in Paris.

The basilica is now known as La Madeleine (after Mary Magdalene). It used to have two towers and two bell towers. The Protestants destroyed half of them. They might have destroyed them all if Théodore de Bèze, Calvin's successor, had not been born in Vézelay! The 13th century **St Anthony's tower** is 30m (98ft)high. Lovely gardens cover the site where the abbey buildings stood. From the tree-shaded terrace behind the church where the abbots' palace stood in the 18th century, you have a fine view of the Cure river and Morvan.

Viollet-le-Duc was criticised, as usual, for using too much of his imagination, but imagination was necessary to complete some sections of the restoration.

Most of the capitals are original and all are absolutely superb. They are well worth studying in detail. The nave is excellent, too, with alternating white and greenish-grey stone in its transverse arches. When we first looked down the **nave**, all 62m (203ft) of it, we were transfixed. It is simple, graceful and peaceful. The light breaks through to the transept and choir at the far end as if it is illuminated by electricity.

A staircase of 200 steps takes you to the top of the tower, from where there are even better views than from the terrace.

From **place Champ de Foire** at the lower end of the town you can follow **Promenade des Fossés**, which is laid out on the medieval ramparts round the town.

Many artists, writers and architects have chosen to live in Vézelay, including the poet, musician, novelist and biographer Romain Rolland (1866–1944) who sought to find in the lives of great men evidence of the greatness and brotherhood of man. He spent the last years of his life at No. 20 Grande Rue. The architect Le Corbusier lived in Vézelay, too, but the daily sight of the basilica did not discourage him from covering acres of earth with heavy masses of reinforced concrete.

The mysticism of Vézelay still attracts pilgrims, but of diverse beliefs. Nuns seek postcards of La Madeleine to send to their sisters; Scandinavian Protestant pastors mix with young modern Catholic priests; middle-aged men and women from all over the world who were the rebels of the 1960s (called *soixante-huitards* in France after the Paris students who rebelled in 1968) now seek modern philosophies and mystic meanings of life; and wearying and ageing pop stars look for a purpose in their lives. All mix in the basilica and the streets, and some outside the city walls in the bars of Champ de Foire.

Down at St Père, near to the workshop of Romain Doré—one of the great wood carvers (and clog-makers) of France—is Marc Meneau's great *l'Espérance* restaurant, Michelin 3 stars, where the rich, great and famous eat. Some arrive in helicopters for lunch. Jacques Delors entertained Europe's leaders there and Mitterand entertained world leaders. They both used also Bernard Loiseau's restaurant at Saulieu.

An attractive route into the river Cousin valley leads to **Avallon**, perched on a granite spur between two ravines. The direct route from Givry is along the N6. Either way, the Cousin valley is certainly worth exploring.

Avallon has traffic problems. The main shopping street from the centre, **rue Aristide Briand**, which runs from place Vauban, past the ancient church to the Promenade de la Petite Porte, high above the Cousin valley, is marked 'Priority for Pedestrians', but visiting drivers rarely give way.

Avallon was very heavily fortified from the Middle Ages, but in 1432 it still fell to a band of freebooters in the pay of Charles VII of France and under the command of Jacques d'Espailly, known as Fortépice. He had captured many castles in Burgundy, and had even threatened Dijon, but the people of Avallon had great faith in their defences and slept soundly behind them. One December night Fortépice and some of his men surprised the guard, scaled the ramparts and sacked the town. He, too, was impressed by the town's walls and decided to strengthen Avallon and use it as a base.

Philip the Good, Duke of Burgundy, was furious. He rushed from Flanders to regain his town, bringing with him a bombarde, a machine for hurling great rocks. It knocked a hole in the walls and the Burgundian soldiers tried to rush through. They were thrown back by Fortépice's 200 men. Philip then sent for more knights and crossbowmen. Fortépice realised that he could not win, so he treated the townspeople of Avallon to a feast. While they were drinking and dancing, he slipped away under cover of darkness, leaving his men to face the Duke's army.

Vauban, the great military architect who was born about 32km (20 miles) away at St Léger, redesigned the defences for Louis XIV. Then Louis decided that Avallon no longer needed defending and gave the ramparts to the town. Vauban's statue is in **place Vauban** alongside the road to Paris. **Grande Rue Briand** passes the **town hall**, the old house of the Princes of Condé and Tour Escalier, the 13th century home of the Dukes of Burgundy. It then runs beneath **Tour de l'Horloge**, a 15th century gate and tower with a fine clock and turret and a slender belfry. The **information centre** is alongside. Go in and get a map of the old town and ramparts. Further along on the left in a cobbled square is the interesting but slightly battered church of **St Lazare**. Underneath it is the original 4th century crypt of a church dedicated to St Mary. The supposed skull of Lazarus was given to the 11th century church by a Duke of Burgundy, Henry le Grand, and it was venerated by people who

The attractive old town of Avallon

believed that it could ward off or even cure leprosy. So many pilgrims arrived that a new church was built, consecrated by a Pope in 1106. The tympana of the two doorways of the façade from 1150 are the great attraction, but they have been so mutilated that it takes an ardent amateur of Burgundy Romanesque sculpture to appreciate them now. But we love the carving on the arches above them, especially above the small doorway. Here is a flower garden in stone—roses, arum lilies, stock and twining vines. The inside is impressive, with a charming rose-window and several 17th century painted wooden statues.

At the end of the road, the wide **Promenade de la Petite Porte** is shaded by tall old lime trees. From the wall you look almost vertically 100m down to the Cousin valley. The road from La Petite Porte runs through the ramparts and takes a hairpin bend by terraced gardens to lead you into a lovely drive through the river Cousin valley.

You can stroll around the ramparts, beginning either way from La Petite Porte. You will pass many towers and interesting old buildings, including Tour du Chapitre (1450), Eperon Gally (a spur flanked by a 1591 watch tower with steps down to a terrace), Tour Beurdelaine (the oldest, built by John the Fearless in 1404 and strengthened in 1590 with a bastion), and Tour de l'Escharguet (the Elected), also called Tour Vachère because it was once the cowherd's tower.

The famous old *La Poste* hotel was already 100 years old when Napoleon slept there en route from Elba to Paris.

South of Avallon are forests, lakes and the winding little roads of the Morvan. There are several ways to Dijon. A fairly straightforward route is along the N6 to Saulieu and Arnay-le-Duc, then the N81 and A38 to Dijon. You could, of course, pick up the A6 motorway near Avallon and switch later to the A38. But we like the really interesting way on minor roads through Semur-en-Auxois, visiting the fascinating Château de Bussy-Rabutin, and finding the source of the river Seine.

SAULIEU, a very Burgundian old town, known as the gateway to the Morvan, was the headquarters of the great Morvan Resistance fighters in World War II, and for centuries a great trading post. It was an important stopping place on the old Paris–Lyon road in the Middle Ages, when merchants traded at its fairs and Rabelais was already praising its cuisine. The old road was restored in 1651 and Saulieu became a trading post again for merchants dealing in wine, corn and wood, a posting stage for horses and later an eating or overnight stop for motorists on the N6. It was renowned particularly for Morvan ham and andouillettes, although between the World Wars Alexandre Dumaine at the *Côte d'Or* restaurant gained worldwide fame for more sophisticated dishes.

Quite recently, the A6 motorway took away much of the traffic and trade. But Saulieu is still holding its own for cuisine. Bernard Loiseau, who now runs the Côte d'Or (tel. 80 64 07 66) is sometimes criticised for his attitude. He has called his own cooking 'cuisine inimitable' (unparalleled) and all gastronomes agree that it is a 'gastronomic experience'. It is also pricey, even by Michelin 3-star standards. Some of the dishes are certainly not everyday fare—like endives with truffles, snail and nettle soup, rabbit livers. As at Vézelay, some customers arrive from Paris by helicopter, disappearing before the last mouthful of dessert is digested. Mitterand used to invite close colleagues. Jacques Delors frequently invited high-powered statesmen. He amused the French press by bringing Soviet leaders here, then flying them off to Chailly, the château converted into a hotel and golf course at enormous expense by the Japanese! For those with less money and Burgundian tastes and appetites, the old *Relais de Poste*, where the coaches once changed horses, still gives a smiling welcome, and truly good meals.

Part of Saulieu's fame rests on its basilica of **St Andoche**, begun in 1112, and the quirk of history that makes the curé of this little town of 3000 people Bishop of the Morvan. The church was started by Stephen of Bagé, Bishop of Autun and Abbot of Saulieu and he bequeathed the title. The church was partly destroyed in wars, but the sculptures of the Romanesque capitals which remain are lovely and imaginative. Even the donkeys truly live and the Devil is certainly a frightening arch-fiend. A later work is a beautiful Virgin and Child given to the church by Madame de Sévigné—perhaps a penance for having got drunk in Saulieu, which she admitted in her writing. It is said that the angel has the face of Sévigné herself.

At the north entrance to the town, in a little square off the N6, is a statue of a bull by a local man, François Pompon (1855–1933), a brilliant animal sculptor. More of his works are in the little **musée Pompon** in a 17th century presbytery beside St Andoche basilica. In the museum, too, are rooms showing a last century Morvan cottage, and a sabot-maker's workshop, flax-weaving room, blacksmith's forge and pottery. (Museum open May–Oct except Tue and Sun; also in Feb and spring school holidays.)

Pompon's tomb is in the charming 15th century church of **St Saturnin** at the south end of the town. Above it is one of his own sculptures of a condor.

Pompon worked for years as assistant to Rodin and used to study animals and their movements in the Jardin des Plantes zoo in Paris. Success came late in life.

Saulieu now has a timber industry which sends more than one million Christmas trees (*sapins de Noël*) each year to cities in France, the rest of Europe and Africa. Large tree nurseries also send hundreds of thousands of saplings all over France and beyond. Furniture is made there, too. The 769 ha (1900 acre) forest, which touches the north and west edges of the town, is owned by the State and is provided with walks and trails, picnic sites, adventure playgrounds and bicycle tracks. You can fish for trout in its small lakes.

The N81 which turns into the A38 to Dijon, meets the N6 at **Arnay-le-Duc**, 27km (17 miles) south-east of Saulieu. Climb the hill at Arnay and you will find pleasant roads and squares of old buildings and tiny shops. The town is known for tableware and the 17th century hospice has become **Maison Régionale des Arts de la Table**—a fascinating show of pottery, crystal, silver and pewter. In the kitchen is a splendid 18th century dresser and pottery dating back to the 16th century (open mid-Apr–mid-Oct; shut Tue, also Mon except July, Aug).

At the bottom of the hill is a hotel which looks like a small-town commercial hotel from outside. Don't be fooled. This is one of our favourites, *Chez Camille*. Armand and Monique Poinsot have made a delicious little hotel from this unlikely building, superbly furnished, well-run and serving excellent meals.

Just before the N81 becomes the A38 motorway to Dijon is **Pouilly-en-Auxois**, exciting for inland-waterway sailors. Here the Burgundy canal goes through a 1.5km-long tunnel. A little road west from Pouilly goes over the motorway to the hamlet of **Chailly-sur-Armançon**, where the fine château has an attractively decorated Renaissance façade, one of the finest in Burgundy. This is now the Hôtel *Château de Chailly* (tel. 80 90 30 30) with a new golf course.

Our wanderers' route from Avallon starts in town on D957 to **Montréal**. This delightful medieval village rising up a hill above the river Serein was the 'Mount Royal' of the notorious Queen Brunhilda, called locally Brunehaut, who died a ghastly death and rated an opera to tell her story. From 1255 it was the favourite hideaway of the Capetian Dukes of Burgundy, who threw out the owner. From Porte d'En-bas, the lower gate with 13th century arcades, the road passes typically Burgundian 15th–16th century houses, some with towers, to **Porte d'En-haut** at the hilltop. The gate is a bell tower to the **church**, founded in 1168, restored last century by Viollet-le-Duc and renowned for its 26 carved-oak choir stalls of the 16th century. Many interesting scenes are shown, such as the carpenter's shop in Nazareth, and the artists themselves, the famous Rigolley brothers, resting from their carving, seated at a table drinking wine from a pot de Bourgogne. The beautiful English 15th century altarpiece was damaged a little when it was stolen in the Revolution.

From the terrace by the cemetery there are splendid views.

The D11 and D954 take you to Semur-en-Auxois. After Toutry you reach the friendly and interesting **Château Epoisses**. To most of us, Epoisses is the name of the cheese which the gastronome Brillat-Savarin called the King of Cheeses and which is still compared, not unfavourably, with Brie. But the pleasant village on the plateau of Auxois, 12km (7½ miles) west of Semur-en-Auxois, is said to be the oldest continuously fortified place in Burgundy. In AD 598 it was a royal seat, where the degenerate King of the Franks, Thierry II (Theodoric) lived with his grandmother, Queen Brunhilda. Thrown out of the kingdom of her other grandson, the King of Austrasia, Brunhilda took refuge in Burgundy and got power over Thierry by pandering to his depraved tastes. The Irish monk Columban (540–615) was an outspoken critic of Thierry's debaucheries and when summoned from the monasteries he had founded in the Vosges to bless Thierry's bastards, he refused to eat the banquet prepared in his honour. The dishes mysteriously shattered. Queen Brunhilda was not amused and Columban had to flee to Switzerland and then Lombardy in Italy, where he founded the monastery of Bobbio.

The château, outside the village, has four towers. The keep is the gate-house. The Condé tower is of brick and stone. The octagonal tower is from the 14th century, the Bourdillon tower from the 10th century. It is all protected by two heavily fortified lines of ramparts and two moats, now dry. Walking between them, you can circle the château. In an outer courtyard are a 12th century chapel and a 16th century dovecote; inside the walls is a balustraded terrace, then the main courtyard with an iron-topped well. The Guitaut family has owned the château since Guillaume de Guitaut acquired it by marriage in 1661.

Inside the château Renaissance paintings are set into panelling and there are richly painted ceilings, as in the room of Madame de Sévigné, who stayed here with her friends because she preferred it to her family château nearby, Bourbilly, which was later damaged during the Revolution and rebuilt in the last century. The King's bedroom is said to have been used by Henri IV. (You can walk round the outside any day, but the inside opens only in July, Aug daily except Tue.)

The meadows around Epoisses are a sanctuary for pied-red cattle in a world of white Charolais beef. From their milk is produced a small cylinder-shaped cheese which is traditionally ripened on straw and washed regularly with white wine and *marc*. The rind turns orange-red, the softish inside is yellow. In the summer this cheese is creamy and pleasant, but left to mature until November, then kept in ashes over the winter, it becomes powerfully savoury, fit to eat with a good Beaune or a Pommard. It has a powerful smell, too! The cheese was abandoned by farmers during World War II and produced only in a factory. Robert Berthaut, a farmer, and his wife now make it the way of their ancestors and you can buy it at their Fromagerie de la Perrière in place-de-Foire, Epoisses.

Château de Bourbilly, south of Epoisses on the D36 over the A6 motorway, is a vast château with four round towers. Originally it was a fortified manor which belonged to Jeanne-Françoise Frémyot de Chantal (1572–1641), who helped St Francis of Sales found the order of nuns called the Order of the Visitation. Her orphaned grandchild, Madame de Sévigné, the writer, lived there as a child and sometimes visited later. The manor was damaged in the Revolution. Last century the present château was built by a man called Darcy who was obsessed by English Victoriana and Victorian Gothic.

Semur-en-Auxois is a most attractive, peaceful old town of cobbled streets, ramparts and four solid, round defence towers, on a high rock of pink granite, almost surrounded by a loop of the river Armançon. From the north approaching Pont Joly, the single-span river bridge, it looks splendid, especially when floodlit in the evenings. From the bridge itself are fine views up and down the river, with old houses and trees beside the water. Little houses are packed on the hillside under the castle keep, beside which the stone spire of Notre-Dame church looks slender and frail.

In the 14th century Semur's ramparts had 18 defence towers and extra walls divided the town into three. The château (dismantled in 1602) was on the western end and you can walk under lime trees round the edge of its ramparts and look into the river below. To reach the promenade you pass a **hospital** which was the handsome 17th–18th century home of the Governors of Semur. The one who sold it, the Marquis de Châtelet, was the husband of the beautiful Emilie de Breteuil, a brilliant mathematician and scientist who seduced Voltaire and became his mistress, only to dump him for a dashing army captain. She also translated Newton into French.

The huge keep which almost covered the spur of rock had a sheer drop to the river valley to the north and south and was flanked by four towers. You reach **Notre-Dame** church through a narrow medieval street leading to a square of old houses. The church was founded in the 11th century by Duke Robert I as recompense for killing his father-in-law. It is attractive, with two square towers and a huge porch at one end and an octagonal tower with the slim stone spire over the transept. Inside, the nave is extraordinarily narrow, so it seems even higher than it is, which is why the church is one of several called a miniature cathedral. Along one side is a row of chapels.

Semur claims to run the oldest race in France, Fête de la Bague. In the Middle Ages it was a foot race for men with a prize of a pair of hose (medieval tights)—of which the men had need, for they ran in the nude. In 1630, the wife of the governor (*not* Emilie!) objected and it became a horse race with the prize of a gold ring inscribed with the town's coat of arms and a pair of gloves. The course is of 2275m between Pont Villenotte and the top of rue Liberté (Course des Chausses). The riders wear period costume.

Three kilometres (2 miles) south by the D103B is Lac de Pont, a 6km reservoir lake made from the river Armançon from Pont-et-Massène to Montigny-sur-Armançon. It has a watersport centre and is very popular on weekends in summer.

Take the D954 to **Alise Ste Reine** and the site of Alésia, where the Gauls made their last stand in 52 BC against Julius Caesar, an event known to modern French children more vividly through the Asterix books. When Caesar thought he had subdued Gaul in 56 BC he sailed to conquer Britain. Gallic tribes started to revolt. Finally the Gauls joined together in a co-ordinated attack under a chieftain called Vercingetorix. Caesar failed to take their stronghold near Clermont-Ferrand, and retreated to regroup with his other forces and German mercenaries. The tribes of Burgundy joined the revolt and Caesar faced defeat. So he started to march towards the Saône, as if fleeing south. Vercingetorix, with a much bigger army, decided to attack him. The Gauls were crushed and Vercingetorix took the remnants of his army to his camp at Alésia.

Using picks and shovels, Caesar's legions built a double line of trenches, palisades, stakes and towers—one to keep the Gauls besieged, the other facing outwards to stop relief forces breaking in. The outer line was 19.5km (12 miles) round. A Celtic army, 250,000 strong, arrived to save Vercingetorix but failed to break through the Roman lines. The Gallic commanders went home and Vercingetorix surrendered. Six years later, when Caesar celebrated his Triumph in Rome, the Gaulish chieftain was paraded through Rome in chains, then strangled to death in a Roman prison.

In the last century, some scholars claimed that the event took place at Alaise, a village in Doubs, south of Besançon. Napoleon III, who was writing a life of Caesar, and fancied himself as a new Caesar, had excavations made at Alise Ste Reine 1861–65, and found bones of men and horses, silver coins and weapons in trenches around Mont Auxois.

A 7m high bronze **statue of Vercingetorix** by Aimé Millet, on a stone plinth by Viollet-le-Duc, was erected on the Mont in 1865. It meant little to locals. Old ladies thought that the statue was of St Gétorix and crossed themselves when they passed. It marks a good viewpoint over the site of Caesar's camp. You can visit the site where excavations continue, but the major finds are in **Musée Alésia** in Alise Ste Reine (open mid-Feb–Nov daily). Excavations include the remains of a basilica dedicated to Ste Reine and a 2nd century tiered Gallo-Roman theatre. Near the statue is **Théâtre des Roches**, built in 1945 on the ancient model. It holds 4000 people and is used for a mystery play on the weekend nearest to 7 September, when a pilgrimage to Ste Reine includes a street procession with people dressed in Gallic and Gallo-Roman costume. The pilgrimage is to a fountain, **Fontaine Ste Reine**, which is said to have gushed from the spot where the orphan girl's head fell as she was beheaded for refusing to go to bed with a Roman local ruler.

A few kilometres north of Alise, near the village of **Bussy-le-Grand**, is the fascinating **Château de Bussy-Rabutin** of a true eccentric, Roger de Rabutin, Count of Bussy (1618–23). It has some of the most striking painted ceilings and walls in France and some of the most sophisticated graffiti in history. While his cousin Madame de Sévigné was writing wittily about the Court of Louis XIV, Bussy's amusing but biting couplets were getting him into all sorts of trouble. He also took part in the notorious 'debauch of Roissy' during Holy Week, when a future Cardinal baptised a frog, and he and other rakes sang obscene songs to hymn tunes. He was exiled to Burgundy and he took with him his mistress, the Marquise de Montglat. There, for her amusement, he wrote *Histoire Amoureuse des Gaules* (A Love History of the Gauls), satirising the love affairs of the Court.

Bussy was allowed back at Court, where his *Histoire* was doing the rounds. The king asked to see one. As there was nothing in it which libelled Louis himself, he and his new mistress, Mademoiselle de La Vallière, thought it very funny. Thanks to this and another of Bussy's writings, *Maximes d'Amour*, the king gave consent for Bussy-Rabutin to be elected to the Académie Française.

Like so many wits, Bussy could not resist a witticism even at the expense of those closest to him. He loved his cousin Madame d Sévigné, but painted a cruel, malicious portrait of her that marred their great friendship for years. Almost fatally, he included the Prince of Condé among his victims—the very man who had backed him in his military career. Condé, who was very powerful and arrogant, threatened to assassinate Bussy in the street, then he and his friends bribed a hack to write satirical couplets about the king, claiming to Louis that Bussy had written them.

Château de Bussy-Rabutin; Roger de Rabutin rebuilt and redecorated the château as a picture gallery of his life

The statue of the nymph Sequana at the source of the Seine

Bussy was sent to the Bastille on Louis' orders and when he came out, he was exiled once again to his château in Burgundy.

It is difficult for us to understand why it should have been such a punishment to be rusticated from Versailles, which was so overcrowded that it was dangerously insanitary and so cold and draughty that the wine froze in the decanters, to a château among beautiful countryside like the Loire valley or Burgundy, where the wine was much better and could be served at the right temperature. Surely the presence of the megalomaniac Sun King was not all that attractive? Perhaps exiles missed the licentious ladies Bussy described in his *Histoire*. Even his beloved mistress forsook him for Versailles and another lover.

He spent most of the rest of his days rebuilding his château and redecorating it as a remarkable picture gallery of his life, loves and of the women who appeared in his *Histoire*. For each picture he composed a caption—many were in verse and often witty and biting.

He went to Paris for the pictures, most of which were copies, apart from one of himself by Le Febvre, pupil of Charles Lebrun, Louis XIV's own artist-decorator and furnisher for Versailles, and a few by Pierre Mignard, the painter of historic scenes and portraits of people in allegorical trappings. Several of the pictures were of the Marquise de Montglat, his former mistress. She was represented as the moon 'with more than one face', as a rainbow, as Zephyr 'lighter than air', and as a swallow who 'flees the bad weather'.

The château is in the woodlands, with trees on three sides and on the fourth a balustraded terrace overlooking Bussy-le-Grand village. Its main building, in limestone, has a tower at each end, and two delicately decorated lower wings in Renaissance style are built at right angles to form a Court of Honour, leading to two more towers with conical roofs. One is a keep, the other a chapel.

Inside, the dining room, called Cabinet des Devises (Room of Mottoes), shows views of the royal châteaux as they were at the time, which are fascinating for architects and historians. Below are allegorical paintings and over the fireplace Bussy himself, by Le Febvre. On the first floor the Salon des Grands Hommes de Guerre is crowded with 65 portraits of great warriors from Du Guesclin to Condé and Turenne; Bussy shamelessly included himself. Most were French but Oliver Cromwell was included—an accolade, no doubt, for Cromwell's having helped the French to beat the Spanish in Flanders and take Dunkirk, so saving Louis from losing Flanders and Picardy.

Portraits of the kings of France decorate an adjoining wing. Bussy's bedroom has pictures of 25 women, including royal mistresses such as Henri IV's Gabrielle d'Estrées, Louis XIV's Madame de Maintenon and the courtesan Ninon de Leclos, with Bussy's second wife and his cousin Madame de Sévigné, with her daughter. Bussy was in love with his cousin, and foolishly had once written asking her to be his mistress, but her husband intercepted the letter and he was banned from her house. Her husband, a dissolute rake, was later killed in a duel.

In the round **Tour Dorée** (Gilded Tower) Bussy excelled himself. The room is covered in paintings. He himself appears again with Louis XIII and Louis XIV, mostly in allegorical pictures of the ladies of Louis' Court, with barbed captions. The notorious Comtesse d'Olonne was 'less celebrated by her beauty than by the use she made of it', and of Madame de la Baume, who had borrowed the *Histoire* and had a copy made, he wrote rather magnanimously, 'The most amiable and prettiest, if she had not been the most unfaithful'. All the Court wanted to know what was written under these pictures and no doubt found out.

Bussy did finally make peace with Madame de Sévigné, and they wrote to each other regularly. He died in 1693 and three years later, volumes of his letters were published. They were regarded as a model of the best French style. Some of Madame de Sévigné's letters were published with them, which were also praised, and more of her correspondence was published, mostly letters to her daughter. It was so witty that her reputation gradually came to excel Bussy's, so that now he has sunk into near obscurity.

The château is open daily April to September, except Tuesdays; late morning and early afternoons the rest of the year except Tuesdays, Wednesdays and Sundays. It has belonged to the State since 1929 and you must wait to join a guided tour (45 min). It is an amusing and most rewarding visit.

From Darcey, close to Bussy, the attractive tiny D103 follows the little river Vau to Vaubuzin, then turns east to St Germain. One-and-a-half kilometres (1 mile) south is the source of the Seine. The beloved river bubbles up from a cave containing the statue of a nymph in a valley of fir trees.

Last century, Napoleon III put a compulsory purchase order on this little piece of land and gave it to the city of Paris. The nymph which was then erected in 1865 is a copy of one sculptured by Jouffroy. Just downstream remains of a Gallo-Roman temple were dug up, with bronzes including the goddess Sequana and a fawn, and wooden statues and votive offerings, including flat sticks carved into human outline. They are in Dijon's archaeological museum.

It seems right that the Seine should be born in Burgundy, for Sequana was the daughter of Bacchus, god of wine. She was one of the loveliest nymphs befriended by Ceres, goddess of corn, and inevitably that old lecher Neptune propositioned her. Refusing, she asked her father and Ceres to turn her to water to escape. It is fitting, we feel, to raise a glass of Burgundy to her when we visit Paris—and to her father Bacchus.

Eleven kilometres (7 miles) down the N71 is **St Seine-l'Abbaye**, where Seine, son of a Count of Mesmont, founded an abbey in the 16th century. The early 13th century abbey church which remains is beautiful. One story says that when St Seine was old, his donkey thoughtfully bent its knees to let the old monk dismount and from the little hole it made sprang the river Seine. But the river was flowing long before his day. So we have settled for Bacchus. After all, at Dijon, only 32km (20 miles) away, the Route des Grands Crus wines begins.

13. Dijon and the wine route to Beaune

When the TGV train from Paris first took passengers to **DIJON** in 1hr 35 min, a Parisian businessman told us delightedly 'It is most convenient. I can complete my business and return without having to stay in Dijon'. An even more delighted Dijon wine négociant said 'I can finish my business in Paris and be home in time for a good meal that evening.' By 'good', of course, he meant a solid, satisfying Burgundian meal.

Henry Miller, the American writer, sneered at Dijon for being 'provincial' and 'bourgeois' between the World Wars. It is certainly provincial, if that means being independently Burgundian rather than falling under the spell of Paris, but no more bourgeois than Paris itself. And although the farmers and vignerons around the city apply their motto that 'a good wine should not be hurried' to life itself, Dijon is at least busy by Burgundian standards.

We find it a delightful place. It is a good place to eat, with many fêtes and fairs based on wine and food. It is rich in truly old buildings, from the Ducal Palace to the delicious little 15th century mansion of a mayor of Dijon, now the restaurant *Toison d'Or*, headquarters of the illustrious wine lovers' society Compagnie Bourguignon des Oenophiles. In recent times open spaces, little parks and flower beds have added to its attraction. It was one of the first towns to protect its old areas by making them pedestrian precincts, but it is also a forward-looking town with new industries, including nuclear research, though food remains by far its biggest industry and its hobby.

There is one great problem still for visitors. Dijon's ancient narrow streets and pedestrian areas have resulted in a one-way traffic system which is a special hell for strangers. But there is a good new underground car park in place Darcy. Whenever you can, park and walk. Happily, walking round the old town is pleasant and entertaining. You can take days browsing among its old buildings without becoming bored. But if you have *very* limited time, it is possible to get a good glimpse of the old city in two or three hours by following the 3km walk which we have suggested (see box, p 160).

When the first of the Valois Dukes, Philip the Bold, took over in 1364, he moved the Burgundian capital from Beaune to Dijon and Dijon's period of greatness began, not only as titular capital of the great Burgundian Empire but

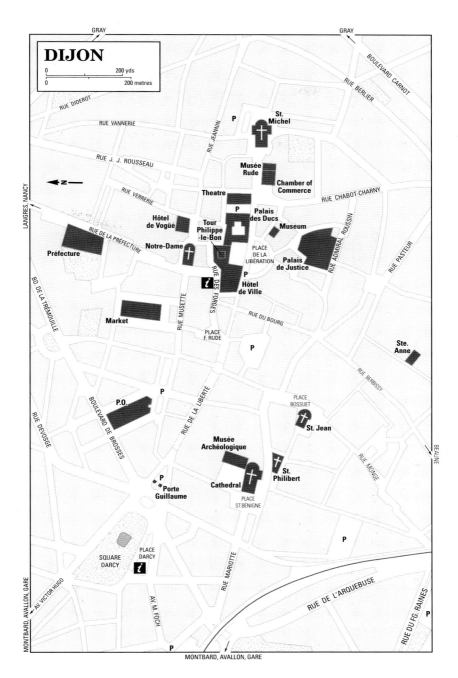

A Walk round Dijon

Walking round Dijon is pleasant and entertaining, which is a good thing, for many pedestrian-only areas and a necessary, complicated one-way system through narrow streets make it impossible to see its multitude of treasures by car.

Start at the railway station and walk along ave Mar. Foch past the information office to place Darcy, overlooked by Hôtel la Cloche. In Darcy gardens, or square Darcy beside a little swan lake is a sculpture of a polar bear by animal sculptor François Pompon. Opposite, the 18th century Porte Guillaume (alongside an underground car park) bestrides rue de la Liberté, the main shopping street. The famous Grey-Poupon mustard shop is at No. 32. Round the corner in rue Bossuet is Coin de Miroir with a Renaissance tower and half-timbered buildings. Further up rue Liberté, turn left into place Rude, where cafés surround François Rude's fountain statue of a vigneron stamping grapes. Rue Rude leads to rue Musette, beyond which is the market district and hall, with many cheap café-restaurants. It is the biggest market in Burgundy. In rue Musette is the 13th century Notre Dame church where the Jacquemart family faithfully strike the hours. Round the corner in rue Chouette is an owl (*chouette*) sculpted on a pillar. Stroke it and you will gain in wisdom and happiness. The superbly elegant 17th century Hôtel de Vogüé is along the road.

Turn left into rue Verrerie, a delightful little street of ancient houses and antique shops. Most impressive of the lovely houses in rue Chaudronnerie is No. 28, Maison des Cariatides. More old houses in rue Vannerie lead to place St Michel, named after the church with a spectacularly ornate Renaissance façade. Take rue Vaillant to place du Théâtre. On the corner is an old abbey church, now the chamber of commerce and housing Museum Rude (closed Tuesday).

Take rue Rameau to the impressive place de la Libération (once place Royale), designed around 1686 by Mansart, part-designer of Versailles. The place leads into the court of honour of the Ducal Palace. A delightful 17th century staircase of 316 steps leads to a terrace with views over town and country. A passage from Cour d'Honneur leads to Salle des Gardes, with a Flamboyant chimney-piece and lovely Renaissance gallery. Across Cour d'Honneur from Cour de Bar is the hall where the States General of Burgundy meet. A pathway from Cour de Flore leads into rue des Forges with wonderful medieval and Renaissance façades. Do see the interior courtyard of No. 34, with a lovely medieval staircase (now the main Dijon tourist office (tel. 80 30 35 39).

Back in place Libération take rue du Palais to the magnificent 16th century Palais de Justice (Law Courts—closed Sunday). Follow rue Amiral Roussin, place J. Mace, rue Piron, then turn left in rue Bossuet to place Bossuet where the big church of St Jean and its curfew tower have found new life as a theatre. Rue Danton leads you to St Bénigne Cathedral, 13th century, with an 11th century rotunda and 93m (305ft) tower. Follow rue Mariotte left under a railway bridge into Jardin de l'Arquebuse, the big botanical gardens. Across ave Albert 1er, a passageway leads back to the railway station.

as a centre of learning and art, with Flemish painters and craftsmen coming to the city. After the last Duke, Charles, was killed and the French took over Burgundy at the end of the 15th century, Dijon lost much of its importance and gradually dropped into a slumber, an attractive small town, dealing in wine but overshadowed in the business by Beaune.

Then came the moment when Dijon's corporation and its chief engineer, Henri Darcy, *grabbed* the new railway. The original Paris–Lyon line was routed direct through Auxerre and Beaune, but the corporation voted for a huge fund to fight for it to go through Dijon. Darcy drew up a plan for a line via Montbard, and on 1 June 1851 the first train came to the town. Dijon became the main junction in Eastern France and its population doubled in about 40 years.

Much the same happened when the fast TGV service was planned in the 1970s. Originally the service from Paris to Lausanne and Berne in Switzerland was to go through Beaune but it was changed to go through Dijon, with a side-line to Beaune.

The engineer Darcy also brought the first modern water supply to Dijon and refused any extra fees, so he has been honoured with the name of the centre of Dijon, **place Darcy**, and a very pleasant garden with fountains. Beside the garden is the elegant renowned hotel of Dijon, *La Cloche*, a national monument. Opposite is the 18th century **Porte-Guillaume**, which replaced an ancient town gate. Here, too, is the new underground car park. From the gate, rue de la Liberté (once called rue Royale) leads to place de la Libération (place Royale), and the Palais des Ducs, the Ducal Palace. **Place de la Libération** is an attractive semi-circular 'square', designed by Jules Hardouin Mansart, designer of part of Versailles, around 1686. Its arcades, topped by a stone balustrade, prolong the Court of Honour which was enclosed by the king's apartments. Originally, a great bronze statue of Louis XIV stood in place Royale, so big that it took 30 years to bring it from Paris. During the Revolution, 60 years later, it was pulled down and melted.

The old Dukes' Palace became empty and neglected when the French took

Saved by Wine

On 7 December 1513, Dijon faced disaster. The Hapsburg German Empire was making a big effort to take Burgundy. The emperor had besieged the city with an army of 30,000 Germans, Swiss and men of Franche-Comté. The Governor of Burgundy, La Trémoille (a local man appointed by King Louis XII of France) had only 7000 men to defend the city. The Swiss breached the city walls. So Trémoille played his trump card. He sent out a group of negotiators to arrange a peace, with a procession of wagons loaded with wine.

The Swiss soldiers got drunk and agreed to lift the siege. In return, France was to pay 400,000 écus and give up the Milanese in Italy. Dijon and Burgundy were saved, but Louis XII said that he did not understand the strange treaty and refused to ratify it.

Louis had to fight the German Empire in Milan and lost the territory anyway.

over but was rebuilt and enlarged towards the end of the 17th century. Philip the Bold's tower remains from the old ducal building and so do the medieval kitchens, with massive fireplaces on three sides to prepare great Burgundian feasts. The chef sat on a big stool in the middle with a huge ladle, to taste the dishes brought to him and to thump tardy underlings.

In the tower Philip the Good imprisoned Good King René—the peace-loving René d'Anjou, Duke of Bar and Lorraine, Count of Provence and of Anjou and titular King of Sicily, a scholar and lover of the arts who preferred poetry to the pomp of being a ruler. The tower was called the **Tour de Bar** after his title and the courtyard beside it is called Cour de Bar. A delightful 17th century staircase leads up the tower.

Part of the palace is used as the town hall. Much of the rest is used for the **Beaux Arts museum** and some of the rooms are so splendid that many visitors admire them more than the exhibits. **Salle des Gardes**, the guard room built by Philip the Good, is exceptionally beautiful, with its Flamboyant chimney-piece and lovely Renaissance gallery. It was used as a banqueting hall on special occasions. The Beaux Arts has been described as one of the best museums outside Paris.

In Salle des Gardes' minstrels' gallery there are two very ornate but majestic tombs of Philip the Bold, whose recumbent figure is protected by two gold-winged angels, and of John the Fearless and his wife Margaret of Bavaria with similar kneeling angels and figures, their feet resting on lions.

Among many treasures on the ground floor are religious paintings by Veronese (Assumption) and Rubens (Virgin and St Francis) and interesting sculptures by Rude and Canova. François Rude (1784–1855) was a Dijon

No. 34 Rue des Forges is Hôtel Chambellan with a magnificent interior including this spiral staircase

The Fighting Canon

When the Germans took Dijon in 1940, the Mayor wisely fled. In his place, the citizens elected a priest, Canon Félix Kir. He was no collaborator, nor did he join any of the Resistance groups. Yet after Dijon was freed he was recognised as one of the great Resistance fighters for the secret work he had done and he remained Mayor and Parliamentary Deputy (Member of Parliament) until 1968.

He was not universally popular. He was described as 'truculent', or, at the best, combative. He had enormous energy and, as one churchman said, more spirit than spirituality. There were those who wanted a quiet life under the Germans, to get on with their business of selling to their victors anything from wine to side-cars for their military BMW motor-bikes. Nor did the Communist Resistance approve of this priest who fought from within the lion's den. The communist steel-workers of Nièvre, the socialists and Gaullistes of the Morvan, the left-wing teachers and intellectuals were already fighting in the forests and hills, supplied with arms by the RAF, who used the Morvan as their dropping zone.

His work to make Burgundy prosperous after the war became legendary—in fact, a book was written entitled *Did Kir Really Exist?* To help the wine and blackcurrant growers recover from the war, he served *blanc-cassis* as the only apéritif on official occasions. It was renamed Kir after him. We feel sure that the Canon would not have approved of the modern snob version Kir Royale, using Champagne as the wine. For when they met, Canon Kir told Arthur two things—that true Kir should be made with Aligoté dry white wine and that in street-fighting against well-armed troops you should try to avoid getting into the streets; you must stay inside buildings even if it means making holes in the walls to get from one to the other.

We wonder how the good Canon knew that? But then, Resistance leaders are not all macho thugs. The Resistance network called Le Loup which finally controlled much of Burgundy was started by Georges Moreau from Clamecy, the old logging town in the north-west of the Morvan. He was a hairdresser. One day a bullying Nazi officer tried to jump the queue. Georges told him to wait his turn. The Germans shut down Georges's salon. So he slid quietly into the forest with friends and started to make himself a nuisance to the Germans. At least he knew how to use a razor.

man who was devoted to Napoleon and fled to Brussels on the Emperor's abdication. He was skilled at getting a look of movement into his sculptures. On the second floor a room is devoted to another Burgundian sculptor, François Pompon (1855–1933), who was a pupil and assistant to Rodin, but only became famous late in life with his magnificent animal sculptures.

Among the Dutch paintings is an excellent Franz Hals' Portrait of a Gentleman (museum shut Tuesday).

On the opposite side of the Cour d'Honneur from the museum is **Salle des Etats**, the great hall of the States General of Burgundy, which has a superb ceiling and a magnificent staircase designed in 1735 by Jacques Gabriel. Through the hall is the Cour de Flore, with decorations glorifying the Prince of Condé, Governor of Burgundy. From the courtyard a passage leads to **rue des Forges**, with fine old buildings, a typical street of old Dijon. No. 34 (Hôtel Chambellan), a Flamboyant Gothic mansion built for a draper, has a magnificent interior courtyard and fine spiral staircase. It now houses the Syndicat d'Initiative and the **tourist office**. No. 40, with a 13th century façade, belonged to bankers in medieval times and Dijon's bankers and traders deposited their reserves, in many currencies, in the vaults, which could be reached only through pavement-level windows.

The **church of Notre Dame** just behind rue des Forges is beautiful and strange. Built in the 13th century, it must have given the architect a headache for it was confined by mansions into a cramped space. The monumental façade which faces the pedestrian rue Musette is original—a flat wall between two beautiful bell turrets, with two thin arcades and three tiers of false gargoyles clamped on as ornament. The present gargoyles, representing lost souls and demons, were added by a 19th century sculptor. The originals had started to fall off centuries before and had been removed for safety reasons. The local story is that a moneylender and his bride stopped outside the church before entering and a gargoyle fell down and killed them—the offending gargoyle represented a usurer with a bag of gold. So the frightened bankers of Dijon paid the Corporation to destroy the other gargoyles. The sculptures on the doorways were destroyed by an apothecary who chiselled them away after the Revolution.

The right-hand bell tower is home to one of Dijon's most popular families, the Jacquemarts. In 1382 Philip the Bold marched to Flanders with an army which included 1000 Dijonnais, to put down a revolt of the Flemings of Ghent and Courtrai, who were objecting to paying punitive taxes to fund the Duke's ostentatious lifestyle. To punish the people of Courtrai, Philip cut the top off their clock tower and sent it by ox cart to Dijon. It contained a pipe-smoking automaton who struck the hours and he settled into his new home contentedly. The people called him Jacquemart. Then one day in 1610 he went on strike and stopped striking. The people decided that he was lonely and gave him a wife. Next century a local wit composed a lament for their sterility and, sure enough, a son was born to strike the half-hours. In 1881 the family was completed with a little girl who strikes the quarter-hours.

Inside the church is a 12th century **Black Virgin statue**, Our Lady of Good Hope, much venerated as the Protectress of Dijon. When the Swiss siege was raised on 11 September 1513, with the help of barrels of wine, Our Lady of

The monumental façade of Notre Dame

Good Hope received the credit rather than St Vincent, and a tapestry given at the time is now in the Beaux Arts museum. Another Gobelins tapestry, given after Dijon was liberated from German occupation on 11 September 1944, is in the church. There are superb medieval stained-glass windows, too. In rue Chouette is **Hôtel de Vogüé**, an early 17th century mansion with colourful tiled roof and Renaissance doorway leading to a courtyard. It is now the town architect's offices.

Rue des Forges and rue de la Liberté both run into **place François Rude**, named after the local sculptor. A very attractive square, it contains the secularised former **Cathedral St Etienne**, now the stock exchange and also containing a museum with reproductions of Rude's work, including a huge relief for Arc de Triomphe in Paris. Local people call the square place du Bareuzai, the Burgundian word for vigneron, after the statue of a naked vineyard worker treading grapes, and they sit outside the cafés drinking coffee or wine.

Close to the rue de la Liberté and place Rude is an unusually interesting and animated **market** area. Besides the biggest market in Burgundy, the area has restaurants serving hearty menus at moderate prices. In the streets across rue de la Liberté is the old **Cathedral of St Benignus**, 13th to 14th century, with a 93m (305ft) high tower, rebuilt in 1896. The remains of the tomb of St Benignus, who is said to have converted much of Burgundy and was martyred in AD 187, still lures pilgrims on 20 November.

To the east of Palais des Ducs is the **church of St Michel**, with a spectacularly ornate Renaissance façade and a most unusual central doorway. It was started in the 15th century in Flamboyant style, then completed in glorious Renaissance style, the French having become enthusiastic about this style after losing a war in Italy. Inside, the church is sober Gothic. The four paintings are by an 18th century German artist, Franz Kraus.

South of Palais des Ducs is the **Palais de Justice** (Law Courts), the old Burgundy parliament building with a Renaissance façade. The chamber of the civil courts has kept its original 16th century decoration and the huge lobby has a superb panelled ceiling. It was once lined with stalls and refreshment bars and fashionable people met there to gossip and parade.

The 15th century **Mayor's house** in rue Ste Anne, which we mentioned earlier, is one of the favourite old houses in Dijon, not only for its superb *Toison d'Or* restaurant serving true old Burgundian dishes, nor because it is headquarters of the Company of Burgundian Wine Lovers, but for its charming atmosphere, its Gothic courtyard where you can drink your Kir and its little museum of wine-making and superb figurines in authentic old costumes. Needless to say, it has a superb wine cellar, with wines chosen at special tastings of the Compagnie.

On the N5 west, past the Arquebuse Gardens, a lake was constructed in the 1960s at the suggestion of Canon Kir, and it is named after him. It is a very popular centre for swimming and watersports. Unfortunately characterless modern apartment blocks have been built around it.

Dijon is a good place to shop especially, of course, for food and mustard.

Mustard

The Romans started the mustard-with-beef habit, possibly because their beef was not always so fresh as it might have been. They just crushed the grains enough to bring out the flavour. Pliny praised it lavishly. The Greeks enjoyed it, too. Crushed grains are now sold as moutarde à l'ancienne. In the 13th century cinnamon and cloves were added. Mustard in Burgundy received its first recorded mention in 1336, when Duke Eudes III gave a banquet to King Philip VI of France, during which 300 litres (66 gallons) of mustard were consumed! Later dukes of Burgundy were accustomed to give important visitors a parting present of a barrel of mustard.

In 1390 Burgundy made regulations to keep up quality, but it was not until 1630 that the Guild of Mustard Makers was founded. Many housewives kept mustard mills in their homes and made their own. They used wine vinegar in those days. Smooth paste mustard was developed in the 17th century. Then, in 1756, a Dijon mustard maker, Jean Naigeon, substituted the juice of grapes still unripe at harvest time, *verjus*, for vinegar. Dijon mustard, already famous, became the most popular mustard in the world. In France, Dijon still provides 70 per cent of the mustard and exports go all round the world. Later, the firm of Grey-Poupon, established 1777, developed a recipe using white wine instead of *verjus* or vinegar. This type of mustard is most popular among gastronomes. The company, whose shop is at No. 32 rue de la Liberté in Dijon, also produces a variety of flavours, including green herbs, tarragon, green pepper and shallots.

Mustard has been used for sauces since the 17th century and has become very popular in 'modern' cooking. If you cook it for any length of time, its pungency goes. So if you want to keep it, you add the mustard towards the end of cooking.

Mustard has been used in medicine since Hippocrates and in the Middle Ages was grown in most monastery gardens, not only to help preserve food but for medical use.

Mustard poultices are still used in many countries, especially in the farming villages, to relieve congestion in bronchitis and pneumonia, and country families still use mustard baths to ease rheumatic and muscular pains and foot baths to soothe tired and aching feet.

Some alternative-medicine practitioners recommend it to relieve asthma.

Rue de la Liberté is the best shopping street, with good fashion and shoe shops. The great mustard shop, **Grey-Poupon**, is at No. 32 and has a choice of various types of mustard and a number of superb old mustard pots on display, and some fine replicas, as well as more modern pots. Grey-Poupon, founded in 1777, developed the most popular modern recipe using white wine instead of vinegar or *verjus* (unfermented grape juice). Dijon not only supplies half of France's mustard but exports a lot, too (see box, p 168). For *pain d'épices*, including the great rounds of honey bread which go so well with Montrachet or goats' milk cheese and a glass of Côte de Nuits or Beaune for 'elevenses', call at No. 16 Mulot et Petitjean. Alas, the great mistress of cheese, Simone Porcheret, is no longer with us, but her wonderful cheese shop and maturing cellars are still at No. 16 rue Bannelier.

There are good food shops around the market area, too and big daily markets.

The combined Fête de Vignes (Wine Festival) and International Folklorique Olympiad in early September is great fun. The International Gastronomic Fair is held for a fortnight in early November. Be prepared to do a *lot* of tasting.

You would need a great deal of time to stop at all the great wine villages on the **Route des Grands Crus**, following the D122 and N74 south from Dijon, but although true wine-bibbers will want to visit every single one, in some there is little to see. So we have written of their wines in Chapter 3 and will now follow those with extra interests.

Marsannay-la-Côte, first stop on the D122, is only 8km (5 miles) from Dijon, but lures people to drive to it for its Thursday market, which has the country-market atmosphere you never find in bigger towns, and for its *Restaurant Les Gourmets* (tel. 80 52 16 32) where, away from Dijon crowds, you can taste Joel Perreaut's classical dishes judiciously enlivened by his own ideas.

We discovered **Fixin** (pronounced Fissin) when looking for a genuine low-priced, old-fashioned Burgundian overnight stop outside Dijon. We found *Chez Jeannette*, with comfortable but simple bedrooms, excellent meals of true old-style dishes, superb cheeses and one of the underestimated wines of Burgundy—gutsy, fruity Fixin, improving until five or six years old. The first time we dined there, we were entertained by a group of celebrating vignerons who managed to sing old songs of the vineyards and caves while doing more than justice to generous portions of *jambon persillé*, various sausages and *boeuf à la bourguignonne*, and draughts of Fixin wine. They seemed to fit into the spirit of Chez Jeannette.

What we did not find until our next visit was the strange **Parc Noisot**. You reach it along an avenue of firs from the little centre village car park. Claude Noisot, major of the Grenadiers in Napoleon's army, followed his idol into exile in Elba, then retired after the defeat of Waterloo. He laid out a park in Fixin, complete with a replica of the fort where Napoleon died in captivity in St Helena. Then he approached another great admirer of Napoleon, the sculptor François Rude, who had fled after Waterloo from Paris to Brussels. Noisot wanted a statue of his hero.

'I'll do you an Emperor,' said Rude, and charged him nothing for it. He produced Napoleon Awakening to Immortality, and you can see it at the top of the hill in the park, reached by steps. Napoleon is leaning on a rock (said to be St Helena), dressed in his cloak, with the Imperial Eagle on the ground. He is raising himself on one elbow.

A pathway leads to a belvedere with Noisot's tomb. He is buried standing, facing towards his Emperor, with sabre in his hands.

There are good views of the Saône valley from the belvedere. The park attendant's house has a small museum of Napoleonic souvenirs. A path from there leads to fountains and 100 steps, symbolising the 100 days between Napoleon's escape from Elba and his second abdication after Waterloo (park closed on Tuesdays).

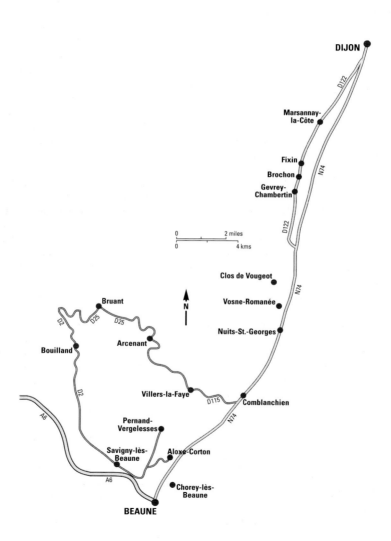

Brochon, a village on the D122 at the boundary of the Dijon and Côte de Nuits vineyards, produces an ordinary Bourgogne Rouge wine. Its château was built in 1900 by a journalist and poet Stephen Liégeard, popular in his day and honoured by the Académie Française, now almost forgotten except for his description of the Mediterranean coast of Provence. He first called it the Côte d'Azur.

Gevrey-Chambertin, squeezed between the D122 wine road and the N74 Dijon–Beaune road, is inevitably long and thin. The old town is grouped round the 13th–15th century church and the château. It was called Gevrey until 1847 when, for publicity purposes, it added the name of its already-famous vineyard, Chambertin, whose deep-coloured intense wines were as appreciated then as they are now. The busier part of the village, where the vignerons live and have their caves, is called **Les Baraques**. Here Gaston Roupnel, the novelist, poet and historian (1871–1946), spent much of his life. His greatest creation, Nono, lived there proudly, too.

Though Napoleon put water in his Chambertin (see Chapter 3) Hilaire Belloc and the great American statesman Thomas Jefferson knew better. Composer Ernst Hoffmann, author of the *Tales from Hoffmann*, called it 'the true poetic wine' and Alexandre Dumas had one of his Three Musketeers say that 'nothing makes the future seem so rosy as looking through a glass of Chambertin'.

Try not to miss the guided tour of **Clos Vougeot**, historic headquarters of the Confrérie des Chevaliers du Tastevin. We have told its story in Chapter 3. The tours begin at 09.00 daily, but the closing times are seasonal (tel. 80 62 82 75). The visit is most rewarding. The respect in which Clos Vougeot has been held for centuries is summed up in a story by Stendhal, who said that on his way back from campaigning in Italy, a Napoleonic colonel named Bisson paraded his regiment in front of Clos Vougeot and made it present arms as a gesture of respect to the great wine.

The château was built in 1551 by Dom Jean Loysier, the 48th abbot of Cîteaux. The massive grape press used by the monks can still be seen in the winery. The monks' abbey of Cîteaux was 13km (8 miles) eastward and in those days the road crossed a marsh, which is still dotted with pools and crossed by little rivers on their way to join the Saône. Rather than risk their precious wine, the Cistercians built a fortress to store it near the vineyards at Gilly-lès-Cîteaux. When this was destroyed in the Thirty Years War, they replaced it with a handsome château in which they entertained lavishly important and influential visitors. The ordinary monks may have lived the simple, harsh life laid down by St Bernard, but the Order knew the importance of good relations with the Establishment, from bishops and governors to kings and popes, and saved their best wine as gifts for such influential people. When Gregory XI became Pope in 1370, the Abbot of Cîteaux, Jean de Brussières, sent him 30 barrels of Clos Vougeot wine. The Pope promised to remember this 'thoughtful' act. Four years later he gave de Brussières a Cardinal's hat. The *Gilly* château is now a luxury hotel (tel. 80 62 89 98).

Cîteaux was founded in 1098 as a breakaway from Cluny Abbey, which the new Order of Cistercians claimed had become decadent, saying that its monks were no longer keeping their vows to live the completely simple, unworldly life. The new Order sought a desolate place where they would have no contact with the outside world and chose this spot among marshes and forest. They started a life of privation, hard labour, the simplest food, much prayer and little sleep. In 1112 Bernard of Fontaine (later St Bernard) joined the Cîteaux community and made it the force behind a campaign of militant unbending Christianity. By 1200 the Cistercians controlled 1000 abbeys and priories and there was a religious rivalry almost amounting to war between Cluny and Cîteaux. As at Cluny, the monks gave up hard labour, leaving that to hired hands. They blamed their hard schedule of prayer. The abbey was suppressed in 1790 in the Revolution.

It is ironic that the one Cistercian house remembered today by most Europeans is the Clos de Vougeot. We wonder what those austere monks who made wine to raise money to spread their gospel of prayer and abstinence and who mostly never tasted the great wines they made would have thought of the bacchanalian feastings and drinking of the Chevaliers du Tastevin who now use the Clos as their headquarters?

Monks are back at Cîteaux. In 1798 Trappists returned to what was left of the old buildings, mostly the ruined library, and built themselves a new monastery in the tradition of Cistercian simplicity, 'de grande sobriété'. It is not open to visitors. But there is a little shop where you can buy books, post-cards and the superb but rare Cîteaux cheese, as rich in smell as in taste.

Directly you enter the village of **Vosne-Romanée**, just off the N74 before you reach Nuits-St-Georges, you know that it is wealthier than most villages of the wine route. It does not flaunt its wealth, but its houses, its school and village hall, its streets and the way people dress all show that there is money somewhere. And, of course, you don't have to look far. Most of its eight grand cru wines are among the best in Burgundy. The 'ordinary' AOC wine is extra-ordinary and fetches high prices. La Tâche and Richebourg are way above most people's pockets but worth every franc of their great price. A wine that we have never tasted, Romanée Conti, is almost unobtainable at any price. Its tiny vineyard produces only 6000 bottles a year. Its neighbour, Romanée St Vincent, was sold in 1990—for about £1 million a half hectare. When the Papacy was due to leave Avignon to return to Rome in the 14th century, cardi-nals delayed their departure, not wishing to give up Vosne-Romanée wine for Italian, and the Pope himself, Urban V, complained about losing his favourite wine.

When we attended the 1992 St Vincent Festival in Vosne-Romanée, we noticed that not only was the wine blended for the occasion by far the best we have been given for drinking the Saint's health, but even the street deco-rations, traditionally made by schoolchildren and ladies of the 'troisième age', were more elaborate than any we had seen. In the village church are the superb wood carvings from the chapel of Cîteaux abbey.

Nuits-St-Georges, 1.5km down the road, is a very commercialised, plebeian place after Vosne-Romanée, but as a wine centre is second only to

Beaune. We have grown to like it, ignoring its warehouses and railway sidings and enjoying it for its friendliness, its alive atmosphere and the excellent value of its wines. It is a place to sit outside a café among families, vignerons and perhaps a local priest, none of them talking in whispers, to eat a hearty meal of Burgundian country dishes at sensible prices, then to wander into a wine shop and find out what wines they are offering 'en vrac'. These are usually sold to you poured from the barrel into smaller plastic barrels which we take home, bottling the wine at an enormous saving. Our best bargain was a year old Savigny-lès-Beaune, which we kept in our own bottles for three years.

Nuits, as the town used to be called, has a huge, austere Romanesque 13th century church, **St Symphorien**, a modern church, **Notre-Dame**, with stained glass by J.J. Borghetto and a 17th century **belfry** of the former town hall.

La Confrérie des Chevaliers du Tastevin was founded in Nuits-St-Georges in 1934. Wine sales, especially exports, had slumped during the Depression and vignerons got together to publicise and improve marketing for Burgundy wines. The brotherhood did not move to Clos Vougeot until 1944.

Nuits-St-Georges was known to gastronomes for years for its *Logis Côte d'Or*, which under the great chef Thierry Guillot became a famous Michelin starred restaurant. Now the star has gone, as so many have recently. Almost opposite is our little hideout, *Les Cultivateurs*, a simple auberge with simple bedrooms, serving excellent value, moderately priced meals of Burgundy dishes, well cooked. Many locals eat there.

Down the N74 is the small town of **Comblanchien**, known not for wine but for a beautiful limestone quarried from local cliffs which is used to face buildings at much cheaper cost than marble. You can see it on many town halls and public buildings in France, including the Palais de Chaillot in Paris, and on apartment blocks from New York to Buenos Aires. A little road right from Comblanchien, the D115j, will start you on a most attractive drive through Villers-la-Faye to Arcenant, then following the D25 for a stiff climb past blackcurrant and raspberry plantations to **Bruant**, with views over the deep gorge of Combe Pertuis.

This is the country where most of the blackcurrants are grown to make Cassis, the liqueur added to white wine to make the apéritif Kir. A sharp turn left on the D2 after Bruant takes you downhill to **Bouilland**, a charming, unspoiled little town in a circle of wooded hills. A short distance along the D104 is a beautiful spot overlooking the town. Most of the cars making their way into Bouilland are heading for the *Hostellerie du Vieux Moulin*, an hotel with a Michelin star for cuisine (tel. 80 21 51 16). Despite international fame, Jean-Pierre Silva's dishes have a strong Burgundian flavour—pasta stuffed with *coq au vin*, the river fish *sandre* braised *à la bourguignonne*, leek and frogs' legs in red wine. The D2 continues downhill between wooded slopes of the narrow valley of the Rhoin river, opening out at the interesting wine town of Savigny-lès-Beaune, with Aloxe-Corton and Pernand-Vergelesses within walking distance.

Savigny-lès-Beaune, a village for people who love motor-cycles, aeroplanes and wine

Savigny-lès-Beaune not only makes one of our favourite reasonably priced Côte d'Or wines, but makes more of it than any other village of the Côte de Beaune. There are 384 ha (950 acres) of vineyards. Traditionally, this wine loosens the tongue into making fine phrases, and even the private houses have inscriptions carved into the stone lintels of their doors.

It is not only a village for wine lovers but for people who love aeroplanes, cars and motor-cycles, and a good centre to stay for a few days away from the overcrowding of Beaune. When the A6 motorway was driven through the end of the vineyards, the precious topsoil was carefully removed and spread around. The little river Rhoin cuts through the vines, too, but is important to the growers, who say that wine from one side is lighter than the other.

There are some spectacular vineyard views from the village, which has a lovely **church** dating back to the 12th century, with a 15th century fresco, and many delightful houses in the centre, including the Manoir Nicolay, which has a formal French-style garden and important cellars. Beyond, begins a sprawl of modern houses towards Beaune.

The 14th century **château** in the centre of the village, built by a Maréchal of Burgundy, has four medieval pepperpot towers, a U-shaped courtyard and an attractive staircase. It was altered in the 17th century. The Duchess of Maine, wife of the favourite son of Louis XIV and of Madame de Montespan, was exiled from Paris to the château by the Duke of Orléans, Regent of France, after Louis' death.

You have to walk to the top of the stairs to find a remarkable **collection of motor-cycles** from 1903 to 1960. There are magnificent bikes with names

The wine village of Aloxe-Corton

almost unknown to young people—Rudge, Velocette, Vincent, NSU—as well as great names like Norton, AJS, Honda, BSA, BMW and Peugeot. We did not know that Blériot's aircraft company made motor-bikes, too. In the stable-end of the château are 15 racing cars, all Abarth, the Italian car with a Fiat engine, all driven in races by the owner of the château, Michel Pont, who won sportscar championships in the 1960s.

In the château park, alongside vines, are more than 20 fighter aircraft, in use from the end of World War II until quite recently—French, US, British and Soviet, including Mirage, Mystère, Sabre, Soviet TF, Gloster Météor, Vampire and Hunter.

Of course, the large château cellars are used to store and mature wine. You can taste and buy (museum open daily; shut for lunch 12.00–14.00).

Aloxe-Corton (pronounced Alosse) is one of the first villages of the Côte de Beaune, and was owned by the Emperor Charlemagne, who gave it to the monks of Saulieu in AD 775. Its vines, from which red and white wines are made, seem to smother the houses. The white Corton-Charlemagne is nectar, rivalling Montrachet, and it seems we owe its very existence to Charlemagne's wife, who nagged him in his old age for drinking so much Corton red wine that it stained his white beard. So he had vineyards planted with white grapes to keep his beard unstained.

Vineyard ownership is very broken up: one owner's parcel is so small that he produces only four cases of 12 bottles a year!

Voltaire was addicted to the red Aloxe-Corton. As he grew older, he wrote to his supplier of Corton Le Bault: 'Your good wine is becoming a necessity

175

to me. I keep quite good Beaujolais to give to my guests, but I drink Burgundy in secret'. The château is now owned by the André family.

Behind the hill of Corton is **Pernand-Vergelesses**, a pretty village with narrow streets, whose wine is good value. New houses fit into the old village, which is one of the most attractive in Burgundy. It still has two *lavoirs* fed by La Mère Fontaine, where women did their washing until someone in the village discovered the washing machine, and where women passed around news long after the radio arrived. The whole village is surrounded by vineyards and woods, as if in a world of its own.

In 1925, Pernand suddenly achieved theatrical fame. Jacques Copeau, director of the Vieux Colombier Theatre in Paris, producer at La Comédie Française, co-founder in 1908 of Nouvelle Revue, and a man who had a profound influence on French dramatic art, decided in 1925, when he was 46, that the French theatre needed to spread way beyond Paris and clear away its cobwebs. So he and his close associates moved to this village in Burgundy and those of his troupe who could not find a place to lodge moved into Aloxe-Corton. They were an international group, some rather strange: there was a Dutchman, a White Russian called Popov, two Americans who climbed the outside staircase of their Burgundian house astride a donkey, and assorted French stage staff, actors and actresses. The big house where Copeau lived is still owned by his family and contains mementos. He died there in 1949.

Chorey-lès-Beaune, once a quiet village producing a simple, quaffable wine, is only about 1.5km (1 mile) form the meeting of the A6 and A36 motorways and is almost a Beaune suburb. But it has a superb and outrageously expensive restaurant with luxurious and very pricey rooms—*Ermitage de Corton* (tel. 80 22 05 28). We have not yet tried its *saumon grillé à la rhubarbe*.

Beaune is only 4km (2½ miles) away.

14. Beaune to Chalon-sur-Saône

Like all fascinating old towns crammed with treasures and magnificent old buildings in narrow streets and busy squares, **BEAUNE** attracts too many people and far too many cars. To enjoy it to the full, it is best to avoid going there if at all possible in late June, July and the first half of August. And it helps to be a true wine lover. Though much of the central area is for pedestrians only, the pavements are still crammed from about 11.00 to around 16.00–17.00 and the café and restaurant tables start serious business at 12.00.

The town is so bound up with wine-making, that wine-makers, *éleveurs* and négociants have taken over, so please read our references to Beaune in Chapter 3, or you might miss the double joy of tasting good wine in a medieval monastery, rampart towers or the ancient caves under the town. Do wander round on foot as much as possible, for you can hardly find a street without fine old stone houses and mansions.

We try to spend at least two nights in Beaune. We like to book into one of the little hotels in the centre, so that we can walk out in the evening to explore, eat (and drink, of course) in freedom. Our old favourite the *Central*, an old-style hotel, round the corner from the Hôtel Dieu in rue Victor Millot (tel. 80 24 77 24) could not be more convenient. When M. Cuny himself was alive and cooking, the little Central had a Michelin star. Under his widow's care, it remains a most friendly family hotel and Jean Garcin cooks most agreeable classic dishes at reasonable prices. Beaune has many good small family hotels. Ask at the **tourist office** in place Halle opposite the Hôtel Dieu (tel. 80 22 24 51).

After the Dukes of Burgundy moved to Dijon, in the 14th century, they kept a mansion in Beaune. It is still there, a 15th century house of stone and wood, with a fine 14th century wine cellar, and it now houses a most interesting **wine museum**.

The history of Burgundian vineyards and of wine-making, from soil to old and new methods, is presented excellently on the ground floor. On the first floor are some fascinating pitchers, bottles, wine-tasting glasses and tastevins, the flat silver cups used by Burgundian vignerons for smelling, judging the

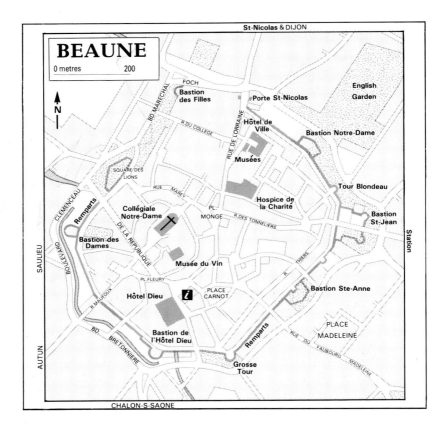

colour and tasting wines from the barrels or vats in their cellars. The grand room is the headquarters of the Ambassade des Vins de France, decorated with three outstanding modern tapestries—a sumptuous Aubusson tapestry called Le Vin, Source de Vie, Triomphe de la Mort by Jean Lurçat, the great rejuvenator of tapestry art, and two by his pupil Michel Tourlière. Tourlière, born in Beaune in 1925, joined Lurçat when that great master was established in Aubusson in 1946. Tourlière has shown scenes from Beaune, Dijon and Clos Vougeot in many of his works.

In the dukes' wonderful old cellars is a collection of vats and wine presses. Beaune was furious when the dukes moved their capital to Dijon. Diplomatically, the dukes made Beaune the seat of the Appeal Courts and the High Court for 400 years more. The High Court (called Les Grands Jours) was a council composed of barons, knights and lawyers. The dukes did not hesitate to bribe courts in their own dukedom and in France by sending presents of Beaune wine. They bribed kings and church dignitaries, too. A bribe is still called *pot de vin* in France.

The town walls, fortifications and towers that still exist were built from the 15th century onwards. After the death of the last Duke, Charles the Bold, in 1477, Louis XI grabbed the dukedom of Burgundy but Beaune resisted until forced to surrender after a five-week siege.

The quarrel between Beaune and Dijon reached comic heights in the 18th century, stirred up by the Dijonnais satirist Alexis Piron, the man after whom Dijon's saddle of hare dish was named. Dijon had been beaten by Beaune in a shooting contest, so Piron wrote a comic poem of revenge, comparing the people of Beaune with the donkeys used on their land and saying that he would starve them to death by cutting down all the thistles on the banks. As Piron almost certainly knew, the important wine merchants of Beaune, the Lasnes brothers, had the sign of a donkey as their trademark. The elders of Beaune pompously banned Piron from their town. Inevitably, he went there, and went to Mass, about which he said 'Those who came to ogle the women were obliged to pray to God, for these ladies would have frightened even John the Fearless'. Then he went to the theatre, where he was recognised and booed and hissed heartily. One poor man trying to hear the play shouted, 'Be quiet—I can't hear anything', whereupon, Piron shouted, 'that's not through lack of ears'. The audience rushed at him and he was saved only by a friend who hustled him away and hid him in his house all night.

The old charity hospital, **Hôtel Dieu**, is indeed a wonderful and remarkable building. From the street it looks austere and dull—a simple façade with a tall, steeply sloped slate roof with dormer windows. The wrought-iron canopy over the gate is the only ornament. Step into the Court of Honour and you are surrounded by a most beautiful mansion, with a magnificent roof of glazed tiles, ablaze with colour and in rich complex geometric patterns— Flemish splendour in Burgundy. A lovely timbered gallery runs around the first floor, and charming arcades of slim pillars around the ground floor. It is indeed 'more like the house of a prince than a hospital for the poor'. Perhaps, despite his life of greed and grabbing, its founder Nicolas Rolin did just about deserve to buy himself a mansion in heaven, as he intended.

Nicolas Rolin was Chancellor to both Dukes John the Fearless and Philip the Good and, as the ducal chronicler Chastellain wrote of him, he governed, managed and looked after Burgundy's business affairs in peace and war on his own. 'He always harvested on earth as if the earth was his abode for ever'. Rolin became fabulously rich, gaining much of his wealth by dubious methods. Growing older, he began to think of his future. When he founded Hôtel Dieu in 1443 as an almshouse and hospital for the poor of Beaune, he wrote quite openly 'I set aside all mortal cares and consider nothing but my salvation, wishing by a happy transaction to exchange for heavenly riches those earthly ones bestowed on me by God's favour, so to make transient riches eternal'. Louis XI of France put it another way: 'It is only right that he who made so many destitute in his life should build them an almshouse before he died'.

Inside, the Great Hall or Paupers' Ward is 52m (171ft) long and has a great timber roof like an upturned ship, supported by chestnut tie beams carved in the shape of monsters' heads and throats. The four-poster beds with side tables and chairs are much like the originals, which were destroyed in the Revolution though the originals were half as wide again—just as well, as two sick people slept in each and in times of epidemics there were four to a bed. The sexes were mixed indiscriminately until Louis XIV, visiting the hospital in 1658, professed himself shocked by such a scandalous arrangement and commanded that the women should be banished to another ward. The Great Hall was used until 1948 when doctors insisted that the patients should be moved to a more modern hospital for treatment.

Patients were not allowed to forget that they would face Judgement Day. The beds were all lined up so that they could see the altar in the chapel at the end of the ward. Over the altar was a truly remarkable picture—a nine-panel polyptych (a painting of four or more panels) by Roger van der Weyden, renowned as a portrait painter. So the sick and old looking down the ward from their beds saw frightening scenes of the final Judgement, with the Just being escorted to the Gates of Heaven and the Damned hurled screaming into the eternal sulphurous pit. The picture is a masterpiece and must have brought many a tough Burgundian transgressor to repentance. It is no longer on the altar. It was hidden in a loft from Revolutionary destroyers and put back in 1836. The nudity of the risen dead scandalised the 19th century sisters, who had them clothed in sackcloth, though happily this was done in watercolours and was removed by Paris restorers in 1877.

The picture was hidden again in the cellars of Château de la Rochepot in 1940. When it returned it was hung in the small Chambre du Roi, where Charles IX and Louis XIV slept on their visits to Hôtel Dieu. Arthur saw it there and through a magnifying glass was shown the extraordinarily careful detail—the great Flemish master had painted every button and jewel exquisitely. But experts said that the room, crowded with visitors, was too humid, so a special museum room was built with automatic temperature, humidity and light controls, and that is where you will find the picture now.

Almost inevitably, the high arched window in the chapel shows Nicolas Rolin himself with two Dukes, Philip the Good and his son Charles the Rash. The floor tiles and walls are decorated with Rolin's motto, *Seule*, followed by a star. Romantics say that it signified to his wife that he loved only her, but in view of his reputation as a womaniser and his lone control over the duchy, it seems much more likely that he himself was the 'only star'. Powerful men of his time adopted the most arrogant mottoes.

Hôtel Dieu is still a rest home for 240 elderly people of Beaune, and the same old kitchen makes their meals—but with modern equipment. You can still see an interesting automatic spit made by a Beaune clockmaker in 1698.

The collection of pewter vessels, bronze mortars and Nevers pottery from the 18th century in the pharmacy is remarkable.

To provide income for the hospice, Nicolas Rolin endowed it with the income of a salt-works at Salins which his wife Guigone de Salins had brought with her as her dowry. It soon proved insufficient, and Nicolas got the Duke's permission to do some fund-raising. Inevitably, he put the squeeze on the vignerons, who donated vineyards. Through the years others followed Rolin's example of investing in their heavenly fortune by leaving more vineyards in their wills. So now the hospice owns 800 ha (2000 acres), of which 50 ha produce the great wine of the Côte de Beaune. The famous auction of these wines on the third Sunday in November used to take place in the Hôtel Dieu, in the *cuverie*, but now only the tasting takes place there. The auction is held in the market hall. The most recent donation to the hospice was a vineyard producing Mazis-Chambertin, from the Côte de Nuits, first auctioned in 1977. A white wine, a Corton-Charlemagne, usually fetches the highest price.

A Son-et-Lumière is held at the Hospice from April–October. Ask at the tourist office opposite the entrance for days and times (tel. 80 22 24 51).

Beaune's **Collegiate Church of Our Lady**, begun about 1120 by the Cluny monks, contains some magnificent tapestries of the life of the Virgin Mary. Made in wool and silk, the five panels were woven from cartoons of a local artist Pierre Spicre, commissioned in 1474 by Rolin's stepson Cardinal Jean Rolin. Incidentally, Chancellor Nicolas Rolin had a picture painted by the great Van Eyck showing himself with the Madonna! It is now in the Louvre. The Cardinal donated corn land to the hospice in return for the sisters' prayers for his soul.

Beaune's **ramparts** are almost continuous for 2km but much is privately owned and other parts are hidden behind greenery or houses. There are eight bastions. The double bastion of St Jean beside the boulevard Maréchal Joffre is the old castle. The moat is now mostly gardens or orchards, with some tennis courts. Following boulevard Joffre north-west to rue de Lorraine, you pass St Jean, Tour Blondeau and Bastion Notre Dame. At rue Lorraine you reach the 18th century town gate of St Nicolas.

The **town hall**, just off rue Lorraine, is in a 17th century former Ursuline convent. It has two museums. The **Beaux Arts museum** contains 16th and 17th century Flemish and Dutch paintings, works of Picasso, Fernand Léger and Marc Chagall and a number by Félix Ziem (1821–1911) who, although born in Beaune, was known for his high-key seascapes in the manner of Turner and, like Turner, for his paintings of Venice. His sunsets are splendid.

The other **museum** is devoted to Etienne-Jules Marcy (1830–1904), local doctor and physiologist, who took the first motion pictures with a single camera. He called the process Chronophotography. An experimental scientist, he invented several things, including a gun-camera, which you can see here, together with some of his films, made from 1888 onwards. He was interested in photographing animal movements, which he studied, and he designed cameras which reduced exposure time to 1/250,000 of a second to photograph insects in flight. (Museum closed Tue and 1 Dec–end Mar.)

Beaune's main **markets** are held on Thursday and Saturday in the big market hall which is almost opposite Hôtel Dieu. The market spreads into the

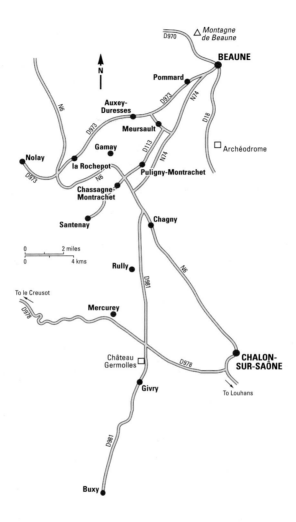

adjoining streets and is one of the genuine old-fashioned food markets where the local people do their main shopping.

Do try to see the vineyards of the **Montagne de Beaune**. Take the D970 north-west towards Bligny-sur-Ouche and a right branch road leads to the top (359m/1178ft). Here is a statue of Notre Dame de la Libération, designed by Albert David in 1946, a war memorial and a viewing table. The view spreads from the brown-tile roofs of Beaune to the vineyards and south to the Mâconnais mountains. It is superb on a fine day in spring or autumn.

When Pope Jean-Paul climbed the Montagne to bless the vines, a Beaune vigneron asked 'Why bless something which is thrice blessed already?'

The extraordinary new **Archéodrome** is much more interesting than it sounds. You will find it 6.5km (4 miles) south of Beaune in a service area alongside the A6 motorway. Take the D18 Chalon road, then go left on the D23 towards Merceuil. It shows a panorama of Burgundy through history to Gallo-Roman times. Stone Age huts have been reproduced, so have burial cairns, a Gallic house, a Roman villa and huge defence works showing a reproduction of Caesar's camp in 52 BC when he defeated the Gauls at Alésia (Alise Ste Reine, p 152).

Though only 3km (2 miles) south-west of Beaune, **Pommard**, astride the D973, seems to be in a different world. It has been a rich village since Americans took to its wine in the 1920s and began to favour it over most Burgundies. A few years back, its ever-increasing popularity led to an annual shortage and some less scrupulous négociants or wine importers blended it with other wines. Pommard got rather a bad name. Jean-Louis Laplanche, owner of the 18th century château de Pommard, fought hard to restore its reputation. Now not only is its wine 'clean' but the village itself has a cleaner look, with its houses scrubbed, its streets paved and flowers blooming—a much prettier picture. Among many famous men who were addicted to Pommard were Victor Hugo (who just liked all good wine) and Erasmus, the great 16th century scholar and religious thinker who, though he exposed the abuses of the church of Rome, refused to join Luther. Though born at Rotterdam, he lived in various parts of Europe and was a Cambridge professor. He said that he wished he could live in Burgundy, not to fight causes but to drink the wine. And when accused of drinking Pommard on a fast day, he said 'My heart is Catholic, but for Pommard wine, my stomach is Reformed'.

We love the village of **Meursault**, not only for its dry, rich white wine but for its truly Burgundian old buildings and its friendly unassuming attitude despite its affluence. A lot of others like it, too, especially since the go-ahead Beaune producers and négociants Patriarche took over Château de Meursault from the Comte de Moucheron and made visits into a very special occasion. But most visitors are there in midsummer or on the Monday in November after the Beaune sales, when the vignerons hold their dinner, to which each brings two bottles of his best wine. They still call it *La Paulée*, but is no longer an old-fashioned *paulée* at which all the vineyard workers used to celebrate the vendange. It is the last of Les Trois Glorieuses (see Chapter 3) and you need to be very influential to be a guest. This prestigious occasion is in strange contrast to the little village shops proudly offering their own products like jambon persillé, the inns where locals drink with tourists, and the travelling shop which parks in the handsome village square opposite the town hall to sell everything from plastic buckets, washing-up bowls and pegs to cheap shirts, braces and safety-pins.

Meursault's agreeable old houses of the 15th and 16th centuries are lived in by local people, not sold as weekend hideouts. Many are around the 15th century church with a beautiful stone spire. Nearby is the delightful **town hall**, a true Burgundian building which was originally a 14th century manor house, altered over centuries. It has a huge square tower and a medieval round tower above ochre walls, which are topped by steep roofs tiled with greeny and yellow glazed slates in zigzag design.

The **château** is an elegant, stately home. It was built in the 16th century by the Moucheron family on the site of a ruined château from 1337 and it belonged to the Comte de Moucheron until very recently. It still has its dovecote, forge, stables and a fine courtyard. There are old wine presses in its huge cellars and in the park are streams with a fishery and orchards. The cellars are incredible. They stretch under the château itself to the outbuildings, which include an old fermenting house. About 500,000 bottles and 2000 oak casks are stored in the cellars. The Moucherons must have liked their own wines. Some of the cellars were originally dug out by the monks of Cluny, who had a big estate at Meursault in the 12th century. The château wines are excellent. (Visits daily, including Sunday 09.00–11.30; 14.30–17.30. Highly organised.)

Meursault misses both the N74 and the D973, which are just over a kilometre away. It shares a little road with Puligny-Montrachet, and Auxey-Duresses is on the D973, so three of the best white wines in the world are within 6.5km (4 miles) of each other. Thomas Jefferson, the US statesman, visited Meursault on a Côte d'Or vineyard tour in 1787 and ordered 250 bottles of premier cru. But the greatest Meursault imbiber must surely have been Cardinal Bernis, French ambassador to Rome under Louis XV. At Communion he served nothing but a good vintage Meursault. When the Vatican expressed rather disapproving surprise, he was unrepentant. 'I wouldn't want our Lord to see me wincing while I take Communion,' he said.

The D973 is an attractive road with many little side roads leading to wine hamlets. The picturesque village of **Auxey-Duresses**, in a deep valley below Mont Melion, is a quiet place with only 350 people, proud of their 16th century church and their wine, especially the rather scarce white which was once sold as Meursault. Very few travellers bother to climb the hill to **St Romain**, another calm village. The ruins of its castle were excavated recently on a rocky spur. There are splendid views from here across the valley to a near-circle of cliffs. Its vineyards, at 300–400m (1000–1300ft), are the highest in the Côte d'Or, so the wine is not great, but is very drinkable and good value.

The D973 climbs past the peak of Mont Melion to **La Rochepot**, which has a delightful 12th century church with a 16th century triptych, and the much restored 15th century **Château de la Rochepot**, one of the symbols of Burgundy, where one of Burgundy's most powerful men, Philippe Pot, was born in 1428. The château, which sits impressively on a hilltop surrounded by trees, is rich in pointed towers, some tiled in blue-grey slate, some, like the main roof, in traditional glazed tiles of zigzag pattern.

Regnier Pot, grandfather of Philippe, was one of 10,000 knights who followed the Duke of Nevers (later John the Fearless, Duke of Burgundy) on a disastrous crusade to Jerusalem against the Saracens in 1396. They went in a spirit of adventure and chivalry, as if going to a joust, and were utterly defeated at Nicopolos. Regnier was one of the lucky ones taken prisoner with the Duke and held to ransom.

The crusaders came back with some tall stories about their adventures and the story told about Regnier is as tall as most. Regnier's bravery had so won the admiration of Sultan Bayazid that he proposed to get Regnier on his side by marrying him to the Sultan's sister. Regnier was already married and anyway did not fancy becoming a Moslem, so he refused. You don't refuse a Sultan who offers you such an honour when you are his prisoner. He was sentenced to fight in the arena the next day, and that night the Virgin Mary appeared to him and gave him some good advice. 'Strike low,' she said, simply. He was at least given a scimitar when he was led into the arena, where he faced a half-starved lion. He struck low, and cut off the poor lion's front legs. The Sultan set Regnier free.

On his return Regnier became chamberlain to the Duke of Burgundy, ambassador to Hungary and a Knight of the Golden Fleece. He bought the castle, then called Roche-Nolay, and spent a fortune improving it.

His grandson Philippe Pot was heaped with even more honours. Of course it helped to be a godson of Duke Philip the Good, who made him a Knight of the Golden Fleece, chamberlain, Steward of the Duke's household, governor of Lille (a very important city in the Duke's Flemish lands) and ambassador to England. But when the last Duke of Burgundy, Charles the Rash, was killed in battle by Louis XI's Swiss mercenaries, he abandoned poor Mary, Charles's only child, and joined Louis XI, who grabbed Burgundy and made him Seneschal of Burgundy and guardian of Louis's son, the Dauphin. At Dijon the Burgundians wiped his name from the rolls of the Golden Fleece, so Louis gave him the Order of St Michael.

A natural diplomat, he used gentle humour as his weapon, pacifying Charles the Rash by jokes when he threw a fit of temper. At the 1454 banquet of the Vow of the Pheasant in Lille (see box, p 14) when Duke Philip the Good announced a crusade and the nobles tried to outbid each other in making extravagant vows (no doubt assisted by good Burgundy wine), Philippe Pot pledged not to eat sitting down on Tuesdays and to fight the Saracen with his right arm bare. Philip the Good seemed to take this second vow quite seriously, for he solemnly rejected it. Luckily for all of them, the crusade never took place.

Later in his life, when the Dauphin was 13 and had become King of France (though his sister, the strong Anne of Beaujeu, was really ruling the country), Pot made a speech which in Louis XIV's day might have cost him his life. The State belongs to the people, he said, and the kings were there by the people's suffrage. They were there not to enrich themselves but to forget their own interests and enrich the people. If they did the opposite, they were tyrants. In fact, he was suggesting a constitutional monarchy, unbelievable in those days. He himself had become very rich indeed. He owned the great château of Châteauneuf-en-Auxois as well as Rochepot and when he died in 1494 he was buried in Cîteaux Abbey in a magnificent tomb by the sculptor who

The Carnots of Nolay

Lazare Carnot (1753–1823), army engineer and scientist, became a member of the Legislative Assembly during the French Revolution. When foreign powers sent armies to destroy the new Republic, he was given the job of raising an army to defend France. He raised 14 armies by mass conscription, fitted them out, planned their campaigns and threw back all the attackers. He was called 'Organiser of Victory'.

It was Carnot who selected Napoleon to command. But he cast the only vote against him when he was made Emperor, and when he saw that Napoleon was fighting wars of aggression to enlarge his Empire, Carnot retired.

He rejoined Napoleon during the Hundred Days between Napoleon's escape from Elba and defeat at Waterloo. When the monarchy returned, he fled to Magdebourg, became a scientist again and died there in 1823. In 1889 his body was brought back to France and buried in the Panthéon. He wrote late in his life of the Revolution: 'We thought that it was possible to obtain an unbounded liberty without disorder, a perfect system of equality without factions. We were cruelly disillusioned by our experience'. And of Napoleon he wrote 'Few men have exercised a more pernicious influence on the fate of their country than Napoleon, despite his prodigious ability, keen judgement, inflexible character and brave heart'.

His elder son Sadi, who died at 36, was called 'one of science's most original and profound thinkers' and did some very important research into thermodynamics. His younger son became Minister of Education, but was forced to resign. He had dared to bring in free and compulsory education for all and (worse still in the eyes of his opponents) to extend secondary education to girls! He also resigned his Parliamentary seat in protest against Napoleon III making himself Emperor. His son, also called Sadi, became President of the French Republic in 1887 but was assassinated by an anarchist in 1894. His wife and family continued his restoration of Château de la Rochepot.

designed the tomb of John the Fearless, now in the Ducal Palace in Dijon, Le Moiturier. Pot's tomb is now in the Louvre.

The château was a wreck after the Revolution, when the stone from one side and the keep were taken for other buildings. But in 1893 it was bought by Madame Carnot, wife of Sadi Carnot, President of France and a member of the great Carnot family of Nolay. He was assassinated the year after. She and her family made a superb job of restoring Rochepot. You can cross the drawbridge to see the courtyard, then the great guard room with a vast fire-place, the kitchens, the sumptuously furnished dining room, a tower, and a

The village of La Rochepot with the château on the hilltop

room with a museum of gifts given to the president on his world travels. (Visits daily except Tuesday from end March to All Saints' Day.)

A few kilometres west of Rochepot, behind a circle of hills, lies the small town of **Nolay**, which gives a taste of peaceful old Burgundy. Its main claim to fame is its talented local family the Carnots, famous in French history from the Revolution. The family still has a house in the square named after them, **place Carnot**, facing a statue called Organiser of Victory, dedicated to Lazare Carnot, engineer and scientist, born in Nolay in 1753 (see box, p 186).

Nolay has an old covered market, old houses with towers and a 15th century church with stone belfry from which a jaquemart of two mechanical figures strikes the hours, reminiscent of Dijon.

A walk of 6.5km (4 miles) north through Tournée valley takes you past **Cormot cliffs**, well-known to climbers. The steepest is called Dame de Paris. Then you reach the village of Vauchignon from where the left fork goes up Cosanne river valley under high cliffs. A steep path left through woods leads to a cave where the river flows attractively in a waterfall. Another meadow path leads to **Cirque du Bout du Monde** (World's End), a beauty spot in a natural amphitheatre where a waterfall of fine spray falls 20m (65ft).

Westward on the N6, where the road from Meursault and Puligny-Montrachet meets it, is the pleasant hamlet of **Gamay**, with a medieval castle and church partly from the 10th century. It gave its name to the Gamay grape, used for making Beaujolais wines. The grape has spread as far as Chinon in the Loire and to vineyards in various places owned by vignerons seeking a highly productive grape making a light, fruity wine which does not have to be kept very long. In the 14th century, Duke Philip the Bold ('le Hardi') banned the grape because he thought it would flood the wine market and put the great Burgundian wines out of business. He called Gamay 'an evil and treacherous plant which produces a very great abundance of wine'.

Chassagne-Montrachet, divided from Puligny by the N6, is a sprawling village with a troubled past. When Louis XI of France was taking over Burgundy, using Swiss mercenaries to do the job, Mary, the only surviving child of Charles the Rash, the last Duke of Burgundy, asked the Prince of Orange, Charles de Chalon, to help her. He was in Chassagne-Montrachet when a big Swiss force advanced and he was forced to flee. When the Swiss found that he had escaped, they burned down the village and killed most of the people.

Santenay is the last of the Côte d'Or wine villages and has something the others do not have—spa water. The spa, in Santenay-le-Bas, has recently regained some of the lustre of olden times. It is used to treat rheumatism and digestive and liver problems. Inevitably, there is a casino. Higher up, from the 13th century St Jean church tucked under cliffs, are spectacular views over the vineyards of Santenay-le-Haut and St Jean, spread along the river Dheune.

Wines are red and can be tannic when young. Of the 12 premiers crus, Les Gravières has the most finesse. Generally the wines are robust. You can taste in the old château built by Duke Philip the Bold (tel. 80 20 61 87) or at Caves Prieuré-Brunet, rue Narosse, in 15th century cellars which has a collection of old tools used by wine-growers (tel. 80 20 60 56).

Chagny on the N6 is a small industrial town where the Côte d'Or wine region meets the Chalonnaise, and there is one very good reason for going there. In a lovely 15th century Burgundian house in place d'Armes, the *Lameloise* family runs a hotel with ten large luxurious bedrooms which earns a place in Relais et Châteaux hotels. In the kitchen, Lameloise Père et Fils cook meals which not only earn them 3 Michelin stars but earn the praise and thanks of gourmets who sometimes find 3-star chefs to be more interested in pleasing the eye than the palate and stomach. The wine list is a joy. Having daydreamed your way through the grand cru wines on the carte du vin you can find a good choice of wines to suit your pocket at the other end. Mind you, eating there is not cheap—just a splendid experience (tel. 85 87 08 85).

For visitors with lighter wallets, Chagny has another very pleasant hotel just 1.5km down the N6 towards Chalon-sur-Saône. *Hostellerie du Château de Bellecroix* (tel. 85 87 13 86) is a fairytale creeper-clad château with two pointed round towers, set in a park away from the traffic of the N6. An old Commanderie of the Knights of St John from 1199, it combines 12th and 18th century architecture with walls 2m thick! The meals are half the price of Lameloise masterpieces and are very agreeable, strongly Burgundian but with imaginative touches. For instance, instead of *jambon persillé* we had *poulet persillé*—chicken meat instead of ham in a white wine and parsley jelly.

Along the D981 south from Chagny are four Côte Chalonnaise wine villages where we used to buy bargain wines until they were discovered by wine merchants seeking refuge from rising prices on the Côte d'Or.

Rully was so quiet the first time we visited it that only a barking dog greeted us for the first hour. There is not much bustle now, but enough to make a visit agreeable. Its old houses are pleasant, its 12th century fortress formidable, its little Commerce auberge where we used to drink with the locals has changed its name to *Le Vendangerot* with a posh menu which includes à la carte dishes and a notice saying that drinks are served only to eaters. Rully's white wine has improved so greatly that it is a possible substitute for AOC Meursault for anyone but the rich.

The bigger village down the road, **Mercurey**, a deadly rival and much more influential, once got a regulation passed to stop Rully using its own name on wines. Wine is made and kept in the fortress château, which you can visit on weekends from mid-April to end October.

Mercurey's wine charter goes back to AD 557 and its growers have a Confrérie-St-Vincent et des Disciples de la Chante Flûté de Mercurey. It meets annually to pick the best wines which are allowed to carry its label 'Chante Flûté', which means a song flowing as softly and sweetly as a flute. You can taste wine in an old chapel in the vineyards, Caveau de Mercurey (open Sat, Sun, also weekdays in July, Aug, Sept).

Despite being sacked often in wars, **Givry** is rare among little wine towns in having some outstanding buildings. Its town hall is in a town gateway of 1771 and its church, a sort of rotunda with domes and half-domes, is regarded by some architects as a masterpiece. It was designed by Emiland Gauthey, an engineer who built Canal du Centre.

Six-and-a-half kilometres miles (4 miles) north of Givry on D981 is **Château Germolles**, a 13th century fortress which, in the 14th century, Philip the Bold, Duke of Burgundy, made into a house for his wife Margaret of Flanders, whom he had married although she was thought ugly, to get control of her vast lands. It is said that he wanted to keep her as far as possible from his palace in Dijon. It is recorded that in 1390, in honour of a visit from Charles VI of France, who was still sane at the time, Margaret topped up her cellars with 60 hogsheads of Givry wine. Gabrielle d'Estrées, favourite mistress of Henri IV, introduced him to the wine after she had stayed at Germolles, and this was the wine which, possibly to please her, he exempted from duty. Inevitably, a flood of wines sheltered under the Givry label and the privilege had to be withdrawn.

The vast old Romanesque cellar at Germolles would certainly have taken a few hogsheads. The château has an impressive entrance gateway with two round towers and a two-storey chapel. There are staircase turrets in the main building (open July, Aug, except Tue).

Buxy (pronounced Bussy) is a very pleasant little town on the D981, and a centre for the white wines of Montagny, which come from a little village to the west and are much underrated. In the centre of Buxy is *La Tour Rouge*, where you can drink the wines with tasty snacks and buy wines to take away. On the edge of Buxy, the Cave de Buxy is a useful and reliable place to buy most Burgundy wines, especially Montagny and other Chalonnaise.

CHALON-SUR-SAÔNE has been an important and busy town since Julius Caesar's conquest of Gaul. Tin from Cornwall used to be landed on boats there and taken down river to the Mediterranean. Chalon is still an important centre for industry and business and a market town for farming, stock-rearing and the vineyards of the Côte Chalonnaise. Yet, being in Burgundy, it does not seem to hurry. If you sit by the river you might mistake it for a holiday town, for pleasure boats are replacing the barges which for so long served the Schneider heavy engineering and arms factories, and even the Canal du Centre, which joins Chalon to Le Creusot, the 'city of steel', is used for pleasure craft.

Chalon's great carnival in March, lasting eight days, draws people from far beyond Burgundy. In June, les Foires Internationales des Sauvagines is a market for wildfowl and game.

The two islands in the river, easily defendable in those days, encouraged Caesar to use Chalon as an important base. The three Roman roads from Boulogne, Trier and Strasbourg met at the town. Not until 1794, when Le Creusot became a steel town, was the Canal du Centre finished as a vital artery serving industrial centres. Modern industries include the making of equipment for the nuclear power industry.

Father of Photography

Using a simple box and the lens from a pair of spectacles, Joseph Nicéphore Niepce from Chalon-sur-Saône, a retired army officer, discovered in 1822 the principle of photography. He succeeded in reproducing on a glass plate an image previously obtained in a dark room. Unlike Fox Talbot Niepce did not manage to insert a 'fixer', so could not reproduce his pictures in large numbers. He took his invention to Paris to enlist the support of Daguerre, who owned a magic lantern entertainment called the Diorama. But Niepce never gained any recognition for his expensive experiments, or made a franc out of them, before he died of a stroke. His wife died destitute.

Daguerre cashed in by getting a hearing from the Académie des Sciences and selling the patent to the French State, thereby gaining large pensions for himself and for Niepce's son.

Niepce's first photograph is now far away in the Gernsheim Collection at the University of Texas. But his home town of Chalon has done him proud, with a statue on quai Gambetta and a fascinating museum of photography in a handsome 18th century post office, Hôtel des Messageries Royales, facing the river. The rooms are excellently laid out. You can see a mock-up of his camera, later equipment used by Daguerre, early colour pictures, the first Kodak camera of 1888, equipment of the Lumière brothers, who produced a cine-camera in 1893, and a copy of a machine carried by the Apollo spacecraft to the moon in 1968 (the original is still on the moon).

A section is devoted to underwater and aerial photography and there is a superb collection of miniature cameras used in criminal investigation, from the Photocravate of 1890 to be hidden under a tie and the Invisible of the same year, to be hidden under the shirt front. Niepce invented other things too, and here you can see his bicycle of 1818, with such revolutionary features as handlebars and a brake. (The museum is shut on Tuesdays.)

Chalon is not an attractive-looking town, but it has some charming old houses, especially half-timbered ones in **place St Vincent** and rue St Vincent. Above all, Chalon has a pleasant atmosphere. The area round place St Vincent has been made into a pedestrian precinct, giving it a most surprising medieval appearance. Alas, the former **cathedral of St Vincent**, named so fittingly for the patron saint of wine and built from the 11th century in a variety of styles, was given a rather hideous neo-Gothic façade last century. Its 15th century cloisters have been restored and at their entrance a chapel has a very attractive early 16th century tapestry. St Vincent was built on the site of a temple to Baco, a Boar god from whom we get the word bacon.

Across the river in the suburb of **St-Marcel-lès-Chalon** is the simple early-Gothic church of the old priory which was attached to the great abbey of Cluny. In a side chapel is the very well into which the Romans tossed St Marcellus to his death. Peter the Venerable, Abbot of Cluny, sent Peter Abelard, the great thinker and bold theologian, to the old priory to die in comfort and peace, which he duly did in 1142. It was Abbot Peter who had saved him from excommunication when his adversary, the bigoted Bernard of Clairvaux (St Bernard) had him declared a heretic by the Pope at the Council of Sens. Abelard had caused a great scandal earlier in his life by running off with his 17-year-old pupil Héloïse, daughter of a Canon of Notre Dame, and giving her a son. When he died, Héloïse, now Abbess of a convent at Paraclete, had his body exhumed from the monks' cemetery at St Marcel and reburied at her convent, where she was later buried beside him.

Denon Museum, in an 18th century building in place Hôtel-de-Ville, is named after Vivant Denon, who organised the museum system, including the Louvre, for Napoleon. He was called Grand Purveyor and Organiser of the Museums of France. An Egyptian scholar, he had accompanied Napoleon on his abortive Egyptian campaign. The museum has a large collection of good but not great paintings, mostly Dutch and French. The best is Study of a Negro by Théodore Géricault (1791–1824), founder of the anti-Classical Realist school, who fled to England after harsh criticism of his work. There are also archaeological collections in the museum and interesting wine-growers' tools and implements (shut Tuesday).

Pont St Laurent joins the two river islands to Chalon. Continue over both islands, then turn left into rue Julien-Lenouveu and you reach the great **rose trail** (Roseraie St-Nicolas) which is 5km (3 miles) long. It winds through a rose garden laid out in a loop of the Saône beyond the golf course, and despite the long walk is well worth visiting any time from June to September. It has 25,000 rose trees set among huge lawns shaded by conifers and apple trees. In June and July the beds are a mass of colour. The September-flowering roses are in separate beds, and there is a rockery of rare plants, an arboretum, bulbs, a water garden and a heather garden. You don't have to walk the *whole* trail, but it is rewarding. And if you want further exercise, there is a 2.5km keep-fit track. (Open early June to early October, for times ask the tourist office in square Chabas, bd République, tel. 85 48 37 97.)

Most of the countryside west and north-west from Chalon to Autun is so seductive that it seems contrary to spend time in the old steel and arms-making town of **Le Creusot**, in the 'basin industriel' where from 1836 local coal was used by the Schneider brothers to fire their great furnaces. But Le Creusot has changed since the steel bubble burst in the 1980s and although we would not describe the town yet as 'a quiet clean backwater' as a French guide did, it has become a much more pleasant town, if no longer so rich. Pleasure boats have joined the barges on Canal du Centre, old industrial buildings have been cleaned up and the spectacular Château La Verrerie, home of the Schneiders and named for the former Queen's Crystal Works founded by Queen Marie Antoinette, has been turned into an industrial heritage museum centre recalling former glories of the steel industry and, believe it or not, a centre for creativity in the *plastic* arts! The two conical furnaces stand in front of the château, one converted into a theatre, the other used for exhibitions.

After the Canal du Centre was opened, joining the river Saône at Chalon to the Loire at Digoin, the population of Le Creusot grew tenfold. One of Schneiders' engineers invented the power hammer in 1867. The Schneiders at Le Creusot rivalled Krupps at Essen.

In 1924 the old 102-tonne power hammer, which now stands symbolically at the southern edge of the town, was replaced by great hydraulic presses. In the heady days after World War II, when steel production was believed to be the magic key to national prosperity all over the world, and Germany, France and Britain were competing to build bigger and better steel works, the Creusot steel empire (Schneider factories) expanded in Le Creusot and set up more factories at Breuil, Torcy and Montchanin. In 1970 it amalgamated with another big steel company to form Creusot-Loire. Arthur can remember Le Creusot in the late 1960s with its steel mills going flat out and looking very dark and satanic! But by 1984, the world was producing too much steel. Creusot-Loire looked for new products and industries.

We confess that until we wandered south-east from Chalon one day looking for a friend's house we thought that all Bresse was in the département of Ain and that those expensive but succulent chickens Poulets de Bresse with an Appellation Contrôlée tag in red on the left leg came exclusively from Bourg-en-Bresse and the farms around. Then we discovered **Louhans** on the banks of the Seille river, 37km (23 miles) south-east of Chalon, and found that not only was this in the Plaine de Bresse but that it shared the marketing of those chickens with Bourg and that it was in Burgundy.

Louhans is very much more attractive than Bourg and just as much a gourmet's delight. To see those chickens, go to the Monday market. Markets on other days specialise in cattle and pigs. The gourmet chickens are handsome white birds with blue feet which must roam free on grass and be fed on maize and milk. Once killed, the chickens are bathed in milk. They cost up to three times as much as a lesser bird but have a lot more flavour. To keep the flavour, most chefs take out the stomach fat to use in other dishes, then simply poach the chicken in cream, serving it with *morilles* (mushrooms) in season. At *Moulin de Bourgchâteau*, Patrick Gonzalez, born in Louhans, also offers the chickens in a delicious chicken liver sauce. This large old mill on the river, with the water under it in two arches, was built in 1778, stopped milling in 1973 and became a delightful hotel in 1986, set in a riverside park (tel. 85 75 37 12). Guests can fish or laze around the river on a barque. One of Patrick's local specialities is sandre from the river cooked in Pinot Noir wine.

Louhans' charming arcaded **Grande Rue** is lined with 17th–18th century houses, and the town has a 14th century church and an 18th century Hôtel-Dieu with a fine collection of 16th century brown glass flagons and Spanish and Moorish pottery.

Early morning fishing in the river Soâne

Canoeists love the river here. The great Ferdinand Point, father of the true modern cooking before 'nouvelle' came to mean mere décor on a plate, and king of *La Pyramide* at Vienne, began in Louhans and is still remembered at the Ferdinand Point Gastronomic Exhibition on the last Sunday in November.

15. Mâcon and Beaujolais

The Mâconnais is a land of good, affordable wine and beautiful scenery. Though the vineyards are only about 16km (10 miles) wide, running from Tournus to St Vérand, the scenery of the uplands is varied and very beautiful with forests on the hill summits, arid slopes and damp rich meadows in the valleys. The vineyards are planted in terraces on the slopes, where morning sunlight falls. Much of the rest is heathland, where goats produce milk for little chevroton cheeses.

There is a wonderful drive from Tournus to Mâcon through the photogenic country of La Montagne and then the vineyards. It misses the historic abbey of Cluny and most of the villages that the poet and writer Alphonse de Lamartine, Mâcon's favourite son, wove into his writing, but it takes you into a world away from that of the direct roads A6 and N6.

TOURNUS is a most likable town, rather neglected by travellers. It was a staging post on the Saône river between Chalon and Mâcon in Roman times and is still a good resting place on a traveller's gentle journey to Provence and the Mediterranean. Apart from its great abbey of St Philibert, it has in its old town cobbled streets with medieval and Renaissance houses, mansions, shop fronts with gables and corbels, several good restaurants, and rather more than its share of antique shops. But the atmosphere of Tournus seems to be dictated by the placid river, running so slowly that Caesar suggested it was standing still. The old bridge was inadequate for binding together the old town on one bank and the new on the 'rive gauche', but a new bridge built in 1988 has made the town easier to explore and has opened up a vista that shows clearly the two Romanesque towers of St Philibert. Much still happens on the river. You can catch boats from quai du Midi to Chalon or Mâcon or take a round river pleasure trip.

St Philibert's abbey is one of the most remarkable, dignified and imposing of Romanesque buildings, described as 'a piece of music in stone'. It seems appropriate that part of it was chosen as the International Centre for Romanesque Studies. It was the church of a 10th century abbey and only after a lot of bickering and ill-will did St Philibert take over from St Valerian, its original patron.

You reach the abbey from the busy traffic of the N6 by taking rue Albert

Thibaudet, which passes between two towers of the medieval Porte des Champs into the quieter old abbey square. The front looks rather like a castle, with loophole slits in bare walls and two towers linked by a fortified parapet. There was good reason. The monks had already had their fill of looting invaders. The parapet was a little bit of extra defence added by a restorer this century.

The whole of the inside of the abbey, from the narthex (the vestibule) with its thick pillars and vaulted roofs and the nave with lighter but still sturdy pillars, to the cool arcades of the cloisters, the 13th century chapter house and the 15th century abbot's lodgings, has an unadorned beauty. Even if you are tired of dragging yourself around churches and cathedrals, try to see this one in its beautiful simplicity.

The missionary Valerian, who came to convert Tournus, was beheaded here in AD 179. He became a Christian cult figure and around his tomb grew up a monastery dedicated to him.

In the 9th century the monks of the Ile de Noirmoutier (now in Normandy) were fleeing with the remains of their patron St Philibert from the invading Norsemen. They moved gradually right across the country as the Norsemen penetrated further and further up the rivers, looting, raping, burning and killing. The raiders found monasteries particularly rich sources of loot. The Noirmoutier monks wandered for 70 years until Charles the Bald, King of France, offered to extend Tournus Abbey to accommodate them.

Tournus now had two saints, St Valerian and St Philibert. But they (or their monks) did not get along very well. And the Noirmoutier monks had still not managed to escape from invaders. The Hungarian Magyars were sweeping westward and in AD 937 they pillaged and burned Tournus. Rebuilding began, but the row between supporters of the two saints flared into open conflict and the Philibert monks moved to St Pourçain in the Auvergne, where they had stayed on their travels. A former abbot, Abbot Stephen, reconciled the two groups of monks. Under the new agreement, Philibert was top saint, with his bones in the church, while Valerian was put down in the crypt, though they were both included in pilgrimages. Craftsmen from Lombardy in Italy contributed to the new abbey.

Though near Cluny, St Philibert's was one of the few abbeys within range that remained independent under the rule of St Benedict and it gradually built up considerable civil power. It was badly damaged by Calvinists in 1562, declined and was secularised in 1627, the monks being replaced by canons who did not live in. The refectory became a tennis court, called Le Ballon. The building survived the Revolution. The abbey was shut down in 1785 and became a national monument in 1841. When the bridge over the Saône was bombed in 1940 and 1944, the stained glass was damaged, but it was reconstructed by Brigitte Simon, one of that family of wonderful craftsmen and artists who restored the glass in Reims Cathedral.

The main **museum** in Tournus in an 18th century convent is named after the local painter Jean-Baptiste Greuze (1725–1805). A popular portraitist and genre painter of everyday scenes, he was driven out of fashion by the neo-

Classicism of David, who used episodes from ancient history to extol civil virtues and had the advantage of being virtual dictator of arts in the Revolution and then Napoleon's official painter until Waterloo. Greuze turned to painting sentimental pictures of little girls. There are several of his paintings in the museum, but there are also works of David and Poussin and of artists more critical of life such as Hogarth. Interesting are the paintings of a lesser known artist Félix Ziem (1821–1911), born at Beaune, a sort of latter-day Turner, with a strong touch of Impressionism, who painted superb sunsets and was brilliant, like Monet, at showing the effect of light on stone. (Museum closed Tue and Nov–Mar.)

The other museum, **Perrin-de-Puycousin**, grew from collections of a local lawyer of that name and is in a 17th century house given for the purpose by a famous literary critic, Albert Thibaudet, who died in 1936. It shows very interesting scenes from the daily life of the past, with wax models in Burgundian clothes, and includes a Burgundian cellar. (Shut Tue, Sun mornings and Nov–Mar.)

Our meandering road to Mâcon, covering about 80km (50 miles), leaves Tournus westwardly by the little D14, which after the A6 motorway climbs quickly, with views over the Saône valley and Tournus, until it reaches Beaufer Pass. Then it winds through valleys between hills of boxwood and pine to **Ozenay**, a hamlet with a church dating from 1180. A little château was built here in the 13th century and extended in the 17th century but it is now a private farm and to see it you must go into the fields behind.

After passing through the Brancion Pass (Col de Brancion) the road turns northward and winds up to the superb medieval fortified old market town of **Brancion**, perched on a spur overlooking two great ravines. Ruined castles, even 10th century ones, do not often interest us very much, but the buildings hidden behind Brancion's ruined ramparts and 14th century gateway are imposing and reveal interesting facts of medieval life. Helped by an excellent leaflet in French or English versions, you discover that what was assumed to be an underground prison was a cunningly constructed food store with an air vent. **Tour de Guet** (watch tower) gives you an insight to medieval sanitary arrangements and in the 14th century **Tour de Beaumont** is an exhibition of life as it was lived here in the Middle Ages.

Many of the medieval houses have been very well restored. The 15th century wooden-raftered market hall is delightful. The little church of **St Pierre** has also been beautifully restored and its 14th century frescoes rescued. The view from its terrace is grandiose. Here in June the village celebrates the feast of St John (St Jean) with a huge bonfire and the church and castle are floodlit. Many houses have flowered balconies and outside stone staircases. The inn is 15th century. The restoration has been done since the family of the Comte de Musard took over in 1860. Members of the original de Brancion family, which owned the castle and village from the 10th to the end of the 13th century, were nicknamed Le Gros and in war and squabbles lived up to their motto 'au plus fort de la mêlée' (in the toughest part of the fight). In 1250 Jocerand de Brancion was killed fighting beside his cousin

St Louis at the battle of El Mansurah in Egypt. His son equipped an army for the next crusade, which bankrupted him, so that he was forced to sell his estates to the Duke of Burgundy. The Catholic League destroyed the castle in the 16th century Religious Wars. We are grateful to the restorers.

Return to the Brancion Pass to take another winding stretch of the D14, which straightens out as it crosses a forest towards **Chapaize**, worth visiting for its beautiful and remarkable church, in the style of Lombardy. It was built as a priory, starting around the year 1100, by Benedictines from Chalon. Its elegant square belfry tower, over 18m (60ft) tall and tapering, which has remarkably survived nearly 900 years of wind and weather, stands above a jumble of irregularly shaped buildings under roofs of different levels. It is charming and a tribute to its 12th century builders. Although **Cormatin** is on the rather busy D981 to Cluny, it is worth the 6.5km (4 mile) drive from Chapaize to see its magnificently furnished and decorated château. Sculptured or gilded French-style ceilings, Louis XIII period furniture, sumptuous Baroque decorations and fine paintings are all so rich and magnificent that they are almost overpowering. The attractive Renaissance château is reflected in the moat, where black swans swim, and beyond is a charming park with ornamental pools, formal gardens, a maze and a walk along the river bank.

The château was built in 1605–8 for the Governor of Chalon, Antoine du Blé. It later belonged to Pierre Dezoteux, who called himself Baron de Cormatin and took part in the US War of Independence. His daughter Nina Dezoteux, wife of Guillaume de Pierreclos and childhood friend of Lamartine, had an affair with the writer and in 1813 had a son by him, Léon de Pierreclos. No wonder Lamartine called Cormatin 'alluring, artistic and delightful'.

In 1888 the author Jacques de Lacretelle whose best work, *Les Hauts Ponts*, is about the decline of a family, was born in the château. At the turn of the century it was owned by Raoul Gunsbourg, director of the Monte Carlo Opera, who built up the fame of the great singer Caruso. He entertained all the great opera, ballet and stage personalities, including Diaghilev, the composer Fauré, Caruso, Sarah Bernhardt, Dame Nellie Melba and the actress Cécile Sorel, who had her own bedroom at the château.

Cormatin was in a sorry state by 1981, when four enthusiasts bought and restored it and its lovely 17th century gardens. (Château open daily 15 June–1 Nov; Sat, Sun 1 Apr–15 June. Even the 19th century kitchen and bathroom are worth seeing.)

Just south of Cormatin is the little village of **Taizé**, renowned for an international religious community visited by thousands of young people every year. Started in 1940 by a Swiss Catholic priest named Schutz, it has become an ecumenical community of men of several religious denominations from 20 countries. Father Schutz has become a monk—Brother Roger. It is a lively place, with young people staying in a bungalow village and tents. Easter brings the big rush. The community's big flat-roofed concrete church of the Reconciliation contrasts with the simple Romanesque village church, lit by

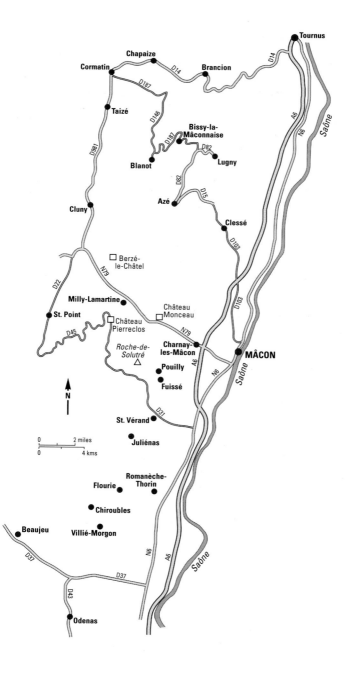

one little stained glass window and with no chairs—just wooden kneeling stools on a bare stone floor. Father Schutz was curé here in 1940 when the village was on the border of occupied and Vichy France. He hid Resistance fighters and fleeing Jews until the Gestapo were on his trail, then he fled temporarily to Geneva.

The site of **Cluny**, once the most powerful centre of religion, learning and art in the world, was 9.5km (6 miles) down the road from Taizé. The abbey's church, built in 1088, was for 500 years the biggest in Christendom, until St Peter's in Rome was built 14m (45ft) longer. Almost nothing remains.

To follow our route, take the D187 south-east from Cormatin to **Chissey-lès-Mâcon**, a hamlet that people visit to see the tower of its 12th century church—tall, square and beautifully proportioned in the Italian style. Fewer people notice the simple line among the names in the memorial of those who died for France in World War I: 'Philibert, Duc, Septembre 1914'. Very typical of the fiercely democratic Mâconnais.

At Prayes, take the D146 through the valley of the little Grison river to the primitive village of **Blanot**—old houses surrounded by dry stone walls in a pleasant setting below Mont St Romain. The remains of a 14th century fortified priory which once belonged to Cluny are now a farm. One round tower and a more military polygon tower still exist. Ancient tombs from the Merovingian period have been found and you can see one near the farm gateway. Follow the D446 northward below the mountain and you reach caves. The network, 76m (250ft) underground, stretches about 1km to Mont St Romain. There are steep stairs and low ceilings. In the 21 chambers, which you can visit, are some big stalactites and stalagmites. Two are massive, but one of them has fallen because of its weight (open Mar–late Oct).

The road becomes most attractive through the Goulaine Forest, then a road left climbs to **Mont St Romain**. Take the road to the tower beside a farm, where you can park. From the top of the tower is a fine panorama, with the Saône, Bresse countryside, and often the Jura mountains and Alps to be seen eastwards, the Mâconnais and Beaujolais to the south and the Charollais to the west.

Back on the D446, turn right very soon on the D187 through the Pistole Pass (Col de Pistole) to **Bissy-la-Mâconnaise**, among the vineyards. Here the scenery becomes less wild and prettier. Follow the D82 to **Lugny**, which produces some of the very best Mâcon wine. The white is outstanding. The wine cooperative (Cave de Lugny, on the D56 in the direction of Tournus) is claimed to be the biggest producers' group in Burgundy. Tastings in the special cave are free (open Mon–Sat mornings and afternoons; Sun afternoons in season; tel. 85 33 22 85).

Return on the D82 to Bissy, then turn south to **Azé**. Here you can visit caves where prehistoric man and wild animals, especially bears, once lived. The Eduen tribe later used these caves as hiding places when fighting the Romans, as did Gallo-Romans after the Roman Legions had left. The first cave is 208m long, the second 800m with an underground river, which you can walk along. The museum has more than 2000 local finds from diggings and the cave.

Take the D15 to **Péronne**, where in the 6th century Gontran, King of Burgundy, decreed that Sunday and Christian feast days should be days of rest. Gontran was one of the few civilised rulers of Burgundy among the Franks, an unsavoury lot given to murdering their parents, children, husbands, wives and in-laws, for political reasons. Péronne is now a wine village. The D103 leads to **Clessé**, a much more important wine village where the co-operative sells not only Mâcon-Clessé but wines from much of the Mâcon region. Tastings are free (open mornings and afternoons except Sun). The church has a magnificent 11th century octagonal bell tower. The D103 continues to Mâcon.

Dukes and counts never made **MÂCON** their capital, and it had no excessively rich merchants to leave a heritage of palaces, big mansions and public buildings. Mâcon has always been a people's town. The people were Protestants in the Religious Wars and they welcomed the Revolution with great enthusiasm, demolishing their cathedral of St Vincent, the great historic abbey of Cluny nearby and 11 other churches.

So Mâcon is not a lovely old town but its riverfront by the Saône is most agreeable and terrace cafés and restaurants along quai Lamartine and quai Jean-Jaurès have good river views. It is a pity that the road along these quais is the N6, but the traffic has at least lessened since the A6 and A40 were built to by-pass the town.

Mâcon's roofs of rounded tiles give it a southern look, as if it is on the outskirts of Provence. It has always been a commercial centre for the wine business of the Mâconnais, but was overshadowed by Lyon industrially and commercially and also had closer links with Lyon, through rivers, road and rail connections, than with Dijon. During the post-World War II boom, a number of Lyon enterprises expanded into Mâcon. Recently TGV fast train routes have tightened the ties with Lyon (now only 15 min away) and with Paris (only 1hr 40 min away).

Mâcon's most important annual event is still the French National Wine Fair in the last two weeks of May. It is the ambition of most French wine-makers, from Languedoc and Bergerac to the Rhône and Alsace, to stick on their bottles a gold and red label marked 'Concours des Grands Vins de France–Mâcon Médaille d'Or 1995', or even 'Médaille d'Argent' or 'Médaille de Bronze'. This means that the wine has been adjudged best in its category. The Wine Committee of Mâcon has excellent cellars for tasting and buying. Maison Mâconnaise des Vins is at No. 484 avenue de Lattre-de-Tassigny (tel. 85 38 36 70) which is the long road which goes north from quai Jean-Jaurès and is, in fact, part of the N6. You can taste a selection of wines from the region or go to the restaurant to taste regional specialities with a selection of local crus (open 07.30–21.00).

One old building which survived the Revolution because it was used as a prison was the 17th century Ursuline convent—a school for daughters of the well-off and well-connected. Now it is a **museum**. It has a room with remarkable exhibits of Burgundian prehistory including local excavations at the famous Solutré site (see below) and other rooms with relics of Celtic, Gallo-

Roman times and the Middle Ages. The paintings are interesting, the ceramics superb. A room of local artists has some interesting paintings by Gaston Bussière, who remained traditional through all the flashy changes in art fashions from the 1890s to 1920s. His sensuous Salammbô was inspired by Flaubert's novel (museum shut Tue).

Mâcon is still obsessed with a local lad born there in 1790, the poet Alphonse de Lamartine, not quite so popular in the rest of France as he was when we were students, but still regarded as second only to Victor Hugo among French Romantic poets. In Mâcon he is admired not only for his poetry but for his political career as a typical Mâconnais—an Independent Radical, totally opposed to the little dictator Napoleon III, who imagined himself to be a new Caesar. Slim, rather humourless and mournful, he was very different from the stereotype jolly, down-to-earth Burgundian, but his love of good wine and handsome young women and attachment to the hills of the Mâconnais, the villages, the houses, even 'the sweet and melancholy voices of the frogs which sing on summer evenings', have endeared him to Burgundians.

He was born in Mâcon into a family that owned several manor houses. Mâcon has a quai Lamartine, a rue Lamartine and a statue of him on the promenade. There is a **Lamartine museum** of documents and souvenirs in Hôtel Senecé, an 18th century mansion, along with period paintings, tapestries and furnishings left from the years when the house was the seat of the Arts Academy of Mâcon. The poet was its president for several years. At **Hôtel d'Ozenay**, 15 rue Lamartine, is the family house where he lived from 1805 to 1820, when he married an English artist, Anne Eliza Birch. He lived his last days in Mâcon in respectable poverty, in spite of being harried by creditors, but died in Paris.

The village homes where he and his friends lived and which appeared in his poems are worth seeing whether you are a Lamartine follower or not. The Mâcon tourist board (187 rue Carnot, tel. 85 39 71 37) will give you a key to the Pèlerinage Lamartine (Lamartine pilgrimage), which is a very good way of seeing the countryside and villages to the west of Mâcon. It is easy to understand why the poet loved them so much. He was an admirer of Wordsworth and showed the same passion for the countryside.

Lamartine's life was divided into two halves. Until he married at 30, he was seen in France as a typical romantic poet, writing beautiful, nostalgic poetry and getting involved in affairs with women of widely different backgrounds, from the daughter of a boatman on Lac du Bourget in the foothills of the Savoy and a 16-year-old tobacco factory worker in Naples to the daughter of a respected Justice of the Peace of Mâcon (an affair which caused his family to send him off to Naples) and the wife of one of his best friends, Guillaume de Pierreclos, by whom he had a son.

He wrote of them all in his poems. But his greatest romance was on Lac du Bourget, where he was sent by his doctor in 1816 to recover from a liver complaint. There he rescued from drowning a girl called Julie Charles, the wife of a Paris doctor. She was staying there to try to cure a lung complaint. He fell very deeply in love. They promised to meet the next year. He kept the promise but she died before she could return. He sat above the lake and wrote his most famous and probably his best poem, *Le Lac*. Four years later he married Anne Eliza Birch and they lived happily together until she died in 1863.

Having entered politics, Lamartine was elected in 1833 to the Assembly as Deputy for Bergues (in Nord) and then for Mâcon. He was much opposed to the reign of the Citizen King, Louis-Philippe, who had virtually stolen the crown from his young nephew, for whom he was supposed to be ruling as Regent. When Louis-Philippe had to abdicate and fled to England to live in Surbiton as Mr Smith, Lamartine became a leading spirit of the Provisional Government which proclaimed the Second Republic. His defence of the *tricolore* as the national flag made him a popular hero. Objecting strongly to the rise of Louis Napoleon, he stood against him for the presidency, but his supporters had joined the clamour for a new Napoleon and Lamartine received only 18,000 votes against 5,500,000 for Louis Napoleon (who was soon to declare himself the Emperor Napoleon III).

Disgusted, Lamartine abandoned politics, returned to Mâcon and wrote *L'Histoire des Girondins* as his contribution to the history of the Revolution. He had got into debt financing his political campaigns and by living the life of a property-owning country gentleman, so that, one by one, he had to sell the family properties, to which he had a passionate sentimental attachment. He died in 1869.

The pilgrimage route starts westward on the N79 through a suburb which is the old wine village of **Charnay-les-Mâcon**. From here, the giant wine-maker Claude Brosse set off with two hogsheads of his wine on a wagon pulled by two oxen to sell his wine to Louis XIV's court. It is a pleasant village of ochre stone houses, with views over the Pouilly-Fuissé vineyards. Brosse is buried in the village church, in a chapel housing the font. To the right, about 6.5km (4 miles) along N79, is the handsome gold-brown **Château Monceau**, left to Lamartine by an aunt. Here he liked to play the great vineyard owner and here he returned after giving up politics, to work in a pavilion among the vines called La Solitude. The château is now an old people's home, so you cannot visit it. Alas, the N79 has become a double-track Route de Vitesse, with no way off it to some minor roads. But happily the old road of N79 has been kept as a Route touristique (D279) to Berzé-le-Châtel.

The house Lamartine loved best is further along the D279 on a road left at Milly, a village set on a hill above a pretty valley which now resounds to fast road traffic and the rush of the TGV trains. The poet lived here, in an old stone house, from the age of seven. He must have been deeply unhappy when debts forced him to sell the house, ten years before he died. There he wrote the first of his *Méditations*, called *L'Isolement*. His most evocative long poem was *Milly ou la Terre Natale*.

> There my heart everywhere finds itself again!
> There everything remembers me, knows me, loves me!
> My eyes find a friend in all this horizon;
> every tree has its history and each stone a name!

You cannot go into the house, but you can see its creeper-clad two-storeyed front with deep windows, the plaque on the gate quoting lines of his poetry and the two cedars he planted when he returned from the East, which are now 175 years old. He used to like to sleep in the house from time to time to recall the sounds of long ago, of his family moving around talking, laughing—'the sounds of youth, of life, of love'. The 12th century church where his family worshipped is still there, and a bust of the poet stands at the top of the village.

The village of **Bussières** is about 1.5km south and you can either walk to it or see it on your return journey to Mâcon. Here young Lamartine was sent for lessons in Latin and French literature from the curé, Abbé Dumont, a follower of Voltaire, who became a great friend of Lamartine. He confessed to the poet that as a young priest he had had a passionate affair with the daughter of the Seigneur of nearby Pierreclos Château, and Lamartine used this as the theme of one of his great narrative poems *Jocelyn*, written after Dumont died in 1832. Near the end of Bussière church is a tomb called 'tombe de Jocelyn' on which you can read the epitaph the poet wrote for his old tutor and friend.

From Milly, cross the new main road and take the Route Touristique to Berzé-la-Ville and **Berzé-le-Châtel**, whose feudal castle once overlooked the most important barony in Mâconnais. It stands attractively on vineyard-covered slopes.

Join the N79 for a short distance until its junction with the D980, turn left, then left again on the D22 towards Tramayes. At **St Point** is the charming house rather grandly called **Château de St Point**, where Lamartine and his wife spent much of their time during their 43 years of contented marriage. This one you can visit. A small door to the left of the village church opens up into the park of the house. Château de St Point was given to Lamartine by his father as a wedding present in 1820. In the little church are two pictures by his wife. Their tombs are in a chapel nearby.

All the rooms in one wing of the house have been redecorated and laid out just as they were in his day. Mementoes include his bed, his travelling writing desk, his top hat, letters from Balzac, Victor Hugo, Châteaubriand and Alfred de Vigny, and even souvenirs of his pre-marital girlfriends, including a bust of Graziella, the young factory girl from Naples, an engraving of the boatman's daughter from Lac du Bourget and the crucifix of his beloved Julie, the doctor's wife. The saddest souvenir of all is a picture by his wife of their daughter Julia, who died at the age of 10 while the family were on a voyage to Jerusalem.

Although Lamartine had his study padded for peace and quiet, he wrote much of his *Meditations* sitting on a stone bench under a lime tree, which is still there, and he wrote *Jocelyn* under the oak tree you can see in the garden. Alongside the D22 just after St Point is a man-made lake now used for water-sports and leisure.

After Tramayes, follow the D45 swinging round to the left. The views are extensive and on the right a little steep road leads to a car park from which

The wine village of St Verand, just across the D31 from Pouilly and Fuissé

you can walk up to the highest point in the Mâconnais, **La Mère Boitier Signal Station** (758m/2487ft). A viewing table directs you to the principal features of a fine panorama. The D45 road takes you over the Col de Grand Vent and winds down on small roads to **Château de Pierreclos**, where Lamartine's friend Abbé Dumont had his love affair. The de Milly family, which owned the château, was related to the Pierreclos family of Château Cormatin (p 198). Lamartine often visited Cormatin to see his childhood friend Nina Dezoteux, wife of his friend Guillaume de Pierreclos and eventually had a child by her—which did not, however, break up her marriage.

The Lamartine trail ends at Pierreclos, but by following through the vineyards to Vergisson, you can visit the great twin wine villages of **Pouilly** and **Fuissé**. Here the superb Pouilly-Fuissé white wine is produced from Chardonnay grapes. Fuissé is the more attractive of the villages. Vines are planted in every square yard of space, narrowing the roads and encroaching to the walls of the church, the little château, and the houses with gold-brown walls and pale terracotta roofs. The one gap in the vineyards is at **Solutré**, whose great rocky escarpment you can see for miles around. To us it is a gruesome rock. For 25,000 years it was a hunting site of palaeolithic man (around 15,000–12,000 BC). Since excavation began in 1866, the bones of about 100,000 horses have been found, with reindeer, lying to a depth of 90cm (3ft) over 1ha (2 acres)—enough to have fed generations. A gentle slope leads to the clifftop. For long we were told that the terrified wild horses were driven up by loud sounds, sticks and fires, then driven over the edge to their death. It is now said that they were slaughtered below the cliff as they sheltered there during their spring and autumn migration. A nightmare scene—but no worse than keeping calves in the dark in a crate too small to move, just to make their flesh whiter and softer for the table.

When he was a prisoner-of-war in Germany, President Mitterand swore that he would climb the rock at Solutré every Whit Sunday. He did, for a number of years. But later he arrived by helicopter for a press photo-call. Who can blame him?

In the village of **Chasselas**, west of Fuissé, grapes were grown on the south-facing walls of the vignerons' houses, to be eaten as dessert grapes. One-and-a-half kilometres down the D31, Beaujolais begins.

Beaujolais wine country is bewitching—a land of hills, packed tightly together with the little valleys between, threaded with streams, with twisting narrow roads made for carts, not cars, and with villages which are mostly just hamlets with a handful of red-roofed houses and a spired church. There is no wine tour of Beaujolais. There are no main roads taking you from one wine village to another. You must try to map read, and you will probably get lost. So the best plan is not to have one, except to decide that you will find by hook or by crook two or three villages which you especially want to visit and see what turns up in between. It is pointless worrying about time—or tyres. About five years ago Arthur (who should have known better) drove his old automatic Jaguar round Beaujolais, and he will never forget it. He spent many a half-hour going backwards along narrow lanes which had become *too* narrow to continue forwards. He recommends hiring a little Renault or a 2cv.

The first village you will find making a cru wine is **St Amour-Bellevue**, whose wine is simply and charmingly called St Amour. They may tell you now that it is named after a Roman soldier called St Amateur, who founded a monastery overlooking the Somme. But we believe the original story we heard 50 years ago in the more rumbustious days of Beaujolais, when we lapped the wine by the litre with local friends in inns that Parisians disdained to enter. The name came to the village because its owners were the canons of Mâcon Cathedral who knew their duty to the community as well as they knew their duty to God. So they did not allow their holy vows to stand in the way of their droit du seigneur and fully instructed the local brides on their wedding nights. Wayward girls must have been very glad of the excuse next night. If you cannot drink the wine with the right companion on St Valentine's Day, do not miss 20 August—St Amour's Day.

Juliénas town was named for Julius Caesar, but it is fitting that the old church, now opened again as a tasting cave (Cellier de la Vieille Eglise) should be decorated with tributes to Bacchus and his followers, for not in the whole of Beaujolais, nor in Burgundy apart from Beaune, have we seen a town so enthusiastically devoted to wine. Every producer has the *dégustation et vente* sign outside, to offer you a tasting (and expect you to buy at least one bottle), hardly a shop does not offer wine and such vital equipment as corkscrews for sale, and the leading local restaurant is not only called *Coq au Vin* but offers its own special version of *coq au Juliénas*. Every old local building, even the 17th century priory, has been pressed into the service of wines.

Clochemerle

Gabriel Chevallier wrote of the people of Beaujolais that they offer their hearts in the palm of one hand '—the hand that does not hold a glass'. Chevallier was a journalist who lived in the little town west of Mâcon, La Clayette, known for horse-racing, making cranes, and for its magnificent riverside '14th century' castle which was, in fact, built in the 19th century. But he spent his holidays in a Beaujolais wine village south-west of Odenas called Vaux-en-Beaujolais. There he noticed that the local people not only consumed a great deal of their own product in their inn but openly and freely relieved themselves of it in public.

Chevallier wrote a joyous book about *Clochemerle*, a fictional village in which the Communist mayor decides that in the name of progress Clochemerle must have a *pissotière*—a urinal—and to annoy his rival, the village priest, he places it in the alley leading up to the church. If you have read Clochemerle, you will know what rumbustious, rollicking, bed-romping, sinful scenes result from this simple attempt to clean up the village. If you have not read it, we do suggest that you hurry to buy a copy. It is superb satire. It has been translated into English, and just about every other language in the world.

The book has made Vaux-en-Beaujolais the most visited village in Beaujolais and Vaux has truly cashed in. It has opened a tasting cave—in fact, this was opened by Chevallier. Its Beaujolais-Villages wine is now called Cave de Clochemerle and the local inn, *Auberge de Clochemerle*. And, of course, the village has built a fine new *pissotière*. Vaux also has a brotherhood called Compagnons du Gosier Sec, or Fellowship of the Parched Throat.

Several places have claimed to be Clochemerle. La Clayette certainly produced some of the characters. But on 20 November 1956, Gabriel Chevallier was asked to open Vaux's wine-tasting caveau. He confirmed that he used to go there on holiday and gave Vaux the right to be Clochemerle.

As a wine critic, he was as down-to-earth as any man of Beaujolais. Of Beaujolais he said 'The more you drink of it, the more delightful you find your wife, the more loyal your friends, the rosier your future and the more bearable the human race'.

Chénas's restaurant, *Daniel Robin*, at Les Deschamps, is run by the wine producer among his vines (tel. 85 36 72 67). The 300-year-old windmill on the hillside between Chénas and Romanèche-Thorins is vaneless and still, but the wine named after it, Moulin-à-Vent, the oldest cru in Beaujolais, remains strong and dark as a Burgundy and it is fitting that there should be tasting cellars on either side of the road to give you strength to climb the path to it for a marvellous panoramic view of vineyards.

All Beaujolais owed a debt last century to a **Romanèche-Thorins** vigneron, Benoît Raclet. In 1830 it seemed that every vine had the pyralid moth blight. Vineyards were devastated. Then Raclet spotted a vine that was still healthy. It grew against the wall of his kitchen where the maid threw out the dirty water. Raclet watered his vines with boiling water and they were cured. Not even his friends took him seriously for 12 years. Finally they realised that he was right and *échaudage* (scalding) became common practice until 1945, when pesticides took over. In Raclet's house in the village is a little **museum** of implements used for this scalding operation, including clothes boilers and even coffee percolators. The fête of new wine in Romanèche is called after him.

Apart from Georges Duboeuf's large and famous winery (see Chapter 3), the little town has a 1-star Michelin restaurant by the station—*Maritonnes* (tel. 85 35 51 70), which has a rather posh version of *coq au vin* called *poulet fermier façon coq au vin*.

Eastward by the N6 and D466E towards St Romain-des-Iles is a 10 ha zoo called **Parc Zoologique Touroparc**, used for breeding rarer birds and animals which (apart from the Big Cats!) wander at liberty. For visitors it has an adventure playground, aerial monorail and picnic area with snack bar.

To the west, the vineyards of **Fleurie** are on a long hill topped by the Chapel of the Madonna, built in 1875 to protect the vines. At the south entrance to the pretty village is the cave cooperative, started in 1927, one of the oldest in Beaujolais. For a small sum you can taste wines there. This was the cooperative run for years by Marguerite Chabert, Queen of Beaujolais. In the village church square, the *Auberge du Cep* still proudly serves the farm chicken cooked in Fleurie wine, as it did in the old days of Gérard Cortembert. Neither modern food fads nor 2 Michelin stars will go to the head of a real Beaujolais village inn. But the other tradition of Fleurie, serving *andouillette* with its charming, seductive wine, pleases us less. You take the sausage, we'll take the wine. Fleurie holds an important International Market of Wines of Beaujolais and Burgundy South on the Sunday after All Saints' Day (1 November).

Southward through the mountains is **Chiroubles**, where there is a statue in the village square of a man to whom all Europe's wine-growers owe a debt, Victor Pulliat (1829–96). When the dread phylloxera had destroyed most of the vines in 1880, Pulliat, a vine scientist, made researches which led to the cure by grafting French slips on to American rootstocks. He planted the first of these hybrids. His statue stands opposite the church and a curious 17th century clock tower. In the Maison des Vignerons you are invited to taste La Tassée de l'Amitié—the cup of friendship.

Planting on the rocky hillside is a tough job. The vignerons have to make individual holes in the granite to plant each vine.

Beside the nearby D26 from Beaujeu in this captivating Beaujolais hill country is **Terrasse des Chiroubles**, 427m (1400ft) high with a magnificent view claimed by locals to be one of the best in France. To help you enjoy it, they have a chalet on top, where you can taste their wine. It is open every afternoon.

After Easter, Chiroubles holds a Fête des Crus—a wine festival at which the Victor Pulliat cup is given to the Beaujolais judged best by a jury of négociants and vignerons.

Locally Morgon wine is said to be 'like granite'. It is more like a Burgundy than a Beaujolais and is best aged for four or five years. But **Villié-Morgon** is one of the most interesting of the Beaujolais villages and a good place to stay if you can get into the pleasant inn, the *Villon* (tel. 74 69 16 16—restaurant shut on Sunday evenings). The tasting caveau is in the Louis XVII château, set in a pretty public park, where there is a zoo (mostly deer) and a display of wine-making tools. A restaurant, *Relais des Caveaux* (tel. 74 04 21 77), is opposite.

The newest Beaujolais cru appellation is Regnié, based on the village of **Regnié-Durette** between Morgon and Brouilly. The village is known for its ambitious 19th century church with two towers and for the Domaine de la Grange Charton, built for Hospice de Beaujeu in 1820, with its classic first floor vignerons' houses reached by typical outside staircases entwined with vines. Its huge *cuvages* can store all the Regnié wine. Vines border the D37 road beside the river to Beaujeu. South of the road, which joins Beaujeu to Belleville-sur-Saône, is the Brouilly wine country, below **Mont Brouilly**, which is capped by a little chapel built in 1857, **Notre Dame du Raisin**, from which are good views over the Saône and the countryside south to Lyon. Each year, Les Amis de Brouilly meet there to pay proper homage to the wine, which means trying to outdrink each other!

Odenas is the biggest village producing Brouilly and Côtes de Brouilly wine. From the village of St Lager on the east side of the mountain a Route des Vins includes a few wine-producing châteaux. The most important, west of Odenas, is the 17th century **Château de la Chaize**, built by the brother of François de la Chaize, Confessor to Louis XIV and the man after which the famous Paris Père Lachaise cemetery was named. If he had broken his vow of confidentiality, he could surely have written one of the bestsellers of all time. The château was designed by Mansart, the huge gardens by Le Nôtre. The château's vaulted wine cellar is the biggest in Burgundy.

Beaujeu is a quiet, most agreeable little town built along the Ardières valley, overlooked by steep hillsides covered in vineyards. Its little shops and tall houses are shuttered much of the day. It has the sleepy, relaxed air of a village in Provence. Beaujolais, the French say, is the start of the south, and Beaujeu was the old capital of Beaujolais. Its Sires owned a large area between Lyon and Mâcon and it acted as a buffer when the two were fighting each other. It held a commanding position on the trade route between the Rhône and the Loire. The Hospice de Beaujeu still holds its wine sales, as it did in the 12th century.

The dukes of Burgundy owned Beaujeu in the 14th century and one of them, Pierre de Bourbon, married the daughter of Louis XI, known as Anne of

Stained glass panel in the cellars of the Château de Foucrenne, Villié-Morgon

Beaujeu. Ironically it was she who took away Beaujeu's title as Capital of Beaujolais in favour of Villefranche. The last Sire of Beaujolais was the Duke of Orléans, who joined the French Revolution and called himself Philippe Egalité (Philip Equality)—but he was still guillotined by Robespierre. His son became King Louis-Philippe, friend of Queen Victoria.

Beaujeu inevitably lives by selling wine, but it is known, too, for its unusual **Museum Marius-Audin** in the town hall. Marius-Audin, a publisher who died in 1951, left to the town his superb collection of dolls, dolls' houses, dolls' furniture and household goods and chattels of the 19th century, with dolls in costumes from different areas of France and Italy. Another section of the museum shows the inside of a peasant's house in the 19th century, and old tools of various trades from shoe-making to wine-making. (Museum open Easter to 1 Nov, afternoons only, all day Sun; rest of year open Sun only.)

Below is a cave, the Temple of Bacchus, where you can taste Beaujolais Villages wines. In December, Beaujolais wines are sold for the hospice. Opposite the 12th century church is the 15th century Maison du Pays de Beaujolais, a lovely wooden building where you can sample wine, honey, cheese and other local products.

Paris. He was staying in Room 215, as he had done for 22 years, when he heard that he had become President of France. But motorists have a good choice of places to stay in towns on the edge of the Morvan—Vézelay, Avallon, Saulieu, Autun, St Honoré-les-Bains. We suggest a number of routes using fairly easy roads. You can explore further by using tiny roads—but not after heavy rainfall!

From Vézelay and St Père, you enter the Morvan along the D958, past the old Roman baths of **Fontaines Salées**, through the wooded gorge of the river Cure valley, to **Pierre-Perthuis**, a village in a lovely spot where the river hurries over rocks through a narrow gorge. Below you is a little 18th century humpback bridge, while from the village a modern single-span bridge of 33m crosses the gorge. On the east bank you can see the **Roche Percée**, a rock forming a natural arch. Turn off the D958 further down, taking the D453 near to Malassis dam, and wind your way round an attractive route overlooking the Cure river, which you cross at St André-en-Morvan. Beyond the little village of Ouches, turn right onto the D944 (a main road from Avallon). As you recross the Cure on a viaduct, you can see to your right the impressive **Château of Chastellux**, on top of a hill above the river, clinging to the rocky slope, its towers in profile against the sky. Claude de Beauvoir, Baron of Chastellux, born here in 1386, was the man who won the Battle of Cravant in 1423, winning also the right for himself and his descendants to attend service at Auxerre Cathedral in full armour, with falcons on their wrists (see Auxerre, p 125). The château has been in the Chastellux family for 1000 years. Alas, it is not open to the public.

Just downstream from where the Cure meets the Chalaux, the Cure is dammed. Crescent dam is 37m high, 329m long and is used not only to generate electricity but, via the Yonne river, to help control the flow of the Seine.

The D944 is an attractive road almost as far as **Lormes**, a charming place in lovely hilly countryside, crossed by many small rivers and lakes. It has fine views and delightful roads leading to Lac des Settons and the dams and lakes of Chaumeçon, Pannesière-Chaumard and Le Crescent. There is good fishing, canoeing, bathing, walking and horse-riding around here.

One-and-a-half kilometres north-west is **Mont de la Justice**, 366m high, with a superb panorama. It is beside the D42, and a path leads to the viewing table at the top. On fine days you can see Vézelay to the north, and across the Yonne depression west, all the way to the hill of Montenoison. South-west you can see to the Bazois and south-east as far as the mountain ski resort of Haut-Folin in the Morvan.

Lormes has a 2-star, 2-chimney logis, the *Perreau* (tel. 86 22 53 21), with 14 bedrooms and good value menus. It is essential to book well ahead for summer. At **Vauclaix**, 8km (5 miles) south, is a similar logis—*Poste* (tel. 86 22 71 38), with 18 rooms. Camping de l'Etang-du-Goulot (tel. 86 20 80 60) has been recommended.

Now continue along the D944, which becomes very pleasant, until you reach a little road left which takes you across the top of the **Pannesière-**

Chaumard dam, only 9.5km (6 miles) from Château Chinon. From here you have an excellent view of the dam, which is 340m long, 50m high. It controls the flow of water in the Seine basin. Its hydro-electric power station produces 18,000,000 kW annually. Its reservoir, which is 8km long, is a beautiful lake among the wooded hills of Morvan. You can drive all the way round it, with many lovely views. The lake is superb for fishing; trout, pike and *sandre* abound. At Chaumard on the east side, *Les Vouas* restaurant serves fresh fish and home-produced meat.

The most attractive near-direct route from the top of the dam to Château Chinon is to return to the D944, turn left, then left again following the little D161 alongside the west edge of the lake until it crosses the tip of the lake onto the D12. This passes Corancy before joining the D37 into Château Chinon.

Château Chinon is not much better off than Lormes for accommodation— a pity, for it is one of the best bases for exploring the Morvan Park. Through history, the rocky hill above it has been an important strategic site. The Gauls and Romans fortified it and there are traces of a medieval fortress. Now there is a simple cross and orientation table, and pleasant walks start here. You can drive along the side of the hill on a road that circles the town, giving rewarding glimpses of the countryside and gorges of the infant Yonne, but the view from the Calvary is best. To the east is the Yonne valley; westward you can occasionally see to the Loire valley (but don't expect too much from a town where it rains 180 days in the year) and to the south-east are Mount Preneley, 853m high, and Haut-Folin, 900m high with a cross-country ski resort and a ski-lift along a forest road reached from the D500 or D179.

In Château Chinon are two unusual museums. The **Musée du Costume** in a fine old house in rue du Château has a most interesting collection of 17th–20th century regional costumes, a cottage-weaver's workshop and souvenirs of Napoleon III, including his two-cornered hat (like Napoleon I's), and the Empress Eugénie's sleigh. **Septennot Museum** in the same road shows gifts given to François Mitterand during his days as president. The town holds a lively Fête of the Morvan and fair on 15 August. A November Fair was attended in the old days by farmers seeking a job in logging to keep their families during the winter.

Our route to Saulieu or Avallon begins by taking the D944 north from Château Chinon, then turning right onto the D37, a winding and zigzagging road which is well worth the driving effort. Just past the village of Planchez, take a small road right which crosses the Cure river on a bridge, then follows the southern shore of **Lac des Settons** reservoir. The lake covers 359 ha in the valley of the river Cure, 573m up in one of the wildest parts of the Morvan, surrounded by oaks, beeches and birch trees. Its beauty, its superb fishing and its watersports have attracted more and more visitors in summer in recent years. The granite dam was built in 1861 to release water to float logs down the river but is now used to regulate the flow of the Yonne, into which the Cure flows.

There are roads and paths all the way round the lake. At the end of the southern shore, turn left onto the better-surfaced D193, which climbs to give

Lac des Settons reservoir is a good place for fishing and watersports

you attractive views of the lake and its wooded islands, until you reach the charming little resort of **Les Settons**. Here are two small hotels, both open from around 1 April to early November—*Morvandelle* (tel. 86 84 50 62) and *Grillons* (tel. 86 84 51 43). Two nautical bases offer sailing, sail-boarding, kayak canoeing, horse-riding and tennis: Les Brantlasses (tel. 86 84 51 98, open Easter–October, also offers water-skiing) and Base Baye (tel. 86 84 51 98).

From near the dam, you can take a pleasant half-hour boat trip aboard the boat *Lac des Settons* (tel. 86 84 51 97) or the *Morvan* (tel. M. Bosset, 86 84 51 99).

Shortly after the dam, the road turns right away from the lake to **Montsauche**, another little resort village, rebuilt after destruction by the Germans in June 1944 to discourage the famous Morvan Resistance. The village is 650m up, with the river Cure running below it, and is only 5km (3 miles) from the lake. It has a campsite (tel. 86 84 51 97) and the *Hôtel Idéal* (tel. 86 84 51 26) on route des Settons.

Leave the village by the D977bis, which drops steeply into the valley of the Cure and crosses the river just before Goulox. On the first bend after crossing the Cure bridge you can leave your car and take a path down to the right which leads you in 8–10 min to the meeting of the Cure and the Caillot rivers, which combine to flow over an attractive waterfall called **Saut de Gouloux** (Gouloux's Leap). In Gouloux village is one of the few surviving sabotiers (clog-makers), Alan Marchand, Mayor of Gouloux for nearly 50 years and old friend of Mitterand. Back on the road you drive through the forest of Breuil-Chenue and then country dotted with pools and woods to reach Saulieu (see p 148).

For the Avallon route, take the D236 north from Montsauche to **Dun-les-Places**. Taking a path leading to the campsite you can walk up to a calvary at 590m which gives good views of the Morvan heights. On 26 June 1944, Germans set fire to Dun and shot 27 Frenchmen in revenge for local resistance. The Romanesque church is not 11th century but was built at vast expense in 1851 by a retired pirate, Xavier Feuillet, to buy peace for his soul. His body lies in the church.

A little scenic road to the north from Dun takes you to the hamlet of Vieux Dun, where a forest track to the right after crossing the river bridge leads to a parking site, from which a path leads up to the summit of Rocher de la Pérouse. Don't attempt this climbing walk unless you are fit. It rises very steeply by 200m. From the top, we are assured, there are fascinating views of this isolated countryside above the Cure valley, with rounded hilltops. From the car park, follow the forest road to join the D10, turning left to reach the mysterious little town with the sombre sounding name of **Quarré-les-Tombes**, which, on a day of dark clouds threatening thunder, seemed to us to fit this attractive but wild part of the Morvan.

The name refers to the 112 limestone coffins or covers (sarcophagi) found near the church and the remains of around 1000 more. They are from the 6th–8th century, Merovingian period, but no one knows why or how they got there. Theories range from the unlikely, such as that pilgrims came to die under the protection of some long-forgotten saint, to the highly improbable theory that after Christians had been slaughtered by invading Norsemen or Saracens, the stone coffins fell from heaven to give them a decent Christian burial. The locals may have been undertakers, of course. St George is now the patron of the church, hardly a long-forgotten saint.

Quarré was a great wartime Resistance centre, where the RAF dropped arms and radio transmitters, and there are many memorials to the men and women who died. By the river Cure bridge is a memorial to 2000 Resistance fighters from the savage battles of 1944. Summer visitors use Quarré and nearby villages as centres from which to explore this land of lakes and forests, and there are a number of pleasant hotels and restaurants which provide for them well. *Hôtel Nord et Poste* in Quarré (tel. 86 32 24 55) has a widespread reputation for Morvandelle and Burgundian cooking. In a rather remote spot, Les Lavaults, 5km (3 miles) south-east along the D10, is a renowned restaurant, *Auberge de l'Atre* (tel. 86 32 20 79), where true local dishes are made with local ingredients—trout, *sandre* (a delicate river fish), beef, mushrooms, wild herbs. At Les Brizzards, south-east, is *Auberge de Brizzards* (tel. 86 32 20 12) in a park with its own little lake and flower garden. The place to buy cheese is from the monks of the Pierre-qui-Vire community, 9.5km (6 miles) east of Quarré in the depths of the St Léger forest (see box, p 218).

St Léger-Vauban, 5km (3 miles) north-east of Quarré, was renamed for the military-engineering genius who was born there in 1633—Sebastian Le Prestre, Marquis de Vauban. A museum, **La Maison de Vauban**, includes a 20 minute audio-visual presentation of his life and work (open mid June–mid-September).

The village **church** is most unusual. Built in the 15th century, it was altered last century and decorated quite recently by the sculptor-architect Marc Hénard, who lived at St Léger for a while. He carved the panels of the doorway and in 1973 designed the attractive blue and pink ceramic tiles around the altar.

From Quarré follow the D10 to Marrault, then drive through wooded country to the D944, which takes you to the Cousin valley and Avallon.

South from Chateau Chinon you climb into some of the most spectacular scenery of Le Haut Morvan (the Upper Morvan). The D27 is a good road to take from the capital, climbing through woods until you reach the St Prix Forest by turning left onto the D197, then taking a very steep forest track to the right. This is one of the routes to Haut-Folin, at 900m (2956ft) the highest peak in the Morvan. Here the French Alpine Club has developed skiing. You can reach the ski-lift here more easily from Arleuf (to the north) by taking the D500, but our route is much more beautiful. Continue along the forest road to La Croisette, where you pick up the D179, which takes you to **Gorges de la Canche**, a very scenic valley whose steep sides are covered with lime trees, sycamores and wych elms. Waterfalls tumble down between brown, green and mauve rocks. The white building at the top is inevitably a hydro-electric power station. You reach the D978 about half-way between Château Chinon

Pierre-qui-Vire

The time to visit this spot in the depths of St Léger Forest 9.5km (6 miles) east of Quarré-les-Tombes is Christmas Eve. Then, we are told, the huge rock of granite, the Rocking Stone (Pierre-qui-Vire), rotates unaided. Midwinter weather is rugged in this remote spot and although you are invited to join the monks in their chapel service, theirs is a closed order, cut off from the world. So not many see the revolving stone. You can rock the stone by hand if you are strong enough, but it is rather mystifying that this Druidic monument should choose Christmas Eve to gyrate.

It seems that Father Muard, returned from foreign missions, was told in 1839 by God 'Je veux que vous soyez saint' (I want you to become a saint). So, with the help of the powerful de Beauvoir family from Château de Chastellux, he founded an abbey beside the river Cousin (called here the Trinquelin) in one of the loneliest spots in the Morvan. There are about 100 monks and both men and women come here on retreat. A particularly large number of people sought refuge in World War II—mainly Resistance fighters on the run. One day the Gestapo burst into the refectory, but the reception from the monks was so icy that they left.

You cannot look around, either, but at the entrance is an exhibition and an audio-visual presentation of the life and work of the monks. They *do* work, as well as attending four services a day and five on Sundays.

They research art and architecture, and print and publish the delightful Zodiac books on these subjects. They also work on their farm and sell a lovely cream cheese made from cows' milk and either eaten fresh or matured on straw, when it is strong in taste and smell. A version with herbs is called Boulette de la Pierre-qui-Vire or Boules des Moines (Balls of the Monks).

Mass is at 09.15 weekdays, 10.00 Sundays. The exhibition is shut in January.

and **AUTUN**, a pleasant, historic town which many people use as a base for discovering Morvan.

It is difficult to believe that this little town, dozing among hills under its beautiful cathedral only 20km (12½ miles) from the Morvan Forest, could have once been called 'sister and rival of Rome', or that until 1957 it produced so much oil from shale that it exported to the United States.

A Gaulish tribe called the Aedui had a capital, Bibracte, on Mont Beuvray, south of what is now Château Chinon. They rebelled against the Romans. To control them and to assert Roman authority in the whole area of Gaul,

Augustus Caesar decided to build a real Roman city to the east. He called it Augustodunum and it became a great centre of Roman law and civilisation, with 100,000 people, 12,000 of them students. It boasted that it was the Rome of the Western Roman Empire. Agrippa's Way, the road from Lyon to Boulogne, ran through it. It flourished in education and commerce, but as Rome's power lessened under attacks from Northern tribes, it was inevitable that Augustodunum would come under attack from 'barbarians' seeking loot. It never recovered from being sacked in AD 270.

Little is left of Autun's days of Roman glory. **Porte-St-André**, with two tall arches for vehicles and two smaller arches for pedestrians, is topped by a gallery of ten arches. Its guardroom alongside was saved by its conversion into a church in the Middle Ages. The gate was restored last century by Viollet-le-Duc. **Senonica Gate** (now Porte Arroux), the entrance from Agrippa's Way, is better preserved. The decorations on the gallery at the top were copied by the architects of Cluny Abbey and then used extensively in Burgundy. The gate was built in the time of the Emperor Constantine. The **Roman theatre** at the eastern end of the town under the medieval ramparts has been extensively restored. It held 15,000 people and is used for summer festivals.

An accident of birth made Autun prosperous again in the 15th century. In 1376 Nicolas Rolin was born there. As Chancellor to the dukes of Burgundy, he became enormously powerful and rich by dubious means, and built the hospice at Beaune to try to buy his way into paradise (see Beaune, p 177). Then his son, Cardinal Rolin, became Bishop of Autun and made it a great religious centre. It already had a famous cathedral, **St Lazare**, with sculptures so superb that they are regarded as some of the finest in Europe.

In 1079 Gérard de Roussillon brought the bones of St Lazarus from Marseille and gave them to the church of St Nazaire in Autun. No one did anything with them, then in 1120 Bishop Stephen of Bagé began to build a new church alongside the old one to house them. The two churches took it in turns to be the cathedral—six months each. St Lazare eventually took over, probably because alms-giving pilgrims made it rich, and St Nazaire was demolished in 1783.

Unlike most church sculptors of the Middle Ages, the sculptor of St Lazare left his name on his work. He was Gislebertus from Rome and he worked, too, on the great church at Vézelay. He is sometimes called Gilbertis France. His masterpiece at St Lazare is the tympanum over the west door, which is of the Last Judgement and one that must have frightened even the toughest medieval peasant into praying for redemption. The evil grimace of Satan trying to cheat St Michael out of a soul, the fiend pushing terror-struck sinners into the flames of hell, the prostitute being devoured by serpents, the talons seizing the head of a man—it is all worthy of a horror film. But it is magnificent. Beneath the feet of Christ in Majesty is the inscription 'Gislebertus hoc fecit' (Gislebertus made this).

The capitals inside, too, show imaginative scenes from the Bible and history. Some are funny. You need to get a plan at the church to follow them. In one Joseph sleeps through the Nativity, in another Simon the Sorcerer tries to fly up to Heaven, key in hand, but, to St Peter's obvious delight, is next seen plunging to earth looking very scared, as one would be without a parachute.

The wonderful tympanum sculptures were saved from mutilation or destruction by the lack of taste of the cathedral's hierarchy. In 1766 the canons decided that Gislebertus's work was barbarous and crude and covered the tympanum with plaster. Because Christ's head stuck out they chopped it off with a chisel. The plaster was taken off in 1837. In 1948, someone noticed that a fine head of Christ in the Rolin Museum was the one missing from the doorway, so it was replaced.

The cathedral canons of 1766 also covered the apse and choir with marble, which was not removed until 1939, and broke up the big medieval tomb of Lazarus. His bones are now in a casket under the altar. On the left as you enter the nave is a painting by Ingres of the martyrdom of St Symphorien at the gate of St André.

From the outside, the cathedral has lost some of its Romanesque character. The belfry and spire fell down in the 15th century when hit by lightning and Cardinal Rolin replaced them with an 80m-high belfry in Flamboyant Gothic style. Climb the 230 steps to the top for views over the rooftops to the outline of the Morvan hills. The two large white slagheaps that you can see are from the schist mines, which produced shale oil.

The two towers over the main doorway were added by Viollet-le-Duc when he restored the cathedral last century. He could rarely resist adding *something* to old buildings, but we do owe him a lot for his restorations of Amiens Cathedral and Notre Dame in Paris.

Rolin Museum is in a wing of Nicolas Rolin's 15th century mansion and a 19th century house next door. It contains Gallo-Roman exhibits, including good mosaics, and Romanesque statuary, including a superb statue of Eve by Gislebertus, saved from St Lazarus's tomb, and showing Eve in her true colours as a slim, nude girl lying among the trees and bushes, plucking the apples nonchalantly. It was rediscovered in 1866, built into a wall, Alas, the other half showing Adam is missing.

On the upper floors are paintings of interest, mostly 19th century French, including one of Anne Boleyn in the Tower by Cibot (museum closed Tuesdays).

A Son-et-Lumière is held at the cathedral daily except Sunday, Monday in July, August, September; Friday and Saturday only mid-May–mid-June.

An attractive and in places spectacular route from Autun takes you to Mont Beuvray and through the south hills of Morvan to the increasingly popular spa of St Honoré-les-Bains, just outside Morvan Regional Park.

Take the little winding, tree-lined D256 south from Autun past **La Croix de Libération**, where it is worth stopping to stand by the great granite cross to look down on the town. The first stone of this memorial was laid to mark the end of German occupation on 9 September 1945, by Mgr Piguet, bishop of Clermont Ferrand, who had survived imprisonment in Dachau concentration camp.

Drive on to Mesvres, turn right on the D61 to Etang-sur-Arroux and across the N81 along the attractive winding stretch of D61 to St Léger-sous-Beuvray. Now turn left along the D3 to follow the one-way road D274 with very steep gradients to the top of **Mont Beuvray**. A path winds through a beech wood to the very top. Here was once the fortified camp of the Gauls, **Bibracte**—a place to which their farmers and families could flee in time of danger. It was here that the great leader of all the Gaullist tribes, Vercingetorix, called a meeting in 52 BC to organise resistance to the occupying Roman legions of Julius Caesar. After the Gauls' defeat at Alésia (see p 152), Caesar went twice to see what was happening at Bibracte. But Augustus Caesar, a wiser man, built Augustodunum down on the plains—a far more pleasant place for the Gauls. We call it Autun.

Virtually nothing remains of Bibracte, although the old ramparts can be traced. In the woodlands, naturalists have put up information boards telling us what birds, creatures and plants we might find here. We were told that from the old beech trees at the top it is possible some days to see as far as the Jura mountains or even Mont Blanc. We have not had such luck with Morvan weather.

Near the road is a mysterious little chapel dedicated to St Martin, the patron saint of travellers until St Christopher took over. The chapel was built in 1876.

You must follow the one-way D274 nearly all the way round Mont Beuvray to pick up our route, the D18 westward to the hamlet of St Puits. Then turn left down the D27 to **Larochemillay**, where an 18th century château stands on a rock overseeing the village and the Roche valley. This is a lovely route—well worth the effort of driving.

Follow the D192 westward to join the D227 to Sanglier, then left on the D299, which passes by the foot of Mont Genièvre. At Niret, turn left down the small D502, taking its left fork to Vieille Montagne. You can park and walk up a path to a belvedere, from which there are extensive views of the hills. The walk takes 30–45 min return. Continue on D502 to Les Montarons, from where the D985 wriggles round to **St Honoré-les-Bains**.

The Romans originally discovered the helpful properties of the sulphurous, radioactive waters of this spa. Unlike most spas, however, it has become increasingly popular recently. The French, of course, believe in spas and regard them as centres for the serious treatment of genuine health problems, and not just fashionable places to laze, swim, be massaged and lose money gambling. The Etablissement Thermal at St Honoré is open 1 Apr–Sep (tel. 86 30 73 27) and its waters are used to treat asthma and bronchitis. It has a casino and sports facilities. A casino seems to be an essential part of the treatment at every spa. We were delighted to see a genuine, classic *Hôtel Bristol* (tel. 86 30 71 12) in St Honoré. No traveller has been honoured for so long as the gourmandising, comfort-loving old Bishop who sent his servant ahead to check that his next stopover hotel was up to his standards. We have had tens of thousands of letters over the years thanking us for recommending hotels—but no one has renamed an establishment Hôtel d'Eperon.

Sixteen kilometres (10 miles) south-west of St Honoré is the little port of

Colette's Country

La Puisaye, the country of woodlands, ponds, marshes and meadows west of Auxerre, is a poor land by Burgundian standards, with few people and fewer visitors. It has been saved in recent years only by the pottery industry. Even the great novelist Colette, who was born there and loved it, wrote honestly of 'a rather sad landscape that casts a shadow over the forests, a quiet but poor village, a watery valley'.

It has always been a land of legend, of stories of ghosts and were-wolves, and a place where the persecuted and law-breakers have run for shelter and safety. Only St Fargeau lures the visitors to its historic château and especially its summer Son-et-Lumière, when 600 actors, 50 horses, dancers, musicians and troubadours contribute to a show which Colette, a musical hall performer as well as a writer, would surely have loved.

Colette was born in the big village of St Sauveur-en-Puisaye in 1873, went to school there and lived there until she was grown up. Her strange life took her to many places, from a fine but lonely castle in the Corrèze to seedy theatre dressing rooms, but her two best-loved novels were set in Puisaye. Her father was an invalided army captain and her sympathetic, country-wise mother was the Sido of the novel of that name. *La Maison de Claudine* (1900) has some fine descriptions of life in a village of La Puisaye and, above all, of the countryside. The house in rue de l'Hospice (now rue Colette) is still there, with a plaque marking her birthplace reading 'Colette est née ici', but it is a private house and you cannot visit it. The whole French nation has been raised on her *Claudine* series of novels and she has a firm place in French literature. In Britain and the US, *Cheri* and *Gigi*, her stories of love, jealousy and sex with a background of music hall life, are better known. The film musical of *Gigi* was a world success, even with people who had never heard of Colette.

Her own story was almost too unbelievable for a novel. As a young, shy country woman, a bit overwhelmed by the literary life of Paris, she allowed her blustering hack-writer of a first husband Henri Gauthier-Villars to have her early novels published under his pen-name of 'Willy' and to take all the plaudits for their success—and to spend the money. For a short time he was regarded as something of a genius for showing such a delicate and acute understanding of a young girl's mind and secret thoughts.

Colette died in 1954. Her home village is creating a Colette museum in the village château.

St Fargeau is reminded of its history by its old château—very impressive, with massive towers over the gateway and solid ones at the corners. It would look forbidding but for the rose-coloured brick from which it was built and the water-filled moat and greenery. Another side of the château opens onto an English-style park of lawns and great trees, where its towers are reflected in a lake fed by a river. The park covers 118ha and includes a horse museum.

Most of the great touches were added to the château by La Grande Mademoiselle, Duchess of Montpensier, daughter of Gaston d'Orléans and first cousin of Louis XIV. She was exiled for five years to St Fargeau for leading a Fronde rebel army against Louis' troops and firing a cannon at the Bastille. Arriving at the château, she found that it had no windows or doors and its courtyard was knee-deep in grass. She began to cry—but soon recovered and had the château completely repaired and modernised. Then she held great parties with theatre and music. Among her guests were Vicomte de Turenne, commander-in-chief of the French Army, the Prince of Condé, Gaston Duc d'Orléans (her father), Madame de Sévigné and the amusing Roger de Bussy-Rabutin, also exiled to Burgundy. Later she was exiled to St Fargeau again for refusing to marry the King of Portugal—sensible of her, for he turned out to be impotent and insane.

The château now belongs to the family of the writer Jean d'Ormeson, who made it a setting for his novel *Au Plaisir de Dieu*, televised here. It is open daily, early April to November. The Son-et-Lumière is shown Wednesday and Saturday in July and August (book at château, tel. 86 74 05 67).

The château farm (274m) shows farm life at the beginning of the 20th century, when Colette started to write about this area.

Cercy-la-Tour on the Canal du Nivernais. Once an important pick-up port for barges on the great network of Burgundy's inland waterways, which were so essential to its trade, it is quite lively in summer now that the canal has become so popular for pleasure cruising.

Pleasure Trips Along the Canals

There are about 120km (750 miles) of rivers and canals in Burgundy, now almost deserted of commercial traffic but very attractive for pleasure boating. During the 17th–19th centuries a vast network of canals was built in Burgundy to link up France's three main rivers, the Seine, Loire and Rhône and the navigable Saône, Yonne and Seille. The barge traffic was of great importance until 50 years ago but is gradually dying, leaving most of the waterways havens of peace.

The **Canal du Nivernais**, which flows through some of the most isolated and rugged countryside of the Morvan, with the occasional red- and brown-

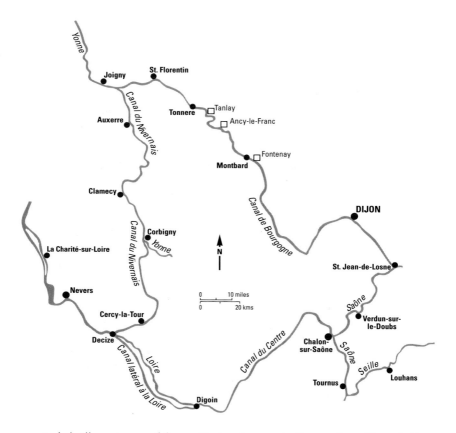

roofed village, is one of the prettiest waterways in France. From Cercy-la-Tour up to Sardy northward it is too narrow for most modern commercial barges, so it has long been dedicated to pleasure boating. Just below Cercy, at Decize, the canal runs into the Canal Latéral à la Loire, and that joins two more canals—Canal de Roanne and the important Canal du Centre.

Decize is a delightful town built on a rocky island of the Loire where it is joined by the Aron river. The high rock at Decize was once the site of a château of the counts of Nevers. The interesting 11th century church was built on a crypt of the 7th century chapel dedicated to St Aré, Bishop of Nevers, who asked that when he died his body should be put in a boat which should be pushed into the Loire. It grounded at Decize.

You can hire boats from several companies in Decize, including Crown Blue Line (Bassin de la Jonction, 58300 Decize; tel. 86 25 46 64). Hirers at Cercy-la-Tour are Croisières du Saussois (Levée du Canal, 58340 Cercy-la-Tour; tel. 85 76 00 77).

The **Nivernais Canal** begins in the north below Auxerre, from which the gentle Yonne river runs to join it. Through Clamecy and Corbigny the canal runs alongside the more winding river, then by means of some clever locks at Sardy and tunnels at La Colancelle, reaches the lakes of Vaux and Baye, which are its highest point. Vaux lake, surrounded by woods, is popular with fishermen and Baye is for sailors and windsurfers. Then the canal descends gently to the Loire valley.

The **Canal Latéral à la Loire** is an attractive and easy canal for people who don't want the bother of too many locks. East of Decize it crosses the town of Digoin, which is at the junction of several valleys, by a canal bridge which joins the Loire to the Canal du Centre. Mostly, it runs through countryside dotted with farming villages, although it does pass alongside Nevers. It is, in fact, the Loire river itself canalised and after Nevers forms the boundary between Burgundy and Cher, passing through the vineyards of Pouilly-sur-Loire (where they make Pouilly-Fumé) on the right bank and Sancerre on the left—a particularly pleasant stretch.

La Charité-sur-Loire, once an important port, is a pleasant town. It was originally called Seyr, but in the 11th century the monks of the local abbey got such a reputation for kindness to poor travellers and pilgrims that more and more people accepted the advice to 'Go to La Charité' and the name gradually changed.

The man who captured the town on behalf of the Burgundians and English, withstanding a siege by Joan of Arc, Perrinet Gressard, took a different view of charity. He sold the town back to the French under the Treaty of Arras for a large ransom and a job for himself for life as Governor. The monks' church, biggest in France next to Cluny when it was built, is now somewhat decayed but still has four of its five original naves. Through traffic was once the curse of the town, with the lorry-laden main road passing along-side the river, but now the big N7 by-passes La Charité and the old *Grand Monarque* hotel on quai Clemenceau (tel. 86 70 21 73) is a peaceful and pleasant place to eat or stay.

Nevers has an excellent choice of boats for sailing the Canal Latéral à la Loire and Nivernais Canal. The Loisirs Accueil organisation (3 rue du Sort, 58000 Nevers; tel. 86 59 14 22) offers a choice of 60 boats. The Canal du Centre, which runs all the way from Digoin to the industrial area of Montceau-les-Mines and close to Le Creusot, to Chagny and Chalon-sur-Saône, does still carry some commercial barges, especially between Montceau and Chalon. In this section the locks are automatic.

The river Yonne runs gently from Auxerre through the north-west of Burgundy right into the Ile-de-France to Montereau, 88km (55 miles) from Paris. Its old port at the head of the Nivernais Canal is now a Port de Plaisance and is a good centre for boat hire, although it is difficult to sail away from a place so pleasant and interesting as Auxerre. The town also contains the offices of an association of boat hirers, Bateaux de Bourgogne (3 quai de la République, 89000 Auxerre; tel. 86 52 18 99), which represents hirers on most of the waterways of Burgundy, with 18 departure bases and a large choice of 'one-way' cruises. You can hire bikes on the quayside to take on your boat. Bikes are almost essential if you want to find fresh bread and crois-sants for breakfast, to visit châteaux or other interesting spots and to find somewhere for a good meal. Such places are rarely placed conveniently within a five-minute walk of the waterway!

North from Auxerre at Joigny the Yonne meets the Canal de Bourgogne, which passes through St Florentin, a good boating base, and sweeps south-east through Burgundy to Dijon and on to the plains of the river Saône, joining the great Yonne and Saône rivers. There are many treasures along the route and many hills and valleys, inevitably meaning many locks in some stretches. Burgundian boating enthusiasts told us that we could easily cover the journey from St Florentin to Dijon in 10 days, including sightseeing, but we should prefer to have a fortnight.

Between Tonnerre and Montbard the two superb Renaissance châteaux of Tanlay and Ancy-le Franc are close to the towpath and the 12th century Fontenay Abbey is 6.5km (4 miles) from Montbard. As the canal climbs through many locks to its 3km-long summit tunnel just after the market town of Pouilly-en-Auxois, it does a huge looping descent past the hill village of Châteauneuf, through the valley of the river Ouche and down to Dijon. This is a lovely stretch of countryside.

Dijon's port, once vital to Burgundy's wine traffic, is now a paradise for pleasure sailors. You can hire boats to drive yourself (Information, Dijon Tourist Office, 34 rue Forges; tel. 80 30 35 39) or join a 'hotel' barge for a cruise of two to seven days, lazing in an air-conditioned barge with good meals and wine, and full hotel service (Continentale de Croisières, 9 rue Jean Renaud, 21000 Dijon; tel. 80 30 42 20).

You can continue by the Canal de Bourgogne south-east to St Jean de Losne, on the Saône, one of the most beautiful rivers in France. St Jean is an excellent boating port, a centre for canoeing, water-skiing, sailing, hiring cruisers (Crown Blue Line, Port de Plaisance, 21170 St Jean-de-Losne; tel. 80 29 12 86) and taking barge trips on the river for an hour to a day (La Béatrice, Tourisaone, 1 place d'Armes, 21170 St Jean-de-Losne; tel. 80 39 22 61).

The journey south on the Saône takes you to Chalon-sur-Saône through the little town of **Verdun-sur-le-Doubs**, a delightful place where the gentle Saône meets the turbulent river Doubs. It is famed for *pôchouse*, a freshwater fish bouillabaisse, and is headquarters of the Confrérie des Chevaliers de la Pôchouse, created in 1949. You can taste the dish in season at its best in *Trois Maures*, place Liberté (tel. 85 91 91 17), a big auberge beside the Doubs, or at the renowned *Hostellerie Bourguignonne*, ave Président Borgeot (tel. 85 91 51 45), where the Lauriot family have made it for generations. (Boats can be hired from Vetus, Capitainerie, place d'Eglise, 71350 Verdun-sur-le-Doubs; tel. 85 91 97 97.)

At Tournus, the Seille, a tributary of the Saône, joins the big river, and between Tournus and Louhans, the pleasant town which is a centre for Bresse chickens, is a beautiful and little known river trip across the tranquil, green Bresse countryside, with only four locks in the 40km (25 mile) journey. (Boats

The woodland setting of Lac des Settons reservoir in the valley of the river Cure (see p 214)

from Croizor, Port de Plaisance, 71500 Louhans; tel. 85 76 04 96.)

From Tournus, the Saône flows south through Mâcon, then never much more than 8–16km (5–10 miles) from the Beaujolais vineyards to Villefranche, though divided from them by the A6 and N6. It joins the Rhône at Lyon.

The great changes of scenery through which these waterways of Burgundy flow show the tremendous variety of Burgundian life and land. Water and wine live together. As the Burgundians say, water and wine make good neighbours, so long as they don't meet in a glass.

Practical Information

Phone Number Changes

France's eight figure phone numbers become ten-figure numbers in autumn 1996. A two-figure prefix will be added to each number according to the first two figures of its present eight numbers. Thus: 31.03.02.00 becomes **02**.31.03.02.00. Paris and Île de France numbers at present beginning (1) will instead begin **01**. These numbers at present start (1) 30, 34, 39, 40, 41, 42, 43, 44, 45, 46, 47, 48, 49, 53, 55, 60, 64, 69.

Present numbers starting	Now begin	Present numbers starting	Now begin	Present numbers starting	Now begin
20	03	47	02	75	04
21	03	48	02	76	04
22	03	49	05	77	04
23	03	50	02	78	04
24	03	53	05	79	04
25	03	54	02	80	03
26	03	55	05	81	03
27	03	56	05	82	03
28	03	57	05	83	03
29	03	58	05	84	03
31	02	59	05	85	03
32	02	60	03	86	03
33	02	61	05	87	03
34	02	62	05	88	03
35	02	63	05	89	03
37	02	65	05	90	04
38	02	66	04	91	04
39	02	67	04	92	04
40	02	68	04	93	04
41	02	69	04	94	04
42	04	70	04	95	04
43	02	71	04	96	02
44	03	72	04	97	02
45	05	73	04	98	02
46	05	74	04	99	02

Tourist Information Offices

Burgundy

REGION OF BURGUNDY **Comité Régional de Tourisme de Bourgogne**: Conseil Régional BP 1602, 21035 Dijon (tel. 80 50 10 20).
CÔTE D'OR **Office du Tourisme**: place Darcy, 21000 Dijon (tel. 80 43 42 12) and 34 rue des Forges, 21000 Dijon (tel. 80 30 35 39).
NIÈVRE **Office du Tourisme**: 3 rue du Sort, 58000 Nevers (tel. 86 36 39 80).
SAÔNE-ET-LOIRE **Office du Tourisme**: 389 ave de Lattre-de-Tassigny, 71000 Mâcon (tel. 85 39 47 47).
YONNE **Maison du Tourisme**: 1–2 quai de la République, 89000 Auxerre (tel. 86 52 26 27).
RHÔNE (for Beaujolais) **Office du Tourisme**: place Bellecour, BP 2254, 69214 Lyon (tel. 78 42 25 75).

Champagne-Ardennes

REGION OF CHAMPAGNE-ARDENNES **Comité Régional de Tourisme de Champagne-Ardennes**: 5 rue de Jéricho, 51037 Châlons-sur-Marne (tel. 26 70 31 31).
ARDENNES **Office Départemental du Tourisme**: 22 place Ducale, 08000 Charleville-Mézières (tel. 24 56 06 08).
AUBE **Comité Départemental du Tourisme**: quai du Comte Henri, BP 394, 10026 Troyes (tel. 25 42 50 50).
MARNE **Office du Tourisme**: 2bis bd Vaubécourt, 51000 Châlons-sur-Marne (tel. 26 68 37 52).
HAUTE-MARNE **Comité Départemental du Tourisme**: Centre Administratif Départemental des Vieilles Cours, BP 509, 52011 Chaumont (tel. 25 32 87 70).

Hotels and Restaurants: Champagne-Ardennes

A = very expensive, B = expensive, C = fairly expensive, D = moderate, E = inexpensive.

Ardennes

BAZEILLES (3.5km/2 miles from Sedan), 08140 Ardennes, **Château de Bazeilles** (tel. 24 27 09 68). 18th century château; luxurious; in fine park; outstanding value. Rooms C. Restaurant, see L'Orangerie below.
L'Orangerie (tel. 24 27 52 11). *Savoureuse* cuisine by renowned *saucier*; excellent fish. In old orangerie of Château de Bazeilles. Meals C.

CHARLEVILLE-MÉZIÈRES, 08000 Ardennes, **La Cigogne**, 40 rue Dubois-Crancé (tel. 24 33 25 39). Simple, generous, classic dishes of old favourites (Ardennes ham; beautiful lamb with *cèpes*). Meals E.

La Côte à l'Os, 11 cours Aristide Briand (tel. 24 59 20 16). 1926 décor, good fish, regional dishes. Meals C–E.

Relais du Square, 3 place Gare (tel. 24 33 38 76). Very convenient hotel, modern rooms, old façade. Restaurant Médicis (independent) nearby, wide choice of menus. Rooms D. Meals C–E.

Auberge de la Forêt, at Montcy-Notre-Dame, 5km (3 miles) on D1, route Nouzonville, 08090 Ardennes (tel. 24 33 37 55). Pleasant small country auberge (booking advised). Classic dishes. Good value. Meals C–E.

DONCHERY, 08350 Ardennes, convenient for Charleville or Sedan. **Château du Faucon** (for phone reservation tel. Loisir-Accueil en Ardennes, 24 56 00 63). Superb turreted 17th century château in big park. Rooms vary. Meals excellent value. Many activities—riding, including lessons, fishing, mountain bikes, tennis, health trail, cooking courses. Rooms B–D. Meals C–E.

FAGNON (8km/5 miles south-west Charleville by D139, D39), 08090 Ardennes, **Abbaye de Sept Fontaines** (tel. 24 37 38 24). Old abbey in parkland with golf course. Comfortable. Rooms B. Meals C.

HAUTES-RIVIÈRES, 08800 Ardennes, **Auberge en Ardennes** (tel. 24 53 41 93). Simple country inn. Garden to river. Traditional dishes; good portions. Rooms E. Meals D–E.

MONTHERMÉ, 08800 Ardennes, **Franco-Belge** (tel. 24 53 01 20). Reliable 2-chimney logis. Regional dishes. Rooms E. Meals D–E.

MOUZON, 08210 Ardennes, **Les Echevins**, 33 rue Charles de Gaulle (tel. 24 26 10 90). Restaurant in a 17th century house (historic monument). Excellent menus and carte of classic dishes. Meals C–E. Shut 1–24 August.

REVIN, 08500 Ardennes, **François Ier** (tel. 24 40 15 88), 46 quai Desmoulins. Beside Meuse river. Hotel renovated, rooms all different. Restaurant-bar; good value meals. Rooms E. Meals D–E. Open every day, all year.

SEDAN, 08200 Ardennes, **Au Bon Vieux Temps**, 1 place de la Halle (tel. 24 29 03 70). Good classic regional cooking; menus from cheap to gastronomic. Meals B–E.

Aube

AIX-EN-OTHE, 10160 Aube, **La Scierie** (tel. 25 46 71 26). At La Vove, 1.5km (1 mile) south. Quiet, pretty, country auberge in park, bordering a river; heated pool. Modernised traditional dishes. Rooms D. Meals D.

BAR-SUR-AUBE, 10200 Aube, **Hotel des Gouverneurs**, 38 rue Nationale (tel. 25 27 08 76). Ex Commerce hotel. New owners. Quiet atmosphere. Unobtrusive service. Classic menus for modern tastes. Rooms D. Meals D–E.

DOLANCOURT, 8km (5 miles) north-west of Bar-sur-Aube, **Moulin du Landion** (tel. 25 27 92 17). Delightful riverside converted mill, trout swim alongside. Fishing. Swimming pool. You eat well. Rooms D. Meals C–D.

MESNIL-ST-PÈRE, 10140 Aube, **Auberge du Lac** (tel. 25 41 27 16). Centre for Lac d'Orient and forest walks. Sailing, wind-surfing, fishing, tennis, bathing nearby. Quiet, comfortable, modernised rooms. Pleasant meals. Rooms D. Meals C–D.

TROYES, 10000 Aube. **Hotel Poste—Table Gourmande**, 1bis rue Raymond Poincaré (hotel tel. 25 73 05 05, restaurant tel. 25 73 84 37). Very comfortable bedrooms. Classic dishes (*filet de boeuf en feuilleté sur beurre rouge*) and interesting (*gaspacho de queues de langoustine*). Rooms B–C. Meals B–D. Also **Bistrot de la Mer** (tel. 25 73 80 78). Meals C–D. **Carpaccio** (tel. 25 73 05 05). Meals D.
Royal Hotel, 22 bd Carnot, near station (tel. 25 73 19 99). Old 'grand' hotel recently renovated. Very good traditional regional dishes. Rooms B–C. Meals C–E.
Valentine, 11 cour Rencontre (tel. 25 73 14 14). Very interesting. 16th century house with 1920s décor. Two courtyard terraces, one delightful, open air, one behind glass. Fine cooking. Well known for fish. Deservedly popular locally. Meals B–D.
Bistroquet, 10 rue L. Ulbach (tel. 25 73 65 65). Wonderful to find an old-style brasserie serving dishes like *pot-au-feu*, roast chicken and *andouillette*. Meals C–D.

STE MAURE, 10150 Aube, 8km (5 miles) north of Troyes by N19, D78, **Auberge de Sainte Maure** (tel. 25 76 90 41). In a garden with a pond beside a river in a forest—a restaurant with a glass-enclosed dining room surrounding a centre fireplace. The new chef has blessedly replaced the excesses of 'modern' cuisine with more satisfying and reliable dishes. Meals B–D.

Marne

AMBONNAY, 51150 Marne, **Auberge St Vincent** (tel. 26 57 01 98). Very likeable village inn among vineyards of Montagne de Reims. Rooms simple but comfortable. Outstanding cooking by Jean-Claude Pelletier, who has refined old country dishes. Rooms D. Meals C–D.

CHÂLONS-SUR-MARNE, 51000 Marne, **Angleterre** et **Restaurant Jacky Michel**, 19 place Mgr Tissier (tel. 26 68 21 51). Pretty bedrooms. A true master chef, Jacky Michel uses a light touch in his classical cooking and follows the seasons, not the fashions. Excellent. Rooms B–D. Meals A–D.
Au Carillon Gourmand, 15 place Mgr Tissier (tel. 26 64 45 07). You can see Châlons' ancient church of Notre-Dame-en-Vaux from the dining room veranda of this pleasant restaurant owned by Jean-Paul Pérardel of Aux Armes

de Champagne at L'Epine. Fine old-style dishes beloved locally. Good value. Shut part of August. Meals C–E.

CHAMPILLON, 51160 Marne, **Royal Champagne**, Relais et Châteaux hotel (tel. 26 52 87 11). Michelin star for cooking. Excellent rooms in bungalows. *Very* expensive. Try good value 'club' lunch (D). Rooms A. Meals A–D.

EPERNAY, 51200 Marne, **Berceaux**, 13 rue Berceaux (tel. 26 55 28 84). Traditionally the leading hotel-restaurant of Epernay. Rooms C. Meals C–D.

VINAY, 6.5km (4 miles) south-west of Epernay, 512000 Marne, **La Briqueterie** (tel. 26 59 99 99). Excellent modern hotel among vineyards. Flower garden. Cuisine full of good ideas without eccentricity. Succulent desserts. Renowned buffet breakfast. Covered and open-air pools. Rooms A. Meals A–B (lunch D).

CUMIÈRES, 6.5km (4 miles) north-west of Epernay on D1, 51480 Marne, **Le Caveau** (tel. 26 54 83 23). Delightful restaurant in old wine cave, very popular with Epernay people. Excellent bourgeoise cuisine, fresh ingredients, sensible prices. We love it. Meals C–E.

L'EPINE, 51460 Marne, 7km (4.5 miles) east of Châlons by N3, **Aux Armes de Champagne** (tel. 26 69 30 30). Restful rooms, immaculate service, nice welcome, superb interesting cooking by Patrick Michelon, thirst-raising wine-list and excellent wine cave for buying take-home bottles. M. et Mme Jean-Paul Pérardel keep one of our favourite hotels in France. Rooms B–D. Meals D (lunch) B–C.

MONTCHENOT, 51500 Marne, **Le Grand Cerf** on N51 between Reims and Epernay (tel. 26 97 60 07). Set in a garden, views of the Montagne de Reims. Some dishes slightly modernised—but not the beef braised in Cumières wine. Wide choice of menus and prices. Meals A–D. Shut part August.

REIMS, 51100 Marne, **Les Crayères** (tel. 26 82 80 80). Old mansion of Madame Pommery. Gorgeous bedrooms. Gérard Boyer's unsurpassed cooking. When we win the National Lottery, our first call will be to book a table and bed at Les Crayères. Rooms A. Meals A.
Orphée Restaurant, Quality Hotel, 55 bd Paul Doumer (tel. 26 40 01 08). Yves Méjean (pupil of Michel Guérard) offers very good meals at reasonable prices. Meals C–D.
Le Chardonnay, 184 ave Epernay (tel. 26 06 08 60). Boyer's famous old restaurant. Meals not quite so splendid but very agreeable and excellent value. Warm atmosphere. Super wine list and wine by the glass. Meals C–D.
Au Petit Comptoir, 17 rue Mars (tel. 26 40 58 58). Boyer's own bistro, so local 'society' haunts it; but its dishes are 'what Grandma used to make', its wine good but unassuming, its décor delicious and prices sensible. Meals D.

Grand Hotel du Nord, 75 place Drouet-d'Erlon (tel. 26 47 39 03). Behind an old stone façade, modernised rooms, near station, in town centre. No restaurant. Rooms D.

Among many Reims restaurants selling agreeable inexpensive meals at very reasonable prices, we suggest, Le Colibri, 12 rue Chanzy (tel. 26 47 50 67). Meals D–E.

STE MENEHOULD, 51800 Marne, **Cheval Rouge**, 1 rue Chanzy (tel. 26 60 81 04). 2-star logis; good value. Rooms D–E. Meals D–E.

SEPT-SAULX, 51400 Marne, in a pretty village equidistant—24km (15 miles)—from Reims and Châlons, **Cheval Blanc** (tel. 26 03 90 27). The Lefèvre-Robert family has cooked here for 125 years and it is 45 years since we had our first plate of crayfish in Champagne here. Really polished traditional regional cooking. Very pleasant bedrooms and garden. Not cheap, but good value. Rooms C. Meals B–C.

SÉZANNE, 51120 Marne, **Relais Champenois et du Lion d'Or**, 157 rue Notre Dame (tel. 26 80 58 03). Attractive new façade with flowery wooden balconies. Good value regional menus. Rooms D–E. Meals C–E.

TOURS-SUR-MARNE, 51150 Marne, **Touraine Champenoise** (tel. 26 58 91 93). Charming river and canalside inn, 11.5km (7 miles) east of Epernay. Friendly ambience, above-average meals. Excellent value. Rooms D. Meals C–E.

Haute-Marne

COLOMBEY-LES-DEUX-EGLISES, 52330 Haute-Marne, **Auberge de la Montagne**, rue d'Argentolles (tel. 25 01 51 69). Converted *fermette*. Pleasant rooms. Good range of menus. Rooms D. Meals C–D.
Les Dhuits, on N19 (tel. 25 01 50 10). New, with spacious rooms. Agreeable, good value meals. Rooms D. Meals D–E.

JOINVILLE, 52300 Haute-Marne, **Soleil d'Or**, 9 rue Capucins (tel. 25 94 15 66). Pretty, cosy rooms. Reliable satisfying meals. Rooms C–D. Meals C–E.

LANGRES, 52200 Haute-Marne, **Cheval Blanc**, 4 rue l'Estres (tel. 25 87 07 00). The White Horse Inn was called St Amâtres Curch for centuries. Became an inn in 1793, with vaulted rooms. Careful classical cooking by Mme Caron. Good value. Rooms D. Meals C–E.

Hotels and Restaurants: Burgundy

Côte-d'Or

ARNAY-LE-DUC, 21230 Côte-d'Or, **Chez Camille** (tel. 80 90 01 38). What a charming, comfortable home! Delicious, unpretentious meals. Rooms C (Annexe D). Meals C–E.

BEAUNE, 21200 Côte-d'Or. Beaune is packed with good hotels and restaurants of all sizes, types and prices. Here are a few which we know well.
Central, 2 rue V. Millot (100m from Hospices and place Carnot car park, (tel. 80 24 77 24). Part of the Beaune scene since Grandpa's days, when Michelin starred it. Simple family hotel; delicious old-style cooking. Rooms C–D. Meals C–E.
Auberge Toison d'Or, 4 bd J. Ferry (tel. 80 22 29 62). Restaurant. New young owners offer good value. Meals C–E.
Le Gourmandin, 8 place Carnot (tel. 80 24 07 88); bistro in the busiest square serving old Burgundian favourites with the patron's own wines until very late. Meals C–E.
L'Ecusson, place Malmédy (tel. 80 24 03 82). Restaurant away from tourist area at end of faubourg Madeleine. Individualistic, modern-style dishes; well-chosen wine list. Meals B–D.
Bernard Morillon, 32 rue Maufoux (tel. 80 24 12 06). Good value weekday menu with Burgundian-style dishes, superb carte with such delicacies as lobster, crayfish, truffles. Meals B–D. Attractive atmosphere.

CHOREY-LÈS-BEAUNE, 21201 Côte-d'Or, 3km (2 miles) north of Beaune by N74, **Ermitage de Corton** (tel. 80 22 05 28). Everything the most opulent, from the *amuse-bouches* to the bathrooms. Beverly Hills among the vineyards. You will either wallow in it or burst out laughing. But the meals, the wines and above all the breakfasts should ensure a return visit. Cash in your share options and go! Rooms A. Meals A–C.

SAVIGNY-LÈS-BEAUNE, 21420 Côte-d'Or, 5km (3 miles) north-west of Beaune, **L'Ouvrée** (tel. 80 21 51 52). Village inn with garden; pleasant welcome. Owner is a wine producer; tastings in the cave. Rooms D. Meals D–E.

DIJON, 21000 Côte-d'Or. Extremely good choice of restaurants. Fair choice of hotels.
La Cloche, place Darcy (tel. 80 30 12 32). Beautiful façade; national monument. Perfect position. Rooms tastefully modernised. Rotonde restaurant. Meals B–C.
Chapeau Rouge, 5 rue Michelet (tel. 80 30 28 10). Charm, comfort, character, convenient position. Very good Burgundian cuisine, modernised a little without upsetting regular customers. Even *jambon persillé* melts succulently on the tongue. Rooms B–C. Meals B–D.

La Toison d'Or, Hôtel Phillipe Le Bon, 18 rue Ste Anne (tel. 80 30 73 52). Apart from a Burgundian life museum, the excellent restaurant of the Company of Burgundian Wine Lovers now has an hotel attached, 15th century, modern comforts. Daniel Broyer cooks traditional Burgundian, classical and inventive dishes. Try his delicious *poulet Gaston-Gérard* (chicken in a sauce of Gruyère cheese, white wine and mustard). Rooms C–D. Meals C–D.

Nord Hôtel, Porte Guillaume, place Darcy (tel. 80 30 58 58). We love this friendly, old-fashioned hotel with comforting bedrooms, conveniently placed, and run by the Frachot family for four generations. Traditional Burgundian dishes the way they should taste. Superb wine list. Wine bar in cellars. Rooms C–D. Meals C–E.

Jacquemart, 32 rue Verrerie (tel. 80 73 39 74). No restaurant. Family mansion in lovely old street near Palais des Ducs. Rooms D–E.

Restaurant J-P Billoux, moved to Le Pré aux Clercs, 13 pl. Libération (80.38.05.05). One of France's best young chefs. Modern versions of classic dishes and personally researched old recipes. Expensive. Jean-Pierre Billoux learned from the great Alexandre Dumaine and still cooks a memorable *poulet au vin rouge*, Dumaine style. Meals A–C.

Bistrot des Halles, 10 rue Bannelier (tel. 80 49 94 15). We thought this was a strangely excellent market bistro—then found that Jean-Pierre Billoux was behind it! Meals D–E.

Le Petit Vatel, 73 rue Auxonne (tel. 80 65 80 64). Good value menus. Meals C–E.

FIXIN, 21220 Côte-d'Or, **Chez Jeannette**, 7 rue Noiset (tel. 80 52 45 49). Genuine little village inn, where genuine Burgundian dishes like *oeufs-en-meurette*, *rognons à l'Aligoté*, *boeuf à la bourguignonne*, taste so much more satisfying than in more pretentious and costlier surroundings. Good, honest cooking with honest portions, lovely cheeses. Simplest, adequate rooms E. Meals D–E.

GEVREY-CHAMBERTIN, 21220 Côte-d'Or, **Rôtisserie du Chambertin** (tel. 80 34 33 20). This restaurant in an ancient wine cave still remains a place of worship in the Côte-d'Or vineyards, although Celestine Menneveau has, alas, left us. Her great Burgundian dishes are still made 'à la façon de Celestine', including light and incomparable *coq au vin*. Certainly not cheap, but for a special occasion. Meals B–C.

Le Bon Bistrot (tel. 80 34 35 14), recently opened above the Rôtisserie du Chambertin, serves good cheaper meals, including *coq au vin*. Meals D.

MEURSAULT, 21190 Côte-d'Or, **Les Arts**, place Hôtel de Ville (tel. 80 21 20 28). Very simple logis in main square where locals drink. Good value, cheap country meals. Rooms D–E. Meals D–E.

Le Chevreuil, facing Hôtel de Ville (tel. 80 21 23 25). La Mère Daugier made it famous for Burgundian cooking long ago. Still above average. Rooms D–E. Meals D–E.

Le Centre, 4 rue Lattre de Tassigny (tel. 80 21 20 75). 2-star Logis de France. Satisfying meals. Rooms D–E. Meals D–E.

MONTBARD, 21500 Côte-d'Or. At Fain-lès-Montbard, south-east by D905 near Fontenay Abbey, **Château de Malaisy** (tel. 80 89 46 54). A country mansion among woods and fields where sheep, Senegalese goats, geese and ducks chatter to each other, unaware that it is a Relais de Silence. Very pleasant. Rooms B–C. Meals C–E.

NUITS-ST-GEORGES, 21700 Côte-d'Or, **Les Cultivateurs**, 12 rue Gén. de Gaulle (tel. 80 61 10 41). Good old-style village auberge used by locals and us. Simple rooms. Good value generous, well-cooked cheap Burgundian meals. Rooms D–E. Meals D–E.
Côte-d'Or, 37 rue Thurot (tel. 80 61 06 10). Days of the très snob, gourmet Crotet cuisine have gone. Young chef cooks with reliable technique. Pleasant welcome and service. Rooms (improved) C. Meals C–D.

PULIGNY-MONTRACHET, 21190 Côte-d'Or, **Le Montrachet** (tel. 80 21 30 06). Burgundian dishes for gastronomes (*blanc de volaille de Bresse au foie-gras*). Super wine cellar. Superior 'rustic' rooms. Cheaper than most Michelin-starred hotels. Rooms B. Meals B–D.

ST JEAN-DE-LOSNE, 21170 Côte-d'Or, **Auberge de la Marine**, on D968 (tel. 80 29 05 11). Generous portions of Burgundy dishes at this comfortable 2-chimney Logis de France, including freshwater fish and *pôchouse*. Rooms D–E. Meals C–E.

SAULIEU, 21210 Côte-d'Or, **Côte d'Or**, 2 rue Argentine (tel. 80 64 07 66). Once the domaine of the legendary Alexandre Dumaine, then of young J.-P. Billoux (Dijon), now of Loiseau. Some call Bernard Loiseau an eccentric, others a genius. He is certainly a brilliant chef cooking some very unusual dishes. Prices too high for most mortals. Rooms are delightful. Rooms A–C. Meals A–B, C (lunch).
Le Relais, 8 rue Argentine (tel. 80 64 13 16). 'Poor' neighbour of Bernard Loiseau. Here we can eat hearty, well-cooked Burgundian dishes at humane prices. Rooms D. Meals D–E.

SEMUR-EN-AUXOIS, 21140 Côtes-d'Or, **Le Lac** (at Lac de Pont, 3km (2 miles) south by D103, tel. 80 97 11 11). Pleasant, well kept traditional hotel. Fishing, bathing. Regional cooking. Rooms D. Meals D–E.

VOLNAY, 21190 Côte-d'Or, **Les Vignes**, N74 (tel. 80 22 24 48). Simple auberge among vines; cheap, good menus. Meals D–E.

VOSNE-ROMANÉE, 21700 Côte-d'Or, **Toute Petite Auberge** (tel. 80 61 02 03). Modest inn on D74 below the village, renowned for the old favourites *oeufs-en-meurette, coq au vin, boeuf à la bourguignonne.* Summer terrace. Big winter fire. Meals C–E.

Nièvre

LA CHARITÉ-SUR-LOIRE, 58400 Nièvre, **Grand Monarque**, 33 quai Clemenceau (tel. 86 70 21 73). The by-pass has added peace to its other advantages. Very pleasant place to stay. Nice Loire river view. High quality classical dishes. Rooms D–E. Meals D–E.

CHÂTEAU-CHINON, 58120 Nièvre, **Vieux Morvan**, 8 place Gudin (tel. 86 85 05 01). In the steps of President Mitterand. 2-star, 2-chimney logis. Rooms D. Meals C–E.

CORBIGNY, 58800 Nièvre, **Chateau de Lantilly**, 3km (2 miles) south-east by D285 (tel. 86 20 01 22). Reasonable prices for a 17th century château, modernised, with swimming pool. Rooms B–D. Meals C–D.

MAGNY-COURS, 58470 Nièvre, **La Renaissance** (tel. 86 58 10 40). Attractive with splendid meals. Called 'the Grand Prix drivers' luxury canteen' and by Gault-Millau, 'the only *grande table* of the Nièvre département'. Certainly Jean-Claude Dray satisfies followers of modern regional and classical cooking. Rooms B–C. Meals A–B, C (lunch).

MONTSAUCHE, 58230 Nièvre, **Idéal Hotel**, on D193, 610m up in Morvan, 5km (3 miles) from Lac des Settons (tel. 86 84 51 26). Quiet. Useful. Rooms D–E. Meals D–E.

NEVERS, 58000 Nièvre, **Hotel Loire**, quai de Médine (tel. 86 61 50 92). Modern; in good position near town centre on the banks of the Loire. Rather 'functional'. Rooms C–D. Meals C–D.

VARENNES-VEUZELLES, 6.5km (4 miles) north by N7, **Château de la Rocherie** (tel. 86 38 07 21). Napoleon III country mansion, terrace for summer, big fire for winter. Sensible yet fairly imaginative dishes. Pleasant rooms. Rooms C–D. Meals B–D.

POUILLY-SUR-LOIRE, 58150 Nièvre, **Relais Fleuri et Restaurant Coq Hardi**, 42 ave. Tuilerie (tel. 86 39 12 99). Delightful old inn we have liked for years. Jean-Claude Astruc's good value regional meals are part of local folklore. He is also a Pouilly-Fumé wine expert. Rooms D. Meals D–E.

ST HONORÉ-LES-BAINS, 58360 Nièvre, **Lanoiselée**, 4 ave Jean Mermoz (tel. 86 30 75 44). Attractive hotel, cosy bedrooms, pleasant garden. Rooms C–D. Meals D.

Yonne

AUXERRE, 89000 Yonne, **Jean-Luc Barnabet**, 14 quai République (tel. 86 51 68 88). In his attractive restaurant on a riverside road, Jean-Luc Barnabet cooks brilliantly, but with modern–size portions and some strange plate-fellows. The result is usually delicious; prices reasonable for a Michelin star. Meals B–C.
Trou Poinchy, 34 bd Vaulabelle (tel. 86 52 04 48). Old dishes like *daube de boeuf bourguignonne* at money-saving prices. Meals D–E.
Le Parc des Maréchaux, 6 ave Foch (tel. 86 51 43 77). Charming Second Empire house with nice garden. Bar; no restaurant. Comfortable. Rooms C–D.

AVALLON, 89200 Yonne, **La Poste**, 13 place Vauban (tel. 86 34 06 12). Hotel since 1707. Napoleon slept here on 16 March 1815. We remember it as one of France's most renowned restaurants. Now recovered from a bad patch. Agreeable meals, well refurbished rooms. Rooms A–D. Meals B–C.
Moulin des Ruats, 5km (3 miles) by D427 in Cousin valley (tel. 86 34 07 14). Delightful converted mill beside river. Trout fishing. Peaceful, shady garden; chef who trained under Boyer. Rooms B–D. Meals C.

CHABLIS, 89800 Yonne, **Hostellerie des Clos** (tel. 86 42 10 63). Part of Chablis's old Hospital, with wine bar in the 18th century chapel. Michel Vignaud's touch of modernism, added to a lot of regionalism and classicism, adds up to delightful dishes. One of our favourite addresses in Burgundy. Excellent pâtisserie. Rooms B–D. Meals B–C.
Vieux Moulin, 18 rue des Moulins (tel. 86 42 47 30). Ancient mill converted into charming auberge. Cheap, good value meals of 'family' cooking. Meals D–E.

JOIGNY, 89300 Yonne. **A la Côte Saint-Jacques**, 14 faubourg de Paris (tel. 86 62 09 70). Over 35 years we have seen Michel Lorain convert his mother's auberge on the N6, known for her solid *coq au vin*, into a white neo-Classical Relais et Châteaux 'palace' with 3 Michelin stars, 19.5 points out of 20 and four toques from Gault-Millau, and praise from all gastronomes. The cooking is magnificent, service arrives with the twitch of a little finger. But, oh, the prices! Near perfection costs too much for us! Rooms A. Meals A.
Hotel Rive Gauche, rue du Port-du-Bois (tel. 86 91 46 66). New; gaining high reputation for looking after passing tourists at moderate prices. Who runs it? Michel Lorain's daughter Catherine! Rooms C–D. Meals C–E.

ST FLORENTIN 89210 Yonne, **Moulin des Pommerats** (tel. 86 35 08 04), 3km (2 miles) north by D30 and D129 at Venizy. Some magic departed from this little mill by a stream with the retirement of Paul Remaux d'Equainville (ex-wartime RAF Wing Commander and a true Frenchman). But young Frédérique Lampart cooked an excellent meal on our visit. Good value. Rooms C–D. Meals C–E.

SENS, 89100 Yonne, **Paris et Poste**, 37 rue République (tel. 86 65 17 43). Traditional old hotel. Fine recipes passed from father to son through generations. Rooms C. Meals C–D.

Saône-et-Loire

AUTUN, 71400 Saône-et-Loire, **Les Ursulines**, 14 rue Rivault (tel. 85 52 68 00). In old convent, now most comfortable hostellerie. Interesting dishes, well cooked. Rooms C–D. Meals C–D.

CHAGNY, 71150 Saône-et-Loire, **Lameloise**, 36 place d'Armes (tel. 85 87 08 85). What a French hostellerie should be! Family run, affable welcome, cosy comfort, brilliant cooking with great finesse of uncomplicated dishes. Worthy of its 3 Michelin stars; worth its *very* high prices. Rooms A. Meals A–C.

CHALON-SUR-SAÔNE, 71100 Saône-et-Loire, **St Georges**, 32 ave Jean-Jaurès (tel. 85 48 27 05). Best hotel in town, with best restaurant. Yves Choux deserves his Michelin star. Rooms B–D. Meals B–D. Also bistro **Petit Comptoir** (tel. 85 93 44 26). Meals E.

ST RÉMY, 5km (3 miles) south of Chalon by N6, N80, **Moulin de Martorey** (tel. 85 48 12 98). Old mill, pretty, shady garden, river alongside, outstanding cooking by young chef. Meals B–D.

LOUHANS, 71500 Saône-et-Loire, **Moulin de Bourgchâteau**, rue Guidon (tel. 85 75 37 12). Large mill (1778) on river Seille. Famous for local poulet de Bresse and river fish (*sandre*, *omble*, and so on). Excellent value. Rooms D. Meals C–E.

MÂCON, 71000 Saône-et-Loire, **Poisson d'Or**, 1km (½ mile) north, allée Parc, near Port de Plaisance (tel. 85 38 00 88). Terrace by river Saône. Regional and fish dishes good. Meals D–E.
Bellevue, 416 quai Lamartine (tel. 85 38 05 07). Classic hotel. Good bedrooms, good cuisine du Marché. Rooms B–D. Meals C–D.

MERCUREY, 71640 Saône-et-Loire, **Val d'Or** (tel. 85 45 13 70). Truly Burgundian, even to speed of service. Big country-style bedrooms. Superb place to eat. Nice Montagny white wines. Rooms D. Meals C–D.

Beaujolais

ROMANÈCHE-THORINS, 71570 Saône-et-Loire, **Les Maritonnes**, near station (tel. 85 35 51 70). Very comfortable, charming garden, pool. No wonder travellers abandon A6 motorway to eat fine old local dishes here. Rooms C. Meals B–D.

CHÉNAS, 69840 Rhône. Restaurant **Daniel Robin**, at Les Deschamps (tel. 85 36 72 67). Taste Robin's own wines on the garden terrace among his vines, then eat local dishes. Meals C–D.

FLEURIE, 69820 Rhône, **Auberge du Cep** (tel. 74 04 10 77). 2 Michelin stars for a Beaujolais village auberge! Justified for Michel Guérin's master touch to classical dishes; spoilt for some by lady owner's 'excessive prices'. Meals A–C.

JULIÉNAS, 69840 Rhône, **Le Coq au Vin** (tel. 74 04 41 98). Old village café, authentic even to its genuine 'zinc', boasts no stars but serves true old dishes like *gâteau de foies grand'mère*, *tripes à la tomate*, *andouillette beaujolaise* and a *poulet de Bresse* simply poached in cream. Chef Claude Clévenot was trained by Georges Blanc! Meals C–E.

Events

Champagne

April	Rethel—Boudin Sausage Fair.
May	Reims—Fête of St Joan of Arc (4th Sunday).
	Renwez—Gastronomic Fair in the forest.
June	Troyes—Champagne Fair.
July	Bogny-sur-Meuse—Festival of the Aymon Brothers.
	Fumay—Fête of the Boudin Blanc and Onion Sausage.
	Langres—Open-air theatre Friday, Saturday evenings (25 87 13 04).
July–August	Reims—Son-et-Lumière at Reims Cathedral.
	Music and Son-et-Lumière at Basilique of St Remi.
	Buxières-les-Villiers—Son-et-Lumière.
	Vendresse—Château Cassine Son-et-Lumière (24 35 44 84).
August	Langres—Ronde des Hallebardiers. Costumed-tour show of fortified town. Friday, Saturday evenings.
September	Renwez—Ardennes ham fair.
October	Reims—Pilgrimage of St Remi.
	Chaource—Cheese Fair.
	Renwez—Apple Fair (early October). Mushroom Fair (late October).
November	Givet Onion Fair.

Burgundy

January	St Vincent Tournante Festival. Big wine festival in different Burgundy village each year, nearest weekend after 22 January.
February	Chablis—St Vincent Wine Festival.
February/March	Chalon-sur-Saône—a week's Winter Carnival, end February to beginning March. Biggest in Burgundy.
Palm Sunday	Nuits-St-Georges—Hospice wine auction.
Whit Monday	Semur-en-Auxois—Fête de la Bague, horse-race around town, oldest horse-race in France.
May	Mâcon—Foire des Vins de France. Contest for wines from all France. Most prestigious in Europe. Nevers—Spring Fair. Saulieu—Journées Gourmandes du Grand Morvan (local food products).
June	Magny-Cours—French Grand Prix Formula 1 cars, usually on 1st Sunday in June. Auxerre—Festival of Jazz.
Mid-June–mid-July	Villefranche-sur-Saône—Festival of Beaujolais.
July	Chalon-sur-Saône—Festival des Artistes des Rues (Street performers all over town).
July/August	St Fargeau (Yonne)—mid-July to end of August—Costume festival with 600 actors, 50 cavaliers on horseback, dancers, musicians, troubadours, etc.
August	Pouilly-sur-Loire—Wine Fair (Pouilly-Fumé). Bouhans—Charolais cattle and horse fair (founded 1645) lively entertainment. Cluny—Festival Les Grandes Heures; five classical music concerts in vaults of abbey cloisters. Glux-en-Glenne, Nièvre—Fête de la Myrtille (Bilberry Fair). Rogny-les-Sept-Ecluses—Fête du Canal du Nivernais, watersports and entertainments.
September	Joigny (Yonne)—Fair of Melons and Onions. Dijon—Fête de Vigne and International Folklore Festival (1st or 2nd week in September). Mâcon—Grape Harvest Festival (first Sunday). Alise-Ste-Reine—Pilgrimage, costume procession, and Mystery of Ste Reine play in open-air theatre. 7 September.
October	Auxerre—Montgolfiades; hot air balloon festival. St Léger-sous-Beuvray—Chestnut Fair.
October/November	Dijon—International Food and Wine Fair, lasting a fortnight.

November	Les Trois Glorieuses Beaune Hospice Wine Auction.
	Vougeot dinner of Chevaliers du Tastevin.
	Meursault wine-producers' dinner.
	Louhans—Fernand Point Gastronomique Exhibition; chefs' contest; raffle of exhibited dishes.
	St Bris-les-Vineux—Auxerre Wine Festival on Sunday nearest to 11 November.
	Chablis—Fête des Vins on fourth Sunday in November.
December	Marcigny—Turkey, Goose and Poultry Fair.

Châteaux, Museums, Castles, Abbeys, Exhibitions: opening times

Champagne-Ardennes

Bazeilles: Musée La Dernière Cartouche (24 27 15 86). 1870 War museum. Open daily except Fri; afternoons 1 Oct–31 Mar.

Belval: Parc Animalier (24 30 01 86). Park with boar, stags, bison, deer, etc. Tour in vehicle except on central paths. Open 4 Jan–30 Aug except Tue, Wed.

Brienne-le-Château: Musée Napoléon I (25 92 82 41). Napoleon at military school. Open daily except Tue and in winter.

Châlons-sur-Marne: Musée Municipale, place Godart (26 68 54 44); museum outstanding in sculptures, paintings; reconstruction of old Champenois room. Daily except Tue.

Charleville-Mézières: Musée de l'Ardenne (24 32 44 60), place Ducal. Lovely building, interesting view of Ardennes life—arms making to stamp collecting and marionettes. Daily except Mon.

Musée Rimbaud, Vieux Moulin (24 56 24 09). Works of poet Arthur Rimbaud. Reconstruction of old room. Daily except Mon.

Musée de la TSF, 184 ave De Gaulle (24 56 12 41); evolution of radio from Eiffel Tower days to today. Daily except Tue, and Sat afternoons.

St Laur Animal Park: 6km (3½ miles) from Charleville (24 57 39 84). Wild boar, deer, stags, wild goats, moufflons in natural surroundings. Open daily afternoons except Thu.

Colombey-les-Deux-Eglises: La Boisserie (25 01 52 52). Général de Gaulle's home. Open daily except Tue.

De Gaulle Memorial (25 01 50 50). Huge Cross of Lorraine in granite. Open all year.

Douzy: Musée des Débuts de l'Aviation, Aérodrome de Sedan, Douzy (24 26 38 70). Early aircraft. Daily May–Sept except Mon; weekends Apr–end Oct.

Epernay: Castellone Champagne Tower and Museum, 55 rue de Verdun (26 55 15 33): includes models to show method of making Champagne; also posters, labels, bottles, and spectacular views over vineyards. Daily 1 May–1 Nov.

Jardin des Papillons, 63 bis ave de Champagne (26 55 15 33): exotic butterflies from round world fly free. Daily 1 May–end Sept.

Essoyes: Maison de la Vigne et Vigneron (25 29 64 64): wine museum, includes souvenirs of painter Renoir. Every day 15 June–15 Sept; weekends Easter–14 June, 16 Sept–1 Nov.

Fleury-la-Rivière: Fresque de Champagne (26 58 42 53). Fresco of 480 sq m showing history of Champagne wine, by the artist Greg Gawra. Commissioned by the Wine Cooperative.

Fromelennes: Grottes de Nichet (24 42 05 54) caves. April–31 Aug.

Givet: Charlemont Fort 1 July–31 Aug. Tour Victoire (24 42 03 54) 15 June–15 Sept.

Joinville: Château de Grand Jardin (25 94 17 54). Superb French Renaissance château of first Duc de Guise (1533), lovely gardens. All summer except Tue.

La Motte Tilly: Château (25 39 84 54). Superb garden and park; rich furnishings. 1 Apr–30 Sept except Tue. Weekend afternoons in winter.

Langres: Hôtel du Breuil de St Germain (25 87 08 05). In beautiful old house, furnishings from Renaissance–18th century. Daily except Tue.

Montier-en-Der: Haras National (Stud farm). (25 04 22 17). Open daily (afternoons only). Displays of stallions and carriage driving Thu (15.00) in Sept, Oct, Nov.

Reims: Palais du Tau, alongside cathedral (26 47 74 39). In banqueting hall of newly crowned Kings of France, relics from cathedral. Open daily.

Musée Beaux Arts, in St Denis' Abbey, 8 rue Chantzy (26 47 28 44). One of France's best provincial museums. Open daily.

Salle de Reddition, 12 rue Franklin Roosevelt (26 47 84 10). School where General Eisenhower, Allied C-in-C, received German capitulation, 7 May 1945. Closed Tue.

Centre de l'Automobile Française, 84 ave Clemenceau (26 82 83 84). Superb collection of classic French cars including Bugattis and Hispano-Suiza. Open Feb–Nov except Tue.

Renwez: Musée de la Forêt (24 54 93 11). Brilliantly presented historic forestry exhibition, inside and out. In forest. Daily Mar–Nov.

Rumigny: Château de la Cour de Pres (24 35 52 66). Elegant Renaissance château. Open midsummer daily except Tuesdays. Spring and autumn, Sun.

Sedan: Château, biggest fort in Europe (24 27 73 73). Daily except Sun; afternoons only 16 Sept–15 Mar.

Troyes: Musée d'Art, place Pierre (25 80 57 30). Great works of art from end 19th–mid 20th century. Daily except Tue.

Villy-la-Forêt: Dernier Fort de la Ligne Maginot (24 22 61 49). Maginot Line Defence of 1940. Open afternoons except Mon in July, Aug. Early Apr–Nov. Sun afternoons only.

Burgundy

Alise-Sainte-Reine: Battle of Alesia (52 BC)—excavations, museum. Daily end Mar–end Sept.

Ancy-le-Franc: Château. Daily 1 Apr–early Nov. (86 75 14 63). Also car and carriage museum (86 75 12 41).

Arcy-sur-Cure: vast caves. Daily Mar–Oct (86 81 90 63).

Arnay-le-Duc: Maison des Arts de la Table (cooking to crockery), 15 rue St Jacques. Daily mid Apr–mid Oct (80 90 11 59).

Autun: Musée Robin (religious art, including tombstones). Daily except Tue (85 52 09 76).

Auxerre: Saint-Etienne Cathedral. Daily except Sun mornings Easter–1 Nov (86 52 31 68).

Leblanc-Duvernoy Museum (beautiful furnishings and porcelain in 18th century museum). Daily except Tue (86 51 09 74).

Beaune: Hôtel Dieu. Daily. Closed Dec.

Musée de Vin de Bourgogne, rue d'Enfer. Daily; closed Tue in winter (80 22 08 19).

Archéodrome (6km/3½ miles south from Beaune at A6 motorway service station. Reached by D18 road). Unique exhibition of early Burgundian history including neolithic huts, Caesar's fortress at Alesia, etc. Open daily.

Buffon: Forges de Buffon. Reconstruction and exhibition of 18th–19th century industrial iron and steel works. Open daily 1 Apr–30 Oct (80 89 40 30).

Bussy-Rabutin: Château of eccentric Count. Fascinating décor. Open daily except Tue, Wed in winter (80 96 00 03).

Château-Chinon: Musée du Septemmat, 6 rue du Château (gifts given to President Mitterand from around world). Open daily 1 May–30 Sept. Sat, Sun rest of year (86 85 19 23).

Costume Museum (French costumes 18th–early 20th centuries), rue Château same opening times.

Dijon: Musée de Beaux Arts, place Sainte-Chapelle (old State Palace). Superb art; furniture, arms museum. Open daily except Tue (80 74 52 70).

Burgundy Wax Museum, 13 ave Albert Ier. Wax figures showing Burgundy's history. Ancient wine cellars. Daily (80 42 03 03).

Cosne-sur-Loire: Farm machinery museum. Les Narcys, St Loup village, old harvesting machines, steam engines, tractors. Demonstrations of old time harvesting, hay-making, threshing, ploughing. Open daily 1 May–30 Sept except Tue.

Fontenay: Cistercian Romanesque Abbey (80 92 15 00). Registered Unesco 'World Heritage'.

Gouloux: Saboterie (Clogmaker's shop). Open daily. (M. Marchand, 86 78 73 90).

Guérigny: Forges Royales. Industrial heritage; blacksmith's forge, naval anchors and chains, old steam engines, power hammers, models of old boats. Open 26 June–18 Sept daily except Tue (86 37 31 98).

La Clayette: Musée de l'Automobile (85 28 22 07). 100 old cars in grounds of château. Open daily except Tue.

Le Creusot: Château de la Verrerie (former royal crystal glass works). Museum of Man and Industry (85 55 01 11). Open weekdays; Sat, Sun afternoons.

Mâcon: Musée des Ursulines, 5 rue des Ursulines (85 38 18 84). From pre-history and medieval art, furniture. Open daily except Tue, Sun mornings.

Magny Cours: Motor-racing circuit Nevers-Magny Cours, France's top car racing circuit, used for French Grand Prix formula 1. Research and production units. Visits by appointment (tel. 86 21 80 00. fax 86 21 80 17). Training sessions available on Renault or Porsche 944 turbo.

Milly-Lamartine: Manor of Lamartine where poet spent his childhood. Open 2 Apr–mid Nov except Tue (85 37 70 33).

Nevers: Ste Bernadette's shrine and museum. Convent of St Gildard, 34 rue St Gildard (86 57 79 99) open daily.

Paray-le-Monial: Musée de la Faïence, Prieuré Bénédictin, ave Jean-Paul II (85 88 83 07), Charolles porcelain collection. Open mid Apr–mid Nov. Daily except Tue.

Pierreclos: Castle of Lamartine's girlfriend, Madame de Milly who inspired the poem 'Jocelyn'. Also wine tasting and sales (85 35 74 60).

Pontigny: Cistercian abbey founded 1114 (Info: Les Amis de Pontigny 86 47 54 99). Open daily except during church services.

Reulle-Vergy: Musée des Arts et Traditions. Life in the old days in vineyards of Hautes-Côtes (80 61 42 93). Open 1 July–mid Sept.

Saint-Brisson: Maison du Parc of Morvan Regional Park. Open daily (86 78 70 16). For all Morvan information. Musée de la Résistance—museum recalling Maquis fight against Nazis in 1940–45.

St Christophe-en-Brionnais: Cattle market with nearly 4000 animals on sale. Thu 6.00–approx 10.00. Countryside fair, regional specialities served.

Saint-Fargeau: Château and park open daily 1 Apr–mid Nov (86 74 05 67). Castle farm showing country life around 1900. Daily 1 Apr–mid Nov (86 74 03 76). Horse team-show Sun afternoons.

Saulieu: Musée François Pompon, Parvis de la Basilique (80 64 19 51). Works of Pompon, animal sculptor, and Morvan history. Open daily except Tue.

Solutré: Musée de la Préhistoire (85 35 85 24). Museum dug into base of Solutré hill where wild-horse skeletons were found, showing prehistoric finds (video film). Open daily except Tue. Closed Jan, Feb.

Tanlay: Renaissance château with magnificent decorations, park, moat. Open daily 1 Apr–1 Nov except Tue (86 75 70 61).

Tonnerre: Hôtel Dieu et Musée Hospitalier (founded 1293) including impressive 13th century ward, patients' room of 1850, old surgery unit. Film of hospital's history. Open daily 1 June–30 Sept; Sat and Sun in Apr, May, Oct (86 54 33 00).

Vézelay: Basilique Sainte-Madeleine (86 33 24 36). Superb Romanesque abbey. Open daily. Lit up Tue and Fri 21.00–22.30.

Vougeot: Château du Clos de Vougeot (80 62 86 09). Open daily. Guided visits (40 min).

Metric and Conversion Tables

All measurements are given in metric units. For readers more familiar with the imperial system, the accompanying tables are design to facilitate quick conversion to imperial unists. Bold figures in the central column can be read as either imperial or metric, e.g.: 1kg = 2.20lb or 1lb = 0.45kg.

mm		in	cm		in	m		yds
25.4	**1**	.039	2.54	**1**	0.39	0.91	**1**	1.09
50.8	**2**	.079	5.08	**2**	0.79	1.83	**2**	2.19
76.2	**3**	.118	7.62	**3**	1.18	2.74	**3**	3.28
101.6	**4**	.157	10.16	**4**	1.57	3.66	**4**	4.37
127.0	**5**	.197	12.70	**5**	1.97	4.57	**5**	5.47
152.4	**6**	.236	15.24	**6**	2.36	5.49	**6**	6.56
177.8	**7**	.276	17.78	**7**	2.76	6.40	**7**	7.66
203.2	**8**	.315	20.32	**8**	3.15	7.32	**8**	8.75
228.6	**9**	.354	22.86	**9**	3.54	8.23	**9**	9.84

g		oz	kg		lb	km		miles
28.35	**1**	.04	0.45	**1**	2.20	1.61	**1**	0.62
56.70	**2**	.07	0.91	**2**	4.41	3.22	**2**	1.24
85.05	**3**	.11	1.36	**3**	6.61	4.83	**3**	1.86
113.40	**4**	.14	1.81	**4**	8.82	6.44	**4**	2.48
141.75	**5**	.18	2.27	**5**	11.02	8.05	**5**	3.11
170.10	**6**	.21	2.72	**6**	13.23	9.65	**6**	3.73
198.45	**7**	.25	3.18	**7**	15.43	11.26	**7**	4.35
226.80	**8**	.28	3.63	**8**	17.64	12.87	**8**	4.97
255.15	**9**	.32	4.08	**9**	19.84	14.48	**9**	5.59

ha		acres
0.40	**1**	2.47
0.81	**2**	4.94
1.21	**3**	7.41
1.62	**4**	9.88
2.02	**5**	12.36
2.43	**6**	14.83
2.83	**7**	17.30
3.24	**8**	19.77
3.64	**9**	22.24

Metric to imperial conversion formulae

cm to inches	0.3937	km^2 to square miles	0.3861
m to feet	3.281	ha to acres	2.471
m to yards	1.094	g to ounces	0.03527
km to miles	0.6214	kg to pounds	2.205

Index